BUSINESS IMPROV

Experiential Learning Exercises to Train Employees to Handle Every Situation with Success

VAL GEE AND SARAH GEE

New York   Chicago   San Francisco   Lisbon   London
Madrid   Mexico City   New Delhi   San Juan
Seoul   Singapore   Sydney   Toronto

1 2 3 4 5 6 7 8 9 10   QFR/QFR   1 6 5 4 3 2 1

ISBN   978-0-07-176821-4
MHID   0-07-176821-1

e-ISBN   978-0-07-176861-0
e-MHID   0-07-176861-0

This publication is designed to provide accurate and authoritative information in regard to the subject matter covered. It is sold with the understanding that neither the author nor the publisher is engaged in rendering legal, accounting, securities trading, or other professional services. If legal advice or other expert assistance is required, the services of a competent professional person should be sought.

—From a Declaration of Principles Jointly Adopted by a Committee of the American Bar Association and a Committee of Publishers and Associations

Library of Congress Cataloging-in-Publication Data

Gee, Val.
    Business improv : experiential learning exercises to train employees to handle every situation with success / by Val Gee and Sarah Gee.
        p. cm.
    ISBN 978-0-07-176821-4 (alk. paper)
    1. Employees–Training of. 2. Business communication. 3. Creative ability in business. 4. Problem solving. I. Gee, Sarah. II. Title.
    HF5549.5.T7G37 2011
    658.3'124–dc22   2011008761

McGraw-Hill books are available at special quantity discounts to use as premiums and sales promotions or for use in corporate training programs. To contact a representative, please e-mail us at bulksales@mcgraw-hill.com.

This book is printed on acid-free paper.

To our amazing family and friends, especially Armando, Syona, and Zane, who inspire and motivate us to always be the best that we can be.

Contents

Acknowledgments

We were not alone in putting this book together. So many people have touched our lives and helped us experience the wonderful world of improv. All the people at the Second City, the Second City Training Center, and Second City Communications: Tom Yorton, John Cates, Caroline Rauch, and Sarah Finch. Also: Charna Halpern, coauthor of *Truth in Comedy* and founder of iO Chicago and Los Angeles. Bob Kulhan of Business Improv. The ensemble members of Valhalla: Molly Erdman, Richard Prouty, John Lutz, Matt Chapman, Jim Carlson, Craig Uhlir, Mike Abdelsayed, Noah Gregoropoulos (coach), and, of course, my amazing coach Liz Allen, coauthor of *Improvising Better: A Guide for the Working Improviser*. Mick Napier, author of *Improvise: Scene from Inside Out* and founder of the Annoyance Theatre. We would also like to thank Richard Kuranda, executive director, and his staff at the Raue Center for the Arts, who brought us in to teach kids improv during the summer. We would also like to thank all the staff at McGraw-Hill Professional who contributed so much in getting this book published, in particular: Senior Editor Donya Dickerson, Editorial Coordinator Tania Loghmani, and Publicist Julia Baxter. Finally and not least, because we would never hear the end of it, … Jeff Gee, husband and dad who read through the manuscript and brought cups of tea when needed.

Business Improv: The Creative Engine behind Productivity

Use Business Improv to Improve Organizational Development and Leadership

There is a popular story about how Sir Isaac Newton sat under an apple tree, when an apple fell on his head and gave him the idea of the universal law of gravity. Business improv doesn't wait for the apple to fall. It inspires people to get up, shake the tree, and eat the apple on the way to the mountainside. In other words, business improv provides the tools and skills that enable people to produce their own chance events.

Organizations thrive by tapping into the creative talents of their employees. Innovation and creativity enhance product quality, accelerate market response capabilities, increase operating system efficiencies, and help sustain the competitive advantage. Companies cannot be innovative without being creative, and improvisation is by its nature creative. Not only is it fun but it also ignites and sustains passion, and it encourages individual choices, exploration, and risk taking.

The culture of business improv instills a safe place for creative change-makers to energize, collaborate, and produce innovations in a meaningful and permanent way for themselves, their team, and the larger organization. In order to do that, it's imperative that leaders work on themselves. People learn by observing behaviors, and so leaders must develop their emotional intelligence; they must understand how they express themselves, relate with others, and cope with the daily demands and pressures. Only then can they build an innovative atmosphere where others can grow and accelerate. Improvisational leaders are able to integrate ideas quickly while balancing reactions to a situation in a thoughtful manner. They discover inner thoughts and behaviors that are effective in a fun, supportive, nonthreatening way.

Another critical component of leadership is relationship management. Improvisation encourages productivity and creativity by increasing the quantity and quality of authentic relationships. In promoting synergy, teams also utilize diversity, face obstacles, empower people, and develop confidence. By fostering dialogue that aligns the goals of all parties involved, people will actually celebrate each other's achievements, which in turn breeds success. Improvisation also creates a less stressful environment and encourages a playful atmosphere. It has been assumed in business that happy people are more productive people. A new study suggests that people who keep busy are more likely to be happy than those who are idle.

In a study published in *Psychological Science*, researchers asked college students to take multiple surveys about their school. After completing the first survey, students could either drop it off right outside the room they were in and then wait idly until the next survey was administered, or they could keep busy by dropping off the survey at a location that was about 15 minutes away. Either way, they were told they'd receive a candy bar when they turned in the survey. Not surprisingly, more students chose the closer location. However, students who kept busy by walking to the farther location reported feeling happier afterward than did the students who remained idle. Business improv is about igniting that flame of energy and enthusiasm that helps people to keep busy and thus be able to:

- Generate ideas
- Build innovative teams
- Leverage the talents of others
- Share and sell ideas
- Solve problems
- Manage emotions
- Gain system support
- Recognize success
- Foster support
- Respond and adapt to change

You Don't Have to Be Funny

We often ask people what they think of when they hear the word *improvisation*. We hear all kinds of things like "spontaneous," "winging it," "creative," and inevitably "hilarious." All of these are true, but *improvisation* and *comedy* are not synonymous. Comedy is just one of the many byproducts and benefits of improvisation. Mostly, improv is a device for expanding comfort zones, learning new competencies, and actively looking for and creating opportunities. The great news is that you do not have to be a funny person to improvise. Anyone can improvise. In fact, you are already doing it in your daily life— when you pick up the phone and talk to someone or when you go to a meeting. In fact, every single interaction you have with a human being is spontaneous improvisation, and like great improvisers, we must train and practice to grow and learn more.

Handle the Unpredictable and Potential Problems and Move Forward

Managing an unpredictable environment is tough because most people are not well equipped for it. There's no normal or abnormal way of reacting to problems. In a business environment that changes instantly with new technology and increasing diversity, business improv provides the tools and skills to help people adapt successfully.

Improvisation helps participants manage change by supporting them through the process. With improvisation skills, they can enter into the unknown equipped with tools to help them deal with the denial, anger, frustration, and apathy that happen in the phases of change. The competencies that improvisation builds on help an organization's support systems create productive environments and encourage curiosity and commitment.

Improvisation has been described as "an intuitive, coordinated, and spontaneous response to a dynamic environment." As such, adaptability, a positive outlook, and communication are vital. Improvisers can smoothly handle multiple simultaneous demands and shifting priorities, and they can adapt their responses and tactics to fit fluid circumstances. They are persistent in pursuing goals despite obstacles and setbacks. Business improv helps employees view challenges as opportunities that encourage success as the operating philosophy.

Discover and Remove Barriers That Keep Organizations Stuck

It's one thing to know what's coming, and another to be able to adjust to it. Improvisation lends itself to productivity and innovation no matter what's going on. It helps remove barriers to teamwork, collaboration, and advancement by:

- Celebrating and recognizing success
- Storytelling
- Building ownership through inclusion
- Soliciting feedback and reviewing suggestions
- Creating a safe place for bold ideas to emerge

The Rules of Business Improv

These tools make us successful improvisers onstage … they will in business too!

- "Yes, and"
- Support and celebrate others
- Suspend judgments
- Take risks and participate energetically

"Yes, and" is the very core of improvisation. It is the springboard from which all other improvisation competencies jump off. It is the first building block—it moves action forward, builds trust, creates acceptance, promotes healthy communication, and supports productive relationships. "Yes, and" provides the framework of innovation, collaboration, and diversity. Teams can't advance without understanding and employing the simple yet wise concept of "yes, and."

Leave all judgments at the door. You can pick them back up when you are finished. I promise they will still be there. Most of us are our own worst critic. This is the biggest challenge that most participants must overcome. "What will my boss think?" "What if I look stupid?" Their inner voice goes into overdrive telling them all sorts of things like they're too old, too young, too serious, too experienced, too educated, too whatever. ... Let it go! In improvisation, these thoughts will keep you stuck. Get out of your head, and get into the supportive nonjudgmental world of improv.

No one cares about what you are doing or saying anyway because the people around you are too worried about what they're doing and saying. People are too busy judging their own level of involvement to worry about yours. So go ahead and contribute, and when you begin speaking, trust that it's right and the appropriate thing will come out of your mouth.

A great way to suspend judgment is tell participants to jump in as fast as possible and be the first ones to volunteer. That way they will stop talking to themselves about all of their judgments! It's always harder to think about doing something than it is to just do it. Always! Plus, it's a team effort. So the team shouldn't rely on a couple of people to do all of the heavy lifting while everyone stands around and watches. It's about sharing the load and contributing even if you don't want to, even if you're scared. Improvisation is one for all and all for one.

As the facilitator, you must set the energy for everyone else. If your energy is low, you're giving everyone permission to do the same. I know that sometimes at certain times of the day your energy can drop, but make it your goal to be the "cheerleader" and encourage yourself and others. It's about practicing the art of energy manipulation. Force enthusiasm and see what happens. Experiment by making yourself go for it. There's nothing to lose and only insights to gain. If your participants need a little energy manipulation, ask them on a scale of 1 to 10 how enthusiastic they were to their team members' offerings. If their answer is low, ask them to commit more.

Support and celebrate those around you. When you encourage people to go for it, the payoff is huge; people become more willing to collaborate and work with you. Improvisation is about making your partner look good. We're taught that our scene partner is God: treat him or her accordingly. That means celebrating each other's offers, ideas, and perspectives. It's about encouraging team members instead of competing with them. Improvisation is inclusive, not exclusive. No one is isolated. There are no silos. Supporting each other's creativity is fundamental.

It is imperative that you as the facilitator support, encourage, and celebrate the participants in every exercise both verbally and nonverbally. Some of the activities will push them out of their comfort zone. You are essentially asking them do things they might perceive as difficult, hard, not appropriate, or not beneficial to the business world. It's your job to generate unconditional support and create an atmosphere of nonjudgmental learning and fun. Every time participants perform any activity, thank them and encourage them with applause and cheers. This will set the tone for all activities to follow, and it will enable them to communicate effectively with people from every walk of life—no exceptions. It's that powerful.

The Steps to Follow

You can modify or change the steps as you feel appropriate. Leave steps out or repeat steps as necessary if they are helping your group reach their potential. The key is to have fun and experience the energy of acceptance, open-mindedness, and encouragement.

The Debriefings

Learning takes place in experiencing the activities, and connecting the competencies of improvisation to their work life and it takes place in the debrief. The questions you ask after every activity are critical to the applicability for the participants.

Business Improv

Business improv is a proven, hands-on training process on how to communicate effectively with people from every walk of life—no exceptions. Today people from every part of the world are communicating with each other face-to-face, via e-mail, and in countless other social networks. Business improv is the one tool that helps people understand how to get the message across in a constructive way that ensures a win-win situation for everyone involved. How we put our ideas across to other people and how we listen can make the difference between a department's being fully functional, productive, and profitable and its breaking down with frontline employees' focusing on what is wrong and what isn't working and senior executives' watching a decreasing bottom line losing ground day by day.

When people learn communication methods in which they can discuss issues, conflicts, and challenging situations as they arise, they become adept at finding solutions and ways to move forward in the moment. When problems of communication between internal and external customers are not solved immediately, they can fester and become so big that managers and department heads may eventually have to intervene. This creates lost time, diminished focus, reduced productivity, and lost revenues. By focusing on specific improv techniques, everyone is heard, everyone has a voice, and everyone takes responsibility for collaborating with everyone else in the moment. Instead of taking days or weeks and sometimes even months to solve a problem, people move forward and get on with doing their jobs in a productive and cohesive manner.

Working with coworkers and customers from different cultures, backgrounds, and belief structures can sometimes create an unpredictable and unplanned framework in which people communicate from a base of fear, anxiety, and worry. This causes people to take things personally and to create rigid and uncooperative triangulation patterns within departments—all of which adversely affect interactions with customers. Business improv provides a proven process with specific rules and characteristics that enable people to explore how to communicate with creativity and spontaneity without fear or apprehension. It opens up possibilities instead of constraints, and it builds an environment in which people enjoy turning up for work and being involved in creating loyal and satisfied customers—both internal and external.

From an employee perspective, one of the reasons for the outstanding results and productive environment provided by business improv is that it is fun, exciting, and innovative. People want to learn, and they are passionate about using their new tools back on the job. Everyone who participates in business improv walks away inspired to communicate and collaborate with coworkers, colleagues, and customers alike. It is similar to learning an exciting new sport: people immediately want to put what they've learned into action. Business improv is the new and exciting communication sport of the century. It is insightful and meaningful, and it provides people with exceptional tools to get their message across no matter what the message, the messenger, or the recipient. Gone forever are the stuffy meetings that take up so much of people's time and a corporation's resources. With business improvisation, people get to the point fast because they are able to think on their feet, take charge of their ideas, and communicate in a language that everyone understands. Business improv is the creation of a universal language that breaks down barriers, builds understanding, and focuses on immediate results.

Managers, supervisors, and business leaders have described business improv as the "communication process of champions." It's not just that people enjoy learning about how to interact with each other and provide their best performance. It is a mechanism that literally lightens up the communication process. As a result, people look forward to collaborating with each other. People are on the same page, communicating within a framework of preestablished rules designed to expand dialogue and encourage feedback. Within the framework of business improv, pushback and shutdown become things of the past because the very rules prohibit inferior dialogue.

Collaboration: The Way Forward to Right Action

One of the reasons that business improv works so well is that it gets people interested and involved. The thousands of people who have learned business improv are always excited to learn new techniques and get involved with the games and exercises. Business improv is fun, interesting, and challenging. People do not have to sit through a day of being lectured at, watching PowerPoints, or even sitting down in groups and going through made-up role-play scenarios that do not reflect real-life situations. Individuals who learn business improv skills become the creators, directors, and actors of their own scenes. They use their own work experiences to create the situations that they come across on a daily basis for which they have had no real tools to utilize. Participants in a business improv class don't just learn about the importance of being spontaneous. They are spontaneous. No longer do they have to try and be creative. They are creative. By the very nature and structure of what we call *resourceful engineering*, people become self-directed and autonomous, which are key principles of adult learning.

People learn by experience. There is no better way to learn how to effectively communicate with other people than to dialogue with other people in unrehearsed and unedited situations. One of the reasons for the outstanding results and productive environments provided by business improv is that it is fun, exciting, and innovative—people want to learn, and they are passionate about using their new tools back on the job. Every business improv exercise is designed to give the learner one key element. It could be, for example, the "yes, and" exercise, which is a key component in creating a profitable discussion with another person. A *profitable discussion* is one in which both parties feel they have been heard and are empowered to move forward with a project instead of coming to a roadblock in which managers, and even department heads, have to get involved.

The entire workforce benefits from business improv because once the rules are learned, they cannot be unlearned. Once people experience and develop the mechanical skills of business improv, it is impossible for them not to use them; being difficult, unreasonable, or uncollaborative no longer works. Perhaps one of the reasons for this is that the rules make sense: they speak to that part within each of us that instinctively *knows* the right and wrong ways to talk to people.

The problem for many people is that even if they know at some level that they are creating a communication breakdown and that they may be right in the middle of a dialogue disaster, they don't know how to stop. Without the skills of business improv, people literally cannot get off the bus that leads to communication collapse. And while a communication problem sounds like a simple thing, it can create such an upheaval that the company can lose thousands of dollars in people-hours trying to find solutions. The best way out of this problem is to give people the skills and knowledge not to get on that bus in the first place.

Self-Directed Practices for Effective Communication

Since respect, support, and collaboration are an intrinsic part of business improv, every participant is treated as an important element within the learning process, and every person walks away from business improv empowered to the best communicator he or she can be.

Adults are autonomous and self-directed, and they need to be free to direct themselves and learn what they need and want to learn. Business improv is founded on a self-directed form of communication. Participants assume responsibility for their part in the communication whether it's listening, responding, or talking. Business improv helps participants use their accumulated knowledge and life experience to enhance communication and build a process in which they can relate to the theories and concepts provided.

Goals and course objectives are clearly defined elements of business improv. Early on participants are encouraged to see how the practical aspects of business improv will enhance every aspect of their life, at home and at work. The wealth of experience that adults bring to the classroom provides a foundation in which all of the participants are treated as equals and are allowed to voice their opinions freely in class.

The Four Critical Elements of Learning

Business improv solves the four critical elements that every manager, frontline supervisor, and facilitator faces: motivation, reinforcement, retention, and transference. Within business improv, there are at least six factors that provide motivation for adult learners:

1. *Social relationships:* Make new friends.
2. *External expectations:* Comply with instructions.
3. *Social welfare:* Improve ability to be of service.
4. *Personal advancement:* Achieve higher job status.
5. *Stimulation:* Provide a break from routine.
6. *Cognitive interest:* Seek knowledge for its own sake.

If adults do not see the benefit of learning, they will not be motivated to learn. People also need sufficient tension and difficulty to challenge them but not so much that they become frustrated by information overload. Right off the bat, business improv motivates people to learn: it is a fun, experiential process that challenges people to communicate in real time, unedited and in a friendly, open atmosphere that creates personal advancement and satisfies an inquiring mind.

Reinforcement is also a very necessary part of the learning process because it encourages correct ways to behave and perform in the workplace. Because of the nature of business improv as an unedited, immediate, and interactive process, positive reinforcement is inherent in the process, and participants are encouraged to continue doing what works best for them. As a result, participants feel encouraged to use the principles back on the job.

Learning concepts are normally retained through practice; the concepts learned during business improv are retained by most participants because the ongoing practice reinforces and supports the learning. Likewise, transference of learning—that is, the ability to use the information taught in the course—is extremely high because participants integrate the new information with what they already know.

Activity 1

"Yes, and"

There was really only one rule I was taught about improv. That was, "yes-and."
In this case, "yes-and" is a verb. To "yes-and." I yes-and, you yes-and, he, she,
or it yes-ands. And "yes-anding" means that when you go onstage to improvise a
scene with no script, you have no idea what's going to happen, maybe with someone
you've never met before…

—Stephen Colbert, host of *The Colbert Report*, a satirical news show

Level of Risk

Low

Background and Purpose

If you are familiar with improvisational theater, you are probably familiar with "yes, and."
"Yes, and" is one of the fundamental ground rules of improv. It's a general philosophy by
which you agree with your partner and then add additional information. It is the best
way to gain trust, acceptance, and mutual discovery and to collaborate.

In improv, "yes, and" is about accepting what's given to you and then adding another
offer to move the conversation, idea, or action along. By acknowledging one piece of
information and adding another, you and your partner work together to advance the
communication. It's a process familiar to creative problem solving: you start with a few
pieces of key information and spend the rest of the time working toward a solution and
defining the various details along the way.

Saying "yes, and" does not necessarily mean that you agree with what the other person
is saying. It is simply a way of ensuring collaboration and moving an idea along. Agreeing
to disagree is still "yes, anding" as long as the intention for both parties is to move forward.

The "yes, and" rule allows people to pick up the ball and run with it. It infuses
energy, it's fun and exhilarating, and most of all it creates an environment in which
people feel empowered to pitch their ideas and thoughts. "Yes, and" is an affirmation
that the person is listening and the offering is being accepted and heard. "Yes, and" does
not mean you agree with or even like the offering. Rather, it means that you are simply
validating that the offering has occurred.

OBJECTIVES

By the end of this activity, people will:

- Encourage the generation of new ideas.
- Use the "yes, and" rule to alleviate difficult communication situations.
- Use communication as a tool to move forward in a positive way.
- Demonstrate the use of the "yes, and" rule.

Mini Lecture

When people first hear an idea or information that they don't understand or agree with, they often blurt out "No!" Maybe it's because "no" is the first word we speak as a way to assert and test our power. As adults, many people say "no" because they don't want to change existing practices or they fear losing the status quo of existing relationships or resources. Onstage, beginning improvisers often say "no" out of fear. They panic and become scared about the unknown, or they don't possess enough knowledge about the situation, or just want to be in control of the scene. Whatever the reason is for saying "no," the communication stops.

Another response to new ideas or information is to say "yes, but," which is just a fancy way of saying "no." At Second City Communications, they say "yes, but" is "no" dressed up in a tuxedo. When people say "yes, but," you know they're going to give you at least one reason why they don't like the information or why the idea won't work, and again the communication breaks down.

Conversely, after working with thousands of people who are learning business improv rules, we've found that some people actually like to say and hear "yes, but" and "no." The people who use "yes, but" feel that it is a polite way of saying "no." They use it as a critical thinking tool to ground the communication while still managing to collaborate. "Yes, but" fuels and stimulates their competitive nature to find the solution. However, the overriding facts are:

- "No" stops communication in its tracks.
- "Yes, but" usually equals "no."
- "Yes, and" moves the conversation forward in a positive, collaborative way.

Overcoming the instinct to say "no" is a major part of learning business improv. The way to cooperate and improve effective communication is to "yes, and." Be a builder, not a destroyer. "Yes, and" allows people to build upon new or existing ideas. It fosters open-mindedness and empowers people to be creative, trust their instincts, and think on their feet.

Overview of Activity

Participants will form groups of two in which one participant is (A) and the other participant is (B). There will be a series of three improv rounds, one after the other. In the first round, the (A) persons will throw out an idea, and their (B) partners will negate it. In the second round, the (B)s will throw out a different idea, and their (A) partners will "yes, but" it. In the third and final round, the (A)s will throw out an idea, and their (B) partners will "yes, and" it.

Time

Instructions—10 minutes
Each round—2 to 3 minutes
Debriefing—10 minutes
Total time—29 minutes

STEPS TO FOLLOW

Round 1
1. Have everyone team up with a partner and decide who is (A) and who is (B).
2. In pairs, the participants hold a conversation about a certain work-related event—for example, a corporate retreat, softball meeting, office party, banquet, or picnic.
3. Person (A) chooses an event to plan with Person (B).
4. Person (B)'s job is to shoot down or negate all of Person (A)'s ideas, saying "no" as often as possible.

Round 2
  Now it's Person (B)'s turn to pitch an idea for a different work-related event. Only this time, Person (A) will respond only with "yes, but" statements.

Round 3
  Now (A) pitches a different work-related event. (B) can respond only with "yes, and" statements.

Round 1 Example

Person A:	"I want to plan the new product launch."
Person B:	"No, I don't think you should be in charge of that."
Person A:	"Well, there's always a first time!"
Person B:	"No, it's just a bad idea."

Round 2 Example

Person B: "I am in charge of the facilities meeting. I was thinking of the executive boardroom."

Person A: "Yes, but it's being used all next week and the week after that."

Person B: "Do you have a venue you can recommend?"

Person A: "Yes, but it's too small."

Round 3 Example

Person A: "I want to plan my birthday."

Person B: "Yes, and let's have it at Restaurant Fajillios!"

Person A: "Cool! I want to have a birthday cake too."

Person B: "Yes, and we'll make the cake look like a big present!"

BENEFITS TO LOOK FOR

The ideas below echo the "Yes, and" approach:

- **Stop the IKTA (*I Know That Already*) disease.** If you walk into every situation thinking you know it all, there will be nothing new to learn. And the only time you should stop learning is when you are six feet under. Be curious. Be willing to try something new even if it doesn't make sense at first. Go in with an open mind and enjoy the learning journey of business improv.
- **Say "yes, and."** Again, you don't have to agree with what is being said. Just acknowledge and authenticate it. If you negate an idea or comment on how bad it is, you are creating conflict and consequences to the relationship, both in the long term and the short term.

Discussion Points

- **Q: What was the effect of the "no" response?** (*I kept trying different ideas, but I felt shut down. I felt powerful getting to say "no," but nothing got accomplished. I was defeated.*)
- **Q: Was there a difference when the response changed to "yes, but"?** (*It was nicer. I liked the fact that I could keep offering up something. It still felt like "no."*)

- **Q: What about "yes, and"?** *(Much more positive. We were able to build on the idea. I felt the conversation was unrealistic. The conversation flowed easier.)*
- **Q: Does "yes, and" mean that you have to agree with everything?** *(No. I can still have a different opinion, and I still want to find a win-win.)*
- **Q: What are some situations in which you could benefit from "yes, and"?** *(It would be a more effective communication process, where everyone felt heard. It would force me to listen more.)*
- **Q: How did your energy and body language change between the rounds?** *(I was closed off in "no." My arms were crossed in "no." I was so energized in "yes, and.")*
- **Q: What are other ways of verbally and nonverbally saying "yes, and"?** *(I can listen better, and I can compliment other people's creativity and thank them for their input.)*

Participant Action Plan

Provide the participants with a copy of the following action plan. Ask them to complete it, and set up a time to review their results one week later. At that time, ask them what has worked and what has not worked. What do they need to do to improve?

"Yes, and" Actions

The actions I will take as a result of the "Yes, and" activity are:

_____

_____

_____

_____

ONE WEEK LATER: What results have I gained from the "Yes, and" activity?

_____

_____

_____

_____

Activity 2

Listen to Understand, Not to Respond

There are people who, instead of listening to what is being said to them, are already listening to what they are going to say to themselves.

—Albert Guinon, French playwright (1863 to 1923)

Level of Risk

Low

Background and Purpose

Listening to your scene partner is another crucial concept to great improvisation. Too many times a player will be in a scene and miss critical pieces of information that could have taken the scene to a more unusual, creative, or thought-provoking place. When I'm in a scene with someone who isn't listening, I think, "This player is clueless, and I'm going to have to carry him on my back the whole way. He has his own agenda, he's on his own planet, and he's not collaborating in the scene." Usually it's because the player was talking to himself about where he thought the scene should go, or he assumed he knew where it was going before the fellow player had finished speaking. As a result, the scene is flat and boring, frustrating to watch, and annoying to perform.

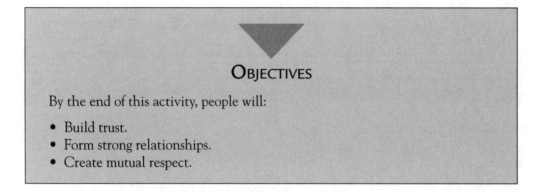

OBJECTIVES

By the end of this activity, people will:

- Build trust.
- Form strong relationships.
- Create mutual respect.

- Be in the moment.
- Listen to understand, versus listening just to respond.
- Listen all the way to the end of what the speakers are saying versus formulating their response while they are talking.

Mini Lecture

"Are you a good listener?" When most people answer this question, they nod their head and say "yes." The problem is, in reality, many of us are not very good listeners. Here's why. As soon as people start talking about particular people, problems, or events, our brain immediately goes into search mode looking for a similar experience to relate to. The people are talking, but we can't hear them because we're so busy inside our own head reliving our own version of the event. "If only they would stop talking for a moment, I could tell them my story." Inevitably we think our story is much more interesting, and so now we are judging the two stories—our and theirs. We may look like we're listening, and if we're really clever, we may even give verbal signals that seem like we're listening such as "ah-ha," "hmmm," "yes," and "okay." In reality, while we are off in our head searching for and reliving our own experience, we have missed crucial pieces of conversation.

Here's a simple exercise to illustrate the point. Please read the following words:

A

BIRD

IN THE

THE HAND

Among the thousands of people who have attended our workshops, when we ask them if this reads "a bird in the hand," most people say "yes, it does." In fact, it doesn't. It actually reads "a bird in the the hand." In other words, many people don't even listen past "a bird" before they think they understand what is being said.

In business as in improv, listening is imperative to good communication. When people are actively listening to understand, instead of listening to respond, real communication occurs and right action is taken. What do we mean by "real communication"? Here's how it sounds:

Jane:

"Can you complete the budget in time for today's meeting at 10 a.m.?"

Sue:

"Yes, I'll have my budget report on your desk by 9:30 a.m."

Jane:

"Thanks. If I get the report on my desk by 9:30 a.m., I'll have time to review it."

Notice how the important criteria about what is needed are repeated so that both Jane and Sue know what is expected and what action will be taken by when and by whom.

In this scenario, if Sue does not have the report on Jane's desk by 9:30 a.m., then Jane will be unprepared for her meeting. The following improv activity will help participants experience the importance of listening to understand versus listening to respond.

Overview of Activity

With a partner, participants have a conversation. The only caveat is that they must use their partner's last word as their first word.

Time

Instructions—3 minutes
One round—2 to 3 minutes
Debriefing—10 minutes
Total time—15 minutes

STEPS TO FOLLOW

1. Have participants find a partner and face that person.
2. In pairs, tell the participants to hold a conversation. They can talk about anything they'd like. The only rule is they must start each of their sentences with the last word their partner just said.
3. Tell them not to worry if their conversation goes all over the place.

Example

Person A: "It's a great day to have a meeting with *everyone*."
Person B: "*Everyone* … here is awake, which is a good *thing*."
Person A: "*Thing* … is I was not expecting to do this *exercise*!"
Person B: "*Exercise* … is not something I enjoy *doing*."
Person A: "*Doing* … is a great verb when used in *conversation*."

▼

BENEFITS TO LOOK FOR

The ideas below echo the Listen to Understand, Not to Respond approach:

- **People don't always need to respond.** Sometimes people just want to bounce ideas around and need a person to listen. Others like the sound of their own voice. This listening activity will show the importance of simply listening.

- **Repeat to increase understanding.** In this game, people must pay attention, listen, and repeat. Obviously, we will never use someone's last word as our first, but as we saw with the Jane and Sue dialogue earlier, repeating back a little bit of what has been said is an excellent way of communicating and a great way to show you are listening.
- **Focus your mind.** Our brain is constantly operating. In fact, it's very hard to stop talking to ourselves or thinking. That's when we miss communication. This exercise reminds us to focus on what the other person is saying all the way through to the very end.
- **Focus on the other person.** There are many different reasons we jump to conclusions and interrupt people's thought process, but the fact is that it doesn't make for great listening. Only after we've listened fully can we contribute something valid.

Discussion Points

- **Q: What did you have to do to make this exercise work?** (*I had to listen to everything they said in order to know what the last word would be.*)
- **Q: Did your conversations make sense?** (*Yes. No.*)
- **Q: Without any judgment, did anyone try to end on an easy or tough word?** (*I preferred to end on an easy word to support people. I did sometimes challenge them with a tough word.*)
- **Q: How did this listening activity show the importance of not immediately searching for a response but actively listening to understand?** (*I realized how easy it is to have my mind wander off. I wanted to interrupt, but I couldn't.*)
- **Q: In the real world, do you find that sometimes you plan your response while someone is talking? And if yes, were you able to do that in this conversation?** (*No, because I didn't know where the speaker would end.*)
- **Q: What kinds of things can we miss if we don't listen to the end?** (*Message, tone, emotion, important information, everything!*)
- **Q: What did this activity have to do with actively listening to understand?** (*Listening is about giving up the control of the conversation for the time the other person is talking; then after I've understood, I can make the appropriate response. In this case, I could make my given word make sense.*)
- **Q: What did this improv activity have to do with the business world?** (*I'm constantly communicating with people all day long. If I want effective relationships, I have to stop talking to myself and really listen.*)

Participant Action Plan

Ask participants to pair up and discuss (a) what they are going to do to become active listeners and (b) how they are going to remind themselves to be active listeners. Ask for volunteers to share their ideas.

Provide all the participants with a copy of the following action plan and ask them to write down their ideas. Set up a time one week later to review their results.

At that time, ask them what has worked and what has not worked. What do they need to do to improve?

Listen to Understand, Not to Respond Actions

The actions I will take as a result of the Listen to Understand, Not to Respond activity are:

_____

_____

_____

_____

The actions I will take to remind myself to be an active listener are:

_____

_____

_____

_____

ONE WEEK LATER: What results have I gained from the Listen to Understand, Not to Respond activity?

_____

_____

_____

_____

Activity 3

Suspend Judgments

We must be willing to get rid of the life we've planned, so as to have the life that is waiting for us.

—Joseph Campbell, American mythologist,
writer, and lecturer (1904 to 1987)

Level of Risk

Medium

Background and Purpose

When people are judgmental, they look at a person, a situation, or an event through their own belief system, which is like looking at life through a distorted lens. Commonly cited synonyms for *judgmental* are *critical, condemnatory, negative, disapproving,* and *disparaging.* I think of this with one player I worked with when I was a founding member of Second City Improv in Las Vegas. The player was smart but über-critical. It made me not want to contribute and instead stand at the back of the stage. I remember going home thinking, "I need to find another profession." Of course, after I *stopped being a victim,* I got on with my work, but the experience still left a bad taste in my mouth.

In improvisation, beginners often fall into the trap of criticizing their scene partner's choice, behavior, or dialogue. Criticism is often born out of fear and a need to control the fear. The effects are serious. As I experienced for myself, the person being criticized may withdraw or attack back and then wither way, and the scene may lose momentum or turn into an unfunny conflict—not good outcomes for any improv scene.

OBJECTIVES

By the end of this activity, people will:

- Actively work to diminish judgmental behavior.
- Learn how to creatively seek alternative solutions to problems.
- Create objective observation skills that enhance a positive work environment.

Mini Lecture

Being judgmental is the opposite of being open and creative. Judgmental people usually think they know the answer because they just do—it's the way it's always been or it's the way people do it around here. One of the antidotes to engaging in destructive, critical thinking is to brainstorm. Brainstorming stops preconceived judgments from hatching into absolute truths. It's a way for creative people and not-so-creative people to have input without fear of rejection.

Without brainstorming, many useful things would not be available today. Think of the Internet. It began with Dwight D. Eisenhower, who created the Advanced Research Project Agency (ARPA) in 1950. He wanted to give the United States a technological edge over other countries, and one important part of his mission was computer science. In the 1950s computers were enormous devices that filled entire rooms. They had a fraction of the power and processing ability that you can find in a modern PC, and there was no way to network computers together. A judgmental mind could not have developed computer science to what it has become today. It required observant and open-minded people to brainstorm a whole new concept and put it into action. Being judgmental reduces creative power and builds a workforce based on fear and negativity. Being open-minded and creative builds a workforce that is successful and innovative and an environment of "can-do" people.

Overview of Activity

Participants will create an ad campaign from the beginning to the very end. Every idea brought forth will be embraced and enthusiastically celebrated. This is an activity in personal energy manipulation, support, and creativity.

Time

Instructions—5 minutes
Each round—2 to 3 minutes
Debriefing—10 minutes
Total time—36 minutes (less if fewer rounds are played)

STEPS TO FOLLOW

Instructions

1. Participants stand in a large circle so that everyone can see each other.
2. Tell the participants they will create an ad campaign starting with an invention of a brand new product. They will then name it, find a target market, choose a celebrity spokesperson, create corporate alliances, and write jingles, commercials, and taglines.
3. The only rule is that everyone must enthusiastically embrace any and all ideas. Any time someone makes an offer, you and everyone else will celebrate and applaud. It doesn't matter if you think it's the worst idea you have ever heard. You are going to unreservedly accept it. You can holler, clap, punch the air, or high five.
4. Ask the participants to practice enthusiastically supporting an offer.
5. Then ask them, on a scale of 1 to 10—1 being a golf clap, 10 being over the top—how they rated their enthusiasm.
6. Tell them this exercise is about energy manipulation—specifically their own and how it affects the group.

Round 1

1. Ask someone to shout out a brand new invention or product—for example, "lemon-scented socks." Usually people will stand and stare at you. *You have to encourage participation.* Say, "It doesn't matter what comes out of your mouth because the whole group will embrace and support you. This activity is not about creating a quality idea. It's about being in the moment and suspending judgments."
2. After the invention or product has been called out, start the enthusiastic applause.
3. Ask someone to please name that product.
4. After an offer, start the enthusiastic applause.
5. Ask someone else to please tell us our target market.
6. Again, after the offer, start the enthusiastic applause.
7. Ask for a tagline from the group.
8. The offer is given, then the applause.
9. Now ask them for a brief overview for a 15-second commercial spot.
10. Applause.
11. Ask them to choose a celebrity spokesperson.
12. Applause.
13. Finally, ask someone to sing the jingle for our product.
14. Applause.
15. Tell participants it's time to take the product to market and end with an enthusiastic applause.

Round 2

Repeat as many times as necessary to make sure everyone contributes.

Note: These steps can be changed as you feel appropriate. You can leave steps out or repeat steps if they are helping the group keep up its energy. You can invent a new product, name it, and create a jingle for it if this is what the group is enjoying most. If the energy drops, tell the participants that this is an exercise in manipulating their own energy. The key is to have fun and experience the energy of acceptance, open-mindedness, and encouragement.

BENEFITS TO LOOK FOR

The ideas below echo the Suspend Judgments approach:

- **Support = trust.** Everyone on the team must participate. There's nothing worse than being the "odd man out." By supporting and encouraging one another, trust is built and a collaborative environment is created.
- **Be enthusiastic.** It's not every day you get to stand up and cheer for someone for no real reason. So go for it! Enjoy the feeling and benefits it gives to your body and mind. Remember what it feels like to be a kid again. You don't have to be childish, but you can be childlike!
- **Laughter improves your immune system.** Apart from the obvious benefits of having fun—enjoying yourself, participating, and helping to build your team spirit—a good hearty laugh relieves physical tension and stress and leaves your muscles relaxed for up to 45 minutes after. Laughter also boosts your immune system and increases immune cells and infection-fighting antibodies. Laughter triggers the release of endorphins, which provides an overall sense of well-being and even temporarily relieves pain. Finally, laughter protects your heart; it improves the function of blood vessels and increases blood flow, which protects you against a heart attack and other cardiovascular problems. So laugh, enjoy, and improve your health as well as your business skills.
- **Have courage to do it differently.** Be willing to go outside your comfort zone. If you are normally quiet, be an inspiration to others. If you are normally the one who inspires everyone else by taking the lead, be willing to support others in doing the same.
- **Have fun.** In business improv, having fun is number one in every activity. If you are not having fun, why not? Is business so serious that you can't have fun for five minutes? If you are a participant in this activity, it is because you are meant to step outside of your normal way of thinking—and to have fun! So go for it and have a laugh.

Discussion Points

- **Q: What did you notice?** *(I had fun. I participated more than I would normally. I let go of my judgments.)*
- **Q: What kind of workplace would suspending judgments provide?** *(We would be more open to listening to others' ideas. We would be more accepting of each other.)*
- **Q: What did you experience about energy manipulation?** *(It felt forced sometimes, but it became real as we went along. The more I put in, the more I got out.)*
- **Q: Were your ideas able to come together?** *(We had to work on it, but when we accepted each other's ideas, it did come together.)*
- **Q: What if there had been lots of eye rolling, or people had said "No" or "That's a dumb idea"? How would the experience have changed?** *(We would not have felt safe to participate.)*

Participant Action Plan

Give all of the players a copy of the following action plan. Ask them to complete it, and set up a time to review their results one week later. At that time, ask them what worked and what didn't work. What do they need to do to improve?

Suspend Judgments Actions

The actions I will take as a result of the Suspend Judgments activity are:

_____

_____

_____

_____

ONE WEEK LATER: What results have I gained from the Suspend Judgments activity?

_____

_____

_____

_____

Activity 4

Be in the Moment

I just hope a third thing doesn't happen.
—Justin Timberlake, *Saturday Night Live*,
American pop musician and actor, six
Grammy Awards and two Emmys (b. 1981)

Level of Risk

Medium

Background and Purpose

Being in the moment requires concentration, the ability to focus, and the skill to prioritize even in the midst of seeming chaos. To practice concentration in the midst of chaos encourages players to be thinking of more than one thing at a time and to act quickly in relation to what is going on around them. In the business world, people who do not have these skills and are able to concentrate on only one specific task at a time may lose focus on other important things that are happening. Being in the moment requires people to see the bigger picture and know what is going on not just in their department but in other parts of the organization. It's having the ability to do their job well, pass the process along to other people who are part of the team, and be able to take care of urgent things as they come up *in the moment*.

The skill needed to do more than one thing at a time is called *multitasking*. While multitasking abilities vary from person to person, everyone in an organization needs to have an eye on the bigger picture. For example, while most people are not required to do the job of every other person in their department, it is critical that everyone in the department understand how his or her job relates to the overall corporate core values. It is also part of a successful company structure that everyone understand how each department is interlinked to every other department and how every job is dependent on others' completing their tasks on time and within budget.

▼

OBJECTIVES

By the end of this activity, people will:

- Have an awareness of their own ability to *be in the moment*.
- Encourage players to think of more than one thing at a time.
- Act quickly in relation to what is going on around them.
- Reinforce focus and concentration.
- Stay open to giving and receiving.
- Be reminded to *be in the moment*.
- Learn the importance of *being in the moment* versus scattering their thoughts.

Mini Lecture

In the business environment, things don't always run smoothly. Consider this example:

1. Sandra is working at her computer finishing an urgent project...
2. When, suddenly, a customer call is escalated to her with a difficult problem that only she can solve...
3. When the boss walks in needing a report from her for a meeting that's being held in five minutes.

The ability to be in the moment will greatly help Sandra in this situation because it will allow her to focus and prioritize. Here's an example of "being in the moment" thinking:

1. Customers always come first.
2. The urgent project on the computer can be put on hold.
3. The escalated customer call must be answered now.
4. After answering the call, the customer can be put on hold for one minute.
5. The boss's needs can be heard.
6. The escalated customer call is handled.
7. The boss's report can be found and delivered to the meeting.
8. The urgent project is resumed.

In the above situation, Sandra may not be able to find the report immediately, the escalated customer call may take longer than expected, and the boss may not be so accommodating. Whatever the situation, when Sandra is in the moment, she will keep herself on task, and she will be able to think on her feet and logically follow the next best steps.

Overview of Activity

All of the participants stand in a circle, and the facilitator mimes having objects that she tosses to a willing player in the group. That player then tosses the object to another player in the group. This is an activity of perpetual motion with multiple objects.

Time

Instructions—5 minutes
Each round—2 to 3 minutes (minimum three rounds)
Debriefing—8 minutes
Total time—22 minutes

STEPS TO FOLLOW

Round 1

1. Gather all of the participants into a large circle where everyone can see each other.
2. Hold an imaginary red ball and say, "I am holding an imaginary red ball. This ball will never change shape or color. It will always be a red ball. I am going to make eye contact with someone in the group and throw it to him or her. When I throw the ball, I will call out, 'Red ball!' The receiver will say, 'Thank you. Red ball!'"
3. Allow the red ball to be tossed around the group until all of the participants are comfortable making eye contact and the givers are calling out, "Red ball" and receivers are saying, "Thank you. Red ball."
4. Continue to toss the red ball and then introduce additional balls of different colors: yellow, green, purple, blue.
5. Allow four to five balls to be tossed around.
6. After a couple of minutes call out, "Freeze!" Ask all the participants to hold up their colored balls. Ask the participants to say the color of their ball. Check to see if some balls are missing. Inevitably there will be.

Debriefing

Debrief using the discussion points below and those later in the chapter:
Q: What can you and your group do to make the activity run more smoothly and make the communication more effective? (*Answers include using eye contact, keeping the integrity of the object, making the object real, and trusting everyone on the team.*)

Round 2

1. Now have the participants do the exercise again and maintain eye contact (*use other answers that the group pointed out*). Continue the game with all of the colored balls, and then add additional objects such as a wet fish, an angry cat, a sleeping baby, a hot potato, a mouth full of marbles. You should end up with 7 to 10 objects.

2. After a couple of minutes call out, "Freeze!" Hold up your object and ask people what they are holding.

    Debrief using the discussion points later in the chapter.

BENEFITS TO LOOK FOR

The ideas below echo the "Be in the Moment" approach:

- **Go outside your comfort zone.** Most people have a comfortable or preferred chair they like to sit in at home; if you have one, you will notice that this chair often makes you feel sleepy. But, while it is good to relax and maybe take a cat nap at home, work is not the place to fall asleep. Go outside your comfort zone, wake up, and let your enthusiasm shine forth!

- **Shine and automatically give permission for others to do the same.** Have you noticed that some people are leaders and shine with a "can-do" or optimistic energy? That's what business improv is all about: giving your time, energy, and support to creative thinking and doing things a bit differently to get the best results by using the best practices. If you are embarrassed to shine and stand out, your team will have a difficult time in reaching their potential.

- **Lead by example.** When people see someone "walking the talk," it makes a big difference in what they are willing to do for that person. If you are asking others to put themselves forward, you have to be willing to do the same.

Discussion Points

- **Q: How important is making eye contact?** (*For effective communication to take place, eye contact is essential. It's important in delegation and making sure that people understand their role.*)

- **Q: Who had more power in this activity: the givers or the receivers?** (*Both had the same power. The givers were looking for people to give eye contact. If they didn't get it, it made the activity impossible. The receivers were also looking for eye contact so they could be effective.*)

- **Q: How was it different when you stopped and refocused on the activity?** *(I was more focused, and I concentrated on the activity.)*
- **Q: How different was it if you were a receiver versus a giver?** *(I was glad that people were looking at me so that I could throw the object to them.)*
- **Q: How did it feel as more and more objects were being tossed around?** *(It made me feel anxious, even though the objects were not real. I didn't want to drop the ball.)*
- **Q: How similar was this to the work environment, when things are being tossed at you all the time?** *(It's the same; people want more and more.)*
- **Q: How can you do it differently as a result of this activity?** *(Prioritize what's important versus what's nice to have. I can use eye contact to communicate whether something is urgent or not.)*
- **Q: How willing are you to use different resources if things get too overwhelming?** *(Very willing. I realize if I communicate with other people, there may be a different or easier way of getting things achieved.)*

Participant Action Plan

Give all of the players a copy of the following action plan. Ask them to complete it, and set up a time to review their results one week later. At that time, ask them what worked and what didn't work. What do they need to do to improve?

Be in the Moment Actions

The actions I will take as a result of the Be in the Moment activity are:

_____

_____

_____

_____

ONE WEEK LATER: What results have I gained from the Be in the Moment activity?

_____

_____

_____

_____

Activity 5

Loosen Up

Throw your heart over the bar and your body will follow.
  —Robert ("Bob") Bruce Mathias, American decathlete, two-time Olympic
  gold medalist, actor, and U.S. congressman for California (1930 to 2006)

Level of Risk

Low

Background and Purpose

This activity is designed to boost people's energy levels. In improvisation it is used as a warm-up right before the players rush onstage. It brings everyone together because of the eye contact given through the exercise. It also brings energy into our bodies, especially if it is a late night performance. And last, it quiets the mind and gets you out of your head. If an improviser was scared, thinking about past performances or troubled by the week's events, this activity helped to ground her and bring her back into the moment. After this activity, she could step onstage with all of her faculties alert and ready to meet the challenges of the show.

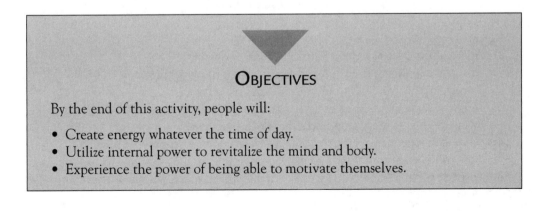

OBJECTIVES

By the end of this activity, people will:

- Create energy whatever the time of day.
- Utilize internal power to revitalize the mind and body.
- Experience the power of being able to motivate themselves.

Mini Lecture

This activity recently won an award in Las Vegas where a large corporation was providing a training conference for its employees. Several teams were asked to compete with each other by demonstrating an activity that would "get everybody involved and energized." The activity had to be one that people could do on their own if they felt tired in the middle of the day or if they needed to get motivated to do a project.

Being able to create energy is vital for those employees who are in a job where they are sitting down or they are isolated at home in a virtual reality setting. The ability to "fire yourself up" is essential when there are intense project deadlines to be met or when the energy slumps in the middle of the day, but the work pace still needs to be maintained. Many people think of motivation as something that someone else does for them. They think of it as an external power source that they can either read about in a book or learn from a class or workshop. When people rely on other people to boost their energy, they disempower themselves of the ability to do it for themselves. This business improv activity is designed to empower people to find the internal energy source within.

Overview of Activity

Participants stand and shake their limbs while simultaneously counting. The facilitator conducts it with increasing speed and volume.

Time

Instructions—2 minutes
Activity—5 minutes
Debriefing—5 minutes
Total time—12 minutes

STEPS TO FOLLOW

Round 1
1. You will need to do a demonstration for this exercise.
2. Ask participants to stand up and find room to move where they will not knock anything down or bump into other players.
3. Tell the participants they will be shaking their four limbs and finally their whole body to the rhythm of their counting up to 8.
4. They will repeat this pattern counting down one less number while increasing each round with speed and volume.
5. Instruct participants to make eye contact with as many people as they can during the exercise.
6. Do a quick demonstration.

Round 2

1. Instruct the participants to raise their right hand to start!
2. Begin shaking your right arm to the rhythm of counting up to 8.
3. Immediately begin shaking your left arm to the rhythm of counting up to 8.
4. Immediately begin shaking your right leg (kicking it in the air while balancing on the left) to the rhythm of counting up to 8.
5. Repeat this with your left leg and finally your whole body.
6. Immediately repeat this pattern with each of your four limbs, and then finally your whole body, except this time, count and shake up to 7 with more speed and volume.
7. Immediately repeat this pattern with each limb, except this time, count and shake up to 6 with more speed and volume.
8. Repeat this pattern counting all the way down to 1. Everyone should be out of breath.
9. Give a round of applause for completion!

▼

BENEFITS TO LOOK FOR

The ideas below echo the Loosen Up approach:

- **Go for it.** This is a go-for-it activity. As the leader, you must be willing to energize yourself and throw your whole self into the activity. And having fun is a great way to boost morale and increase team collaboration. Bringing out the shy people on a team will create more solutions and options when problem solving.
- **Get oxygen to the brain.** Unfortunately, we spend most of our days sitting at our desk. Our energy goes straight into our chair. Our brain needs oxygen to think, and exercise is a great way to pump blood up there. This exercise teaches people a quick, painless, and fun way to energize themselves and get "pumped up" and ready to rock 'n' roll at any time: at the beginning of a meeting, during an after-lunch food coma, and at any other point in the day that they feel the need to recharge.

Discussion Points

- **Q: How did that feel?** *(I felt silly to begin with, but once I got going with it, I had a lot of fun.)*

- **Q: How will this help you at work?** (*I can do this any time I feel myself lagging or drained of energy—it will help me remotivate myself.*)
- **Q: What did you think about the others taking part in the activity?** (*I liked the fact that everyone was so willing to join in—we are a great team.*)
- **Q: Can you see yourself using this activity when other people are around?** (*I am not going to leap up and start shaking my hands and feet in the middle of the office, but I will definitely do it in my own cube.*)
- **Q: Did anything surprise you about this activity?** (*We usually have meetings that are serious. This was a great diversion and a reminder that we can have fun and be energized at work.*)

Participant Action Plan

Give participants a copy of the following action plan. Ask them to complete it, and set up a time to review their results one week later. At that time, ask them what worked and what didn't work. What do they need to do to improve?

Loosen Up Actions

The actions I will take as a result of the Loosen Up activity are:

_____

_____

_____

_____

ONE WEEK LATER: What results have I gained from the Loosen Up activity?

_____

_____

_____

_____

Activity 6

Thank You

Every interpersonal situation has a solution in which everyone wins.

> —Del Close, considered one of the premier influences on
> modern improvisational theater, actor, improviser, writer,
> teacher, and coauthor of the book *Truth in Comedy*
> (March 9, 1934, to March 4, 1999)

Level of Risk

Low

Background and Purpose

This activity is about supporting communication and creating a safe environment in which people can take risks and know that whatever they say is going to be accepted. We don't actually go onstage and say, "Thank you!" every time someone does something great or says something witty or even supports us by leaping into a scene. But in our minds we are all saying, "Thank you, thank you, thank you!" Saying "thank you" creates validation and a positive environment in which communication is accepted. It acknowledges and validates the message of others.

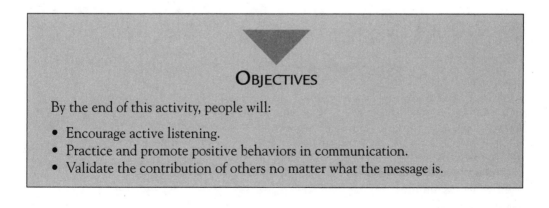

OBJECTIVES

By the end of this activity, people will:

- Encourage active listening.
- Practice and promote positive behaviors in communication.
- Validate the contribution of others no matter what the message is.

Mini Lecture

In the business environment, "offer and acceptance" has the same positive effect that players experience when performing improv onstage: it establishes an environment in which ideas can be put forward without fear of disagreement. This, in turn, builds an atmosphere of creativity and collaboration. In many ways being at work is not much different from being onstage: people are watching the way others perform. In large corporations, managers are actually required to give *performance reviews*! If employees are seen to be difficult, thorny, or negative, it not only disrupts their relationship with colleagues but it also has a trickle-down negative effect on the customers.

"Thank you." These two words are so commonplace that it's sometimes easy to forget to say them, yet saying these words is one of the simplest ways to make people feel valid, important, and respected. Saying "thank you" is a great way to start, grow, and keep relationships. Consider this story about Charles Plumb, a U.S. Navy jet pilot who served in Vietnam. One day, he and his wife were in a restaurant when a man came up and said, "You're Plumb, aren't you? You flew jet fighters in Vietnam from the aircraft carrier USS *Kitty Hawk*, and you were shot down."

"How in the world did you know that?" asked Plumb.

"I packed your parachute," the man replied. Plumb gasped in surprise and gratitude. The man pumped his hand and said, "I guess it worked!"

Plumb assured him, "It sure did. If your chute hadn't worked, I wouldn't be here today."

Plumb couldn't sleep that night, thinking about the man who had had his fate in his hands. "I wonder how many times I might have seen him and not even said 'Good morning, how are you?' or anything because, you see, I was a fighter pilot and he was just a sailor. Sometimes in the daily challenges that life gives us, we miss what is really important. We may fail to say hello, please, or thank you, congratulate someone on something wonderful that has happened to him or her, give a compliment, or just do something nice for no reason. As you go through this week, this month, this year, recognize people who pack your parachutes."

Overview of Activity

Participants will find a partner and have a conversation. The only instruction is that they must say "thank you" to start each sentence.

Time

Instructions—4 minutes
Each round—2 to 3 minutes
Debriefing—8 minutes
Total time—18 minutes

STEPS TO FOLLOW

Round 1

1. Have all the participants team up with a partner whom they do not know that well.
2. In pairs, the participants will hold a conversation about any topic.
3. The only rule is that they must say "thank you" before responding to their partner.

Round 2

Repeat the exercise, only this time, use different words or sounds to convey the spirit of "thank you."

Round 3

Repeat the exercise, only this time, use nonverbal ways to say "thank you."

Round 1 Example

Person A: "I went to Greece for my vacation last year, and I tried parasailing for the first time."

Person B: "Thank you. I've never done that. How was it?"

Person A: "Thank you. It was really scary to begin with, but once I was up there, I felt really safe."

Person B: "Thank you. I'm afraid of heights. I prefer being on land."

Round 2 Example

Person A: "I just bought a new puppy. She barked all last night."

Person B: "I am grateful to you. That must have driven you crazy. Have you had a dog before?"

Person A: "I appreciate you. It's my second dog, I got her because the other one is getting old. What about you? Do you have pets?"

Person B: "Couldn't have done this without you. Yes, I'm a cat person … cats and fish."

Round 3 Example

Person A: "Did you see our new product range? It's really cool."

Person B: (Nods head approvingly) "Yes, I've used it a couple of times. It cuts downtime in half."

Person A: (Open-palms hand gesture) "Yes, the customers love it. The price point is good also."

Person B: (Raises eyebrows and smiles) "I agree. We're way ahead of the competition."

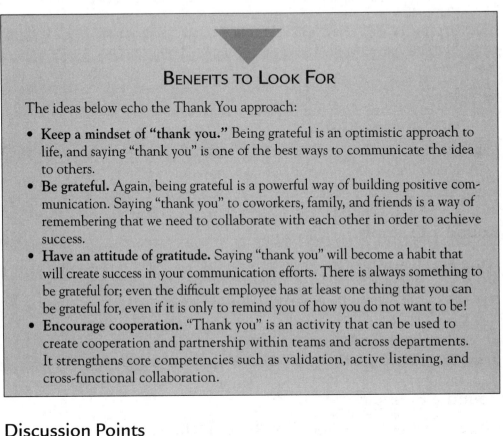

Benefits to Look For

The ideas below echo the Thank You approach:

- **Keep a mindset of "thank you."** Being grateful is an optimistic approach to life, and saying "thank you" is one of the best ways to communicate the idea to others.
- **Be grateful.** Again, being grateful is a powerful way of building positive communication. Saying "thank you" to coworkers, family, and friends is a way of remembering that we need to collaborate with each other in order to achieve success.
- **Have an attitude of gratitude.** Saying "thank you" will become a habit that will create success in your communication efforts. There is always something to be grateful for; even the difficult employee has at least one thing that you can be grateful for, even if it is only to remind you of how you do not want to be!
- **Encourage cooperation.** "Thank you" is an activity that can be used to create cooperation and partnership within teams and across departments. It strengthens core competencies such as validation, active listening, and cross-functional collaboration.

Discussion Points

- **Q: How did it feel when saying "thank you" did not seem to fit?** (*It was distracting because I felt I wasn't being truthful. I decided to play along anyhow, and my partner didn't seem to notice.*)
- **Q: How did it feel when someone said "thank you"?** (*I felt valued. I felt good. I could relate to my partner when I felt I was being understood and validated.*)
- **Q: How did it feel to say "thank you" without using words?** (*It was easy; I use hand gestures a lot anyway.*)
- **Q: How can we keep the spirit of the activity alive without saying "thank you"?** (*Body language. Emotional tones that are thankful and supportive.*)
- **Q: What if "thank you" doesn't fit the conversation?** (*Sometimes saying "thank you" does feel awkward, but the more I use it, the more it becomes a habit of being grateful and accepting what others have to say.*)

- **Q: Did any of you sometimes not agree with your partner but you had to say "thank you" anyway?** (*Saying "thank you" doesn't mean that I necessarily agree with or go along with what the other person is saying. "Thank you" is simply a way of acknowledging the other person's communication and validating that I am listening.*)
- **Q: Did any of you find the nonverbal "thank you" hard?** (*Body language and tonality have enormous power in communication. Nonverbal cues can have a huge impact in sending out my message of thanks. A smile really can say a thousand words.*)

Participant Action Plan

Think about the last time you did a favor for someone or gave time or money to a charity or an organization. Did the person you were working with say "thank you"? If you gave money, did you get a thank-you note in return? If you didn't get a note, you probably remember, and you were not very happy that your generosity, however big or small, did not get acknowledged.

When you show appreciation to fellow employees, you invite them into your "organizational family" and increase their commitment and their feelings of validation and respect.

Whether your organization is all volunteer or it has paid staff, the people that bring your programs to life are people that spend a lot of time together. The first opportunity to build a habit of saying "thank you" is within this group.

Provide all of the participants with a copy the following action plan. Ask them to complete it, and set up a time to review their results one week later. At that time, ask them what has worked and what has not worked. What do they need to do to improve?

Thank You Actions

Here are a few simple and creative ways to say "thank you":

Give praise. Praise something your colleague or coworker has done well. Identify the specific actions that you found admirable and tell the entire staff, not just the person you are appreciating.

Share food. Almost everyone loves food. Take coworkers to lunch to express your appreciation for all of their hard work, or bring homemade cookies or cupcakes into the office to share.

Make a tradition. Create a fun tradition. Whether your tradition falls around a holiday or you make up your own, getting everyone involved brings the group together.

Share stories. Share success stories with your coworkers. Letting them know what their work means to someone else can have more impact than anything you might say.

Based on the above ideas, the actions I will take as a result of the Thank You activity are:

_____

_____

_____

_____

ONE WEEK LATER: What results have I gained from the Thank You activity?

_____

_____

_____

_____

Activity 7

Gratitude

All of us kids ended up "doing Mom." There are four of us who've tried show business. Five if you insist on counting my sister the nun, who does liturgical dance.

—Bill Murray, improviser, actor, author

Level of Risk

High

Background and Purpose

As a player, I am so thankful when another player comes onstage to support me in the performance. If the other player didn't appear, I would be standing alone, and the audience would be disappointed, I'd be disappointed, and the relationship with my team would be badly affected! The feeling we give each other as an ensemble is the spirit of thanks, and it's one of the most important concepts in improv. When players know that the communication they offer will be accepted by other players, it is liberating and provides the freedom to be creative and spontaneous. The concept of "offer and acceptance" and being thankful creates an environment of support and validation, which enables all the players to know that whatever they put forward as an idea, they do not have to fear rejection, denial, or a negative response.

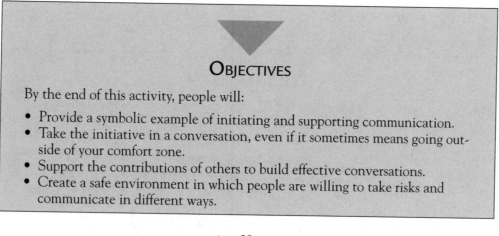

OBJECTIVES

By the end of this activity, people will:

- Provide a symbolic example of initiating and supporting communication.
- Take the initiative in a conversation, even if it sometimes means going outside of your comfort zone.
- Support the contributions of others to build effective conversations.
- Create a safe environment in which people are willing to take risks and communicate in different ways.

Mini Lecture

In the work environment we are often put into uncomfortable positions such as presenting a new initiative to the team, managing change, and handling difficult customers. When we are uncomfortable, we often become embarrassed because we are afraid of rejection, failure, and in some cases even losing our job. The problem, however, with being uncomfortable is that we often want to hide away and not be seen; in the workplace this does not help us. For one thing, everyone knows when a person is hiding, and for another, it does not help the other team players who are also, in one way or another, pushing through their own barriers.

When we stay in our comfort zones, we are in danger of becoming the kind of people who don't like change, who don't like to use new systems, and who don't care much for new employees. When we step outside our comfort zones, we build our strength and become the optimistic innovators of change. Instead of turning into an experienced employee who doesn't like to share information with the new employees, we expand our horizons and as a result have more to offer in terms of skill, talent, and collaboration.

Overview of Activity

Participants form a circle. In the middle of the circle, participant (A) will strike and hold a pose, like a statue. Another participant (B) will join (A) and strike a complementary or supportive pose. (A) thanks (B) and returns to the outer circle. (B) remains, and a new participant (C) steps out and the process begins again. As the exercise continues, multiple participants enter and everyone suggests titles for the statue.

Time

Instructions—5 minutes
One continual round—5 to 10 minutes
Debriefing—10 minutes
Total time—25 minutes

STEPS TO FOLLOW

1. Have participants form a circle and ask for a brave volunteer (A) to step into the middle of the circle. Make sure you and the rest of the people standing in the circle support (A) by thanking and applauding (A)'s courage. These responses create a supportive environment.
2. Ask (A) to strike and hold a pose as if (A) were a statue. It can be any type of pose (A) wishes to pick. An example to use is a weight lifting pose. Whatever pose (A) chooses, tell (A) it is "perfect."

3. Now ask someone else (B) in the circle to join (A) in the middle. If no one moves, say, "Not everyone at once!" Remind them of the poor person (A) who needs their support.

4. As (B) walks into the center, ask (B) to strike a pose that complements or supports (A)'s pose. For example, if (A) is lifting weights, (B) can also lift weights or be a spotter.

5. After (B) strikes a complementary or supportive pose, (A) says "thank you" to (B) and returns to the outer circle. Now (B) is posing alone in the middle.

6. Ask for a new volunteer (C) to step out into the middle of the circle and strike a complementary pose to (B). (B) says "thank you" and leaves, and the process continues.

7. Remember to encourage the group to step out quicker and not leave people alone in the circle, just to jump in, and so on. Everyone in the circle should have stepped into the middle and posed as a statue at least once.

8. You can also bring two people into the middle of the circle or even several people.

9. You can also have three or four people standing on the outside to title the statue. For example, titles might be "The Weight Lifting Competition!" or "Pumped Up!"

▼

BENEFITS TO LOOK FOR

The ideas below echo the Gratitude approach:

- **Initiate a conversation.** If you ask a group of people to raise their hands, even if they are shy, most people raise their hands. The way to get around being shy is to participate and initiate conversation. Take the lead, ask questions, actively listen, and be curious and interested about your team.

- **Build rapport.** One of the best ways to build rapport is to support other people in what they are doing. Communicate through eye contact and *reframing* (that is, repeating back in your own words) what they just said.

- **Create a safe environment.** Some people think it's up to others to create a safe environment—"if other people start doing it, then I will too." Creating any kind of supportive environment begins by having a willingness to do something different—in this case to support your team and not allow anyone to stand alone feeling uncomfortable.

Discussion Points

- **Q: How did it feel being in the middle?** *(It was really uncomfortable when no one joined me. After someone joined me, I felt supported. The more we did the activity, the easier it felt.)*
- **Q: How did it feel being on the outside?** *(I felt bad that no one went forward. I found myself going out just so other people wouldn't be alone. I didn't have a good idea so I didn't go out.)*
- **Q: Did you not act on an idea you had, and why?** *(I didn't feel creative. Everyone else's ideas were much better. I wasn't quick enough.)*
- **Q: How do you stop your own critic from preventing action?** *(Stop telling myself I can't do it or I'm not good enough or that my ideas suck.)*
- **Q: How did it feel to "go for it" and improvise?** *(It was nice. I like to push myself to do things when I feel scared.)*

Participant Action Plan

Provide all of the participants with a copy of the following action plan. Ask them to think of one thing that they will do differently as a result of this activity. If possible, set up a time to review their results one week later. At that time, ask them what has worked and what has not worked. What do they need to do to improve?

Gratitude Actions

The actions I will take as a result of the Gratitude activity are:

_____

_____

_____

_____

ONE WEEK LATER: What results have I gained from the Gratitude activity?

_____

_____

_____

_____

Activity 8

Buzzwords, Acronyms, and Jargon

You can discover more about a person in an hour of play than in a year of conversation.
—Plato, 428 BC, classical Greek philosopher, mathematician, writer of
philosophical dialogues, and founder of the Academy of Athens, the first
institution of higher learning in the Western world

Level of Risk

Low

Background and Purpose

Jargon and buzzwords are a special language used by people who work in a particular area or who have a common interest. In improv, buzzwords are like inside jokes, and they can isolate the audience because the improvisers are then communicating in their own language. It's not manipulative or done on purpose; sometimes improvisers actually forget that there is an audience sitting there. We are in our own little world, laughing and having fun in our scenes, oblivious to the fact that the audience might not understand. In improv we have lots of jargon words, such as *calling out* and *pimping*. It seems like any time people work closely together, they use buzzwords and jargon. It's great to make strong connections, but for the outsiders it's not so much fun. Calling out is a fun way of saying you made a mistake. Pimping is the opposite, where you force someone to be a character or do something that he or she doesn't want to do—like sing or dance.

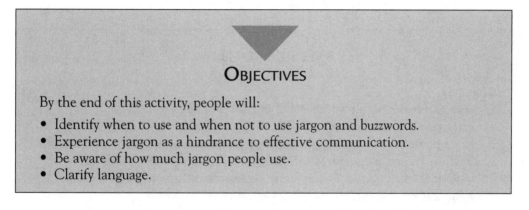

OBJECTIVES

By the end of this activity, people will:

- Identify when to use and when not to use jargon and buzzwords.
- Experience jargon as a hindrance to effective communication.
- Be aware of how much jargon people use.
- Clarify language.

Mini Lecture

There is no doubt that jargon is useful for keeping things short and simple. Three letters like "FBI" are much easier to say than the "Federal Bureau of Investigation." Public jargon is useful because most people understand what it means, but within a company or an organization, the jargon is known only to the people within it, and even then, the jargon may not cross divisional or departmental boundaries. Cross-functional teams may not understand each other's jargon. As Sue in a large pharmaceutical company said, "I hate going to some meetings because I don't know what the jargon means in my own company. I switch off and start doodling, texting, or doing other work."

There's nothing wrong with using jargon as long as it is at the appropriate time and place. As one manager said, "They just changed the jargon. Everyone knew what things used to mean, but now, no one has a clue what anyone is talking about." In order to learn, adults have to know what terms mean and why they are important. Many times they can figure things out, but unless people are told or have read what the latest buzzword means, it's impossible to decipher. In reality, most adults don't ask. They would rather nod their head and pretend they understand than appear stupid and out of the loop!

Overview of Activity

Have enough space for players to team up. Have players team up with people they don't know very well. In round 1, groups of four to five people will strike up a conversation in which the participants pitch in as much jargon and as many buzzwords and acronyms as they can possibly use. In round 2, the same people will each explain what they were talking about, using plain language as if they were brand new employees, fresh into the system, or just out of college.

Time

Instructions—5 minutes
Each round—3 to 4 minutes
Debriefing—10 minutes
Total time—23 minutes

STEPS TO FOLLOW

Round 1
1. As a group, discuss all work-related buzzwords, jargon terms, and acronyms. (Write them on a flip chart if necessary.)
2. Have participants form groups of four to six people.
3. In these groups, participants will have a conversation about work and include as much jargon and as many buzzwords and acronyms as possible.
4. After a few minutes, call out, "Freeze!" and explain round 2.

Round 2

Now have the groups hold another conversation, but this time have them speak as if their partners were brand new employees, fresh into the system, or just out of college.

▼

BENEFITS TO LOOK FOR

The ideas below echo the Buzzwords, Acronyms, and Jargon approach:

- **Be aware of your speech.** Jargon is a great tool for connecting people who are working on similar projects, but it is not useful when other people are present who do not possess the same type of knowledge.
- **Regulate language.** Buzzwords can help generations feel connected. But they can also make different generations feel unconnected. Awareness is the first step in knowing when and when not to use buzzwords.
- **Think before you speak.** When customers do not understand the jargon, they won't ask for an explanation. They'll just go to the competition where they hope to understand what everyone is talking about.

Discussion Points

- **Q: If the conversation got confusing, how did you handle it?** (*I had no idea what was going on, but I didn't like to ask and appear dumb. Sometimes I got confused about what I was saying.*)
- **Q: What do you do if you don't understand your own company jargon?** (*Sometimes it happens in meetings, and I just start talking to myself or texting under the table.*)
- **Q: What are some ways to overcome jargon?** (*I can let people know that I don't understand. I can ask for the full words to be written out in the meeting agendas.*)

Participant Action Plan

Ask participants to partner up and give them five minutes to discuss what actions they will take as a result of this activity. Provide participants with a copy of the following action plan and ask them to complete it. Set up a time to review their results one week later. At that time, ask them what has worked and what has not worked. What do they need to do to improve?

Buzzwords, Acronyms, and Jargon Actions

The actions I will take as a result of the Buzzwords, Acronyms, and Jargon activity are:

_____

_____

_____

_____

ONE WEEK LATER: What results have I gained from the Buzzwords, Acronyms, and Jargon activity?

_____

_____

_____

_____

Activity 9

The Interrupter

When your work speaks for itself, don't interrupt.
> —Henry J. Kaiser, an American industrialist who became known
> as the father of modern American shipbuilding (1882 to 1967)

Level of Risk

Low

Background and Purpose

I can't even begin to tell you how terrible a crime it is to interrupt a fellow improviser on stage. It's hammered into us at the very earliest stages of learning. The reasoning behind it is simple: basically, when you interrupt people you are saying that (a) you are not listening, (b) you are somewhere else, (c) what they have to say is irrelevant to you, and (d) you think your thoughts and ideas are better than theirs. It does not bode well for creating a trusting collaborative relationship. People who interrupt would not last long in any improv group because they are not team players, and improv is all about being on a team.

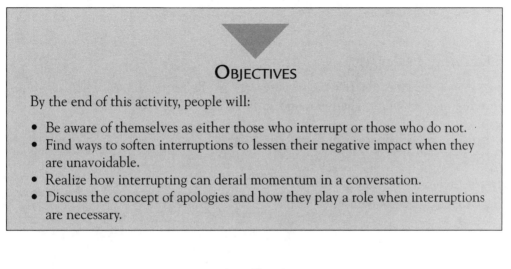

OBJECTIVES

By the end of this activity, people will:

- Be aware of themselves as either those who interrupt or those who do not.
- Find ways to soften interruptions to lessen their negative impact when they are unavoidable.
- Realize how interrupting can derail momentum in a conversation.
- Discuss the concept of apologies and how they play a role when interruptions are necessary.

Mini Lecture

When an angry customer needs to vent, one of the worst things you can do is interrupt. Sometimes, however, interruptions are necessary, especially if you have a customer telling a long story and you have other customers waiting. When we designed a telemarketing workshop for an airline company, we learned that one of its big problems was that many customers talked for too long; the customer service representatives didn't have enough time to answer all the calls, and having lengthy conversations with some customers meant that other customers were put on hold—not a good plan for any company that is interested in providing excellent customer service.

The best way to use interruption as a way to steer the conversation is by *reframing* what the customer just said:

Mr. Long: "… and my dog is coming with us, our cat couldn't come because she doesn't travel well, but our dog …"

Ms. Short: "That's wonderful. I love dogs too, so tell me what date are you returning with your dog?"

Interruptions have advantages and disadvantages, and knowing the power of an interruption is an important part of this activity. Interrupting a colleague who is describing an idea or asking for support is a way of saying that you are not interested in what she has to say. This has an adverse effect on collaboration, team building, and creating a supportive work environment.

Maybe the best thing we can do to be a better listener is to imagine that we have a drop of glue on our lips keeping our mouth closed—that would definitely keep us from interrupting. Think about listening more than talking; make the conversation about the other person. When you do this, you will interrupt less, because all of the reasons we interrupt are about us; when we make the conversation about the other person, we naturally interrupt less.

Overview of Activity

In pairs, participants will have a conversation. In the first round, they will take turns interrupting each other. Then in round 2, they will practice apologizing.

Time

Instructions—3 to 4 minutes
Each round—2 to 3 minutes
Debriefing—5 minutes
Total time—18 minutes

STEPS TO FOLLOW

Round 1

1. Have all the participants team up with a partner, preferably someone they don't know very well.
2. Ask one person in each pair to raise his or her hand. They will be the (A)s. The others will be the (B)s.
3. Tell the participants, in pairs, to have a conversation about anything they like. The (A)s will begin the conversation.
4. The (B)s' role is to be the interrupter, meaning their job is to frequently interrupt.

Round 2

1. Say, "(A), it is time for revenge. You will now be the interrupter with the added stipulation of apologizing after the interruption. You will frequently interrupt your partner, then quickly apologize and let him or her continue."
2. Give an example of how this might sound by demonstrating with a participant. Ask your partner to start talking about anything; then you interrupt and apologize.

Round 2 Example

Person A: "I went to Mexico for my vacation …"

Person B: "Vacation! Let me tell you about the best vacation ever! Oh, gosh, I'm sorry. Please continue …"

Person A: "I was just saying that it was a blast. We swam in the …"

Person B: "I love to swim! I almost made it to the state finals back in high school. Whoops! Please forgive me."

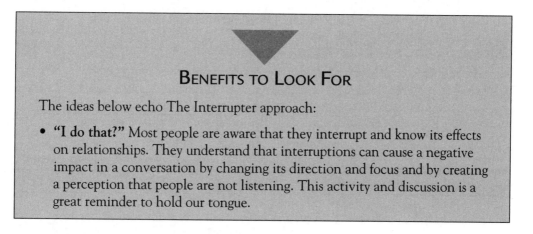

BENEFITS TO LOOK FOR

The ideas below echo The Interrupter approach:

- **"I do that?"** Most people are aware that they interrupt and know its effects on relationships. They understand that interruptions can cause a negative impact in a conversation by changing its direction and focus and by creating a perception that people are not listening. This activity and discussion is a great reminder to hold our tongue.

> • **Make apologies.** When an interruption is unavoidable, whether it's to clarify or add on, sometimes we have find ways to soften the interruption to lessen its negative impact. Acknowledging the fact that you are interrupting has amazing benefits. It shows that you respect the thoughts and ideas of the person you are communicating with and that you do want to hear that person. Just don't use apologies too much!

Discussion Points

- **Q: How did you get through your conversations despite being interrupted?** (*I found it hard to focus. Our conversation was all over the place and sent me off on tangents.*)
- **Q: How did the first apology feel? And after a while?** (*The first few times it made me feel better. After a while it was annoying and sounded false.*)
- **Q: Why do people interrupt?** (*Triggers ... something triggers a thought and they want to share it. They stop paying attention. Interruptions bring attention back to themselves. Our brains operate faster than we can speak, and we want to get out all our words.*)
- **Q: When are there times when interrupting is necessary?** (*I'm short on time. I don't understand what was said. A decision needs to be made. We need to find a different time to talk.*)
- **Q: What are some ways you can manage interruptions?** (*I can be understanding. I can say something like "Before I forget, ..."*)

Participant Action Plan

Ask participants to pair up and discuss what they are going to do in order to know the advantages and disadvantages of interruptions. Provide participants with a copy of the following action plan. Ask them to complete it, and set up a time to review their results one week later. At that time, ask them what has worked and what has not worked. What do they need to do to improve?

The Interrupter Actions

The actions I will take as a result of The Interrupter activity are:

_____

_____

_____

_____

ONE WEEK LATER: What results have I gained from The Interrupter activity?

_____

_____

_____

_____

Activity 10

Offering Support

If the community is happy, then they support your business, and if your business is doing well, then you can give back even more to the community.

—Magic Johnson, a retired American professional basketball player who played point guard for the Los Angeles Lakers and won the All-Star MVP Award

Level of Risk

Medium

Background and Purpose

There are many times in improvisation when players draw a blank or feel stuck in a scene. Thank goodness there are people around to jump in and save the day. It can happen at any time during a show, even right at the top when the audience provides a suggestion. At the beginning of every improvisation show, the players ask the audience for a word or phrase to start the scene—*then the audience knows that the show is completely made up right in front of their eyes*. But if someone from the back row yells, "Simile!" Bam … you're done for. You're standing right there onstage in front of an entire audience stuck in your head thinking all kinds of things like, "What is a simile again?" Before you know it, five seconds have gone by, which onstage feels like an eternity, and you still haven't moved or started a scene. That's when you just need to start speaking and trust that you will support the offer in an intelligent way; that's also when other players jump in and make the scene come alive in a new and unexpected way.

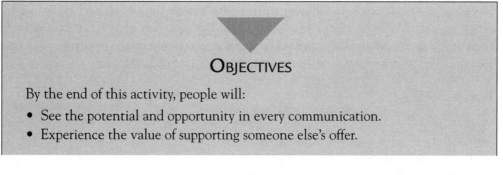

▼ Objectives

By the end of this activity, people will:

- See the potential and opportunity in every communication.
- Experience the value of supporting someone else's offer.

- Experience the value of initiating offerings that enable support.
- Explore different ways to indicate your support by keeping the communication process positive and moving forward.

Mini Lecture

There is no one on the planet who does not need support in one way or another—in our personal lives and our work lives, we all need people. Imagine, for example, if no one had invented electricity, gasoline, or elevators: most of us would be walking everywhere, going to bed early when the candle was finished, and walking up flights of stairs. The laptop would never have been invented without the support of many people.

At work we rely on others to such a huge degree that we almost forget the level of support that we receive every day. For example, we rely on people to clean our offices, provide maintenance and service, and create change initiatives, strategies, and core values. Many companies provide health insurance and other benefits, all of which are designed to support the employees so that they can come to work free of anxiety and worry. But this activity is not about the support that the company provides, because people have different points of view about that; some think it's wonderful, and others think it is not enough.

This activity is about you supporting your colleagues, coworkers, and customers—the people you come into contact with every day. We were recently providing training at the Veterans' Association, and we noticed that all of the employees had a very clear and definite view of why they were working there. When asked, "What is your mission?" they all said, "To provide service to the veterans." And what they all discovered was that the more they supported their colleagues in doing their job, the more services they were able to provide to the veterans.

Whatever your job and wherever you work, you can depend on the fact that what you do makes a huge difference. If you support your colleagues, coworkers, and customers, you are making a positive difference; if not, then you are making a negative difference. The real question is this: what kind of a difference do you want to make in the world? With this activity you will understand the importance of making a positive difference.

Overview of Activity

Standing in a circle, each participant turns to the person on his left and gives him an imaginary gift. Whoever opens the imaginary gift has to decide what it is and announce it to the rest of the circle. The giver of the imaginary gift then has to justify why he gave the gift. The pattern repeats until everyone in the circle has had a turn.

Time

Instructions—5 minutes
Each round—5 to 10 minutes
Debriefing—5 minutes
Total time—15 minutes

STEPS TO FOLLOW

1. Have everyone get into a circle. If there are more than 20 participants, you will want to divide them into two groups.
2. Have one person raise her hand. She will be Person A and start the activity.
3. Person A will give an imaginary gift to the person on her left, Person B.
4. Person B will open the gift and thank Person A for giving him the imaginary gift, labeling what it is by saying, "Thank you for the XXX."
5. Person A will need to justify why she gave Person B the XXX. (You might want to demonstrate this with a participant.)
6. After Person A has finished explaining her reason for giving Person B that particular gift, B will then turn to the person on his left, Person C, and give her a different imaginary gift.
7. Person C will then open the gift and thank Person B for giving her the imaginary gift, labeling it like this: "Thank you for the XXX."
8. Person B will then justify why he gave Person C an XXX.
9. This repeats until everyone has had a turn.

Example

Person A gives Person B an imaginary gift:

Person B: "Thank you for the … sweater!"

Person A: "Well, I know you have an iron deficiency and you're always cold. I got it from North Face so you could go climb Mount Everest and never get sick."

Immediately, Person B then gives Person C an imaginary gift:

Person C: "Oh, thank you for the … pink lipstick!"

Person B: "Well, I know you love the color pink, and it really does match your eyes. And I know how you hate to have chapped lips so I got you this L'Oréal lip schmeer."

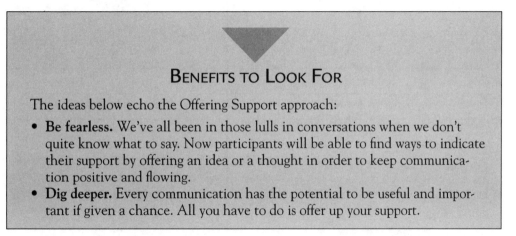

▼ BENEFITS TO LOOK FOR

The ideas below echo the Offering Support approach:

- **Be fearless.** We've all been in those lulls in conversations when we don't quite know what to say. Now participants will be able to find ways to indicate their support by offering an idea or a thought in order to keep communication positive and flowing.
- **Dig deeper.** Every communication has the potential to be useful and important if given a chance. All you have to do is offer up your support.

Discussion Points

- **Q: Which did you enjoy more: receiving the gift or having your gift idea validated? Why?** (*When they confirmed my offer, it made me feel brilliant! And vice versa!*)
- **Q: Which did you find more difficult: coming up with a gift or justifying a gift? Why?** (*Both were equally difficult. I found giving the gift was difficult because I was judging my idea too much. I found the justifying difficult because I literally blanked.*)
- **Q: What can you do to offer support in a conversation to help stimulate it?** (*Politely try and remind the people I'm talking to of what they were saying to see if they remember. I can direct the conversation to a different topic.*)
- **Q: How does this activity translate to business?** (*It's a metaphor for open communication. I have to offer support to my customers and validate their needs, wants, and questions.*)

Participant Action Plan

Have everyone work in groups of four to five people and discuss what they will do differently as a result of this activity. Provide all of the participants with a copy of the following action plan. Ask them to complete it, and set up a time to review their results one week later. At that time, ask them what has worked and what has not worked. What do they need to do to improve?

Offering Support Actions

The actions I will take as a result of the Offering Support activity are:

_____

_____

_____

_____

ONE WEEK LATER: What results have I gained from the Offering Support activity?

_____

_____

_____

_____

Activity 11

Acceptance

Acceptance is not love. You love a person because he or she has lovable traits, but you accept everybody just because they're alive and human.

—Albert Ellis, American psychologist and founder of
cognitive-behavioral therapies (1913 to 2007)

Level of Risk

High

Background and Purpose

I don't have to like what my fellow improvisers say or do, but I do have to accept it. If I don't, the scene stops or turns into a conflict. For example, imagine if my fellow improviser comes onstage and says, "Hello, Dad!" and I say, "I'm not your dad." Where can the scene go from there? Where can the conversation go? Nowhere!

It doesn't matter what I have going on in my head. I could have a completely different story. I could be thinking that I am a mother or I am a horse, but if my scene partner speaks first and says, "Hello, Dad!" I have to drop what I am thinking and go along with the scene: I am now a dad.

What if instead I were to say, "I'm not your dad"? Then my scene partner would have to say, "Oh, okay, I'm sorry. What are you?" If at this point I said, "I am a horse, and you're a horse," then the audience would be watching a very disjointed scene, which would be boring and uncomfortable.

And, apart from the audience's losing out, the ramifications of nonacceptance would be huge to the improv team. I would know that my scene partner only wanted to play by her rules, which would mean that I couldn't add any creativity and I would have to go with whatever she said. Let me tell you, that would not be fun. I will not want to work with this person anymore because she doesn't want to collaborate. She wants to work by herself.

▼

OBJECTIVES

By the end of this activity, people will:

- Be willing to receive information and messages more easily.
- Trust themselves and strengthen their team connections.
- Take risks and tune in to their spontaneous nature.
- Be encouraged to take the initiative within a group environment.

Mini Lecture

In business improv, acceptance is essential to collaborative teamwork, innovative change, and creative problem solving. Acceptance is a written or verbal indication that somebody agrees to an invitation; it is the willingness to believe that something is true or sufficiently tolerable that we can listen to it without protesting. When people experience change, they often go through a period of anger, denial, or upset, but if the situation cannot be changed, then acceptance is a big key to moving forward. Change the things that you can change and accept the things that you cannot.

Acceptance is also a willingness to treat somebody as a member of a group, or allow somebody to join in. In the workplace, acceptance helps coworkers, colleagues, and customers get along and create new opportunities. Not only that, when we accept other people, we can more easily overcome conflict, upset, and worry.

It's not always obvious in the workplace when we don't fully accept other people, but we can easily make other people feel uncomfortable and not accepted when we don't listen to them, when we interrupt, or when we roll our eyes when they bring new ideas to the table even though the new and creative ideas might actually work.

Some reasons that acceptance may be difficult for some people is that they like to be in control, they fear losing job security, or they hold beliefs that are so different from those of the other people they work with that they just can't tolerate the differences. The problem with nonacceptance in today's world is that the marketplace is so diverse— our customers, coworkers, and colleagues come from many different cultures and ethnic backgrounds—that if we don't accept each other, then we are in danger of losing not just our business but also our sense of well-being and our sense of support. In business improv, acceptance is essential to collaborative teamwork and innovative change.

Overview of Activity

This is a physical exercise. The facilitator will shout a location or environment, and the participants will all respond with "yes, let's" and then populate that environment, becoming people or objects active in the new environment. The participants will keep adapting to the new environment as the locations continue to change.

Time

Instructions—4 minutes
Each round—30 seconds to 1 minute
Debriefing—5 minutes
Total time—10 minutes

STEPS TO FOLLOW

1. Instruct the participants to walk around the room.
2. Tell them you will shout out a location, and they must respond by saying, "Yes, let's go to the ... *location!*" and immediately populate that environment and either become something or someone within that environment. For example, if you say, "Let's go to the beach," they would respond, "Yes, let's go to the beach!" and instantaneously they'd become a swimmer, a volleyball player, a shark, or a sand castle. Other locations can include: fairgrounds, convention center, library, gym, cafeteria, the moon, golf outing, trade show, center of the earth, wedding.
3. The only stipulation is that there can be only one of each object or person in any environment. For example, if they are a sunbather and see another person sunbathing, they must change what they're doing or find a way to collaborate with that person.

▼

BENEFITS TO LOOK FOR

The ideas below echo the Acceptance approach:

- **Practice "yes, and."** Employing the "yes, and" philosophy will help you in taking risks and initiating communication so you can grow more and more effective relationships.
- **Take initiative.** You can take charge even when responding to a message.
- **Risk it.** Communication within a group can require you to jump in and put your contribution out there, even if you think it's not worthy or even if you think someone else will think it's not worthy. The point is to contribute.

Discussion Points

- **Q: How did you feel as you listened to the instructions?** (*I didn't think it was a smart idea. I was excited. I was a little judgmental but ready to do it.*)
- **Q: What did you do if you had a great idea and someone was already doing it?** (*I thought of something else. I thought of what would be unexpected.*)
- **Q: How did you adjust to other people's ideas?** (*They inspired me, and I thought of something to go with them, something new; for example, I thought of sunbathing on the beach but someone else was sunbathing, so I became a beach umbrella.*)
- **Q: How does this exercise relate to your customers?** (*I need to be supportive and helpful with them.*)

Participant Action Plan

Have participants pair up and discuss the actions they will take as a result of this activity. Provide all the participants with a copy of the following action plan. Ask them to complete it, and set up a time to review their results one week later. At that time, ask them what has worked and what has not worked. What do they need to do to improve?

Acceptance Actions

The actions I will take as a result of the Acceptance activity are:

_____

_____

_____

_____

ONE WEEK LATER: What results have I gained from the Acceptance activity?

_____

_____

_____

_____

You Should, You Could, You Would

My ideas about how to command respect have changed. … I've learned that you can't demand it, or whack it out of people with a two-by-four. You have to cultivate it, in yourself and those around you.

—Pat Summitt, women's basketball coach, University of Tennessee

Level of Risk

Low

Background and Purpose

Advice is like opinions: everyone's got one. We seem to love giving it and rarely follow it. In improvisation we tend to make strong declarative statements building as we go with as few questions as possible. We are taught to initiate statements with a lot of specific detail in them.

But if we notice that our scene partners are on a different page, lost, or confused and need our help, we try and communicate in a way that allows them to be creative. We empower them to solve their own problems with as few directives as possible.

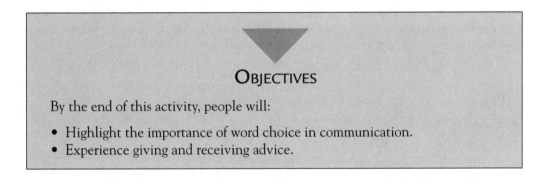

OBJECTIVES

By the end of this activity, people will:

- Highlight the importance of word choice in communication.
- Experience giving and receiving advice.

Mini Lecture

Good coaches empower people by treating them as being whole and already having the answer within themselves. Coaches who are realistic and honest about what people can achieve—even when it's hard—are the kind of coaches people look up to. Good coaches have the ability to speak the straight truth or facts without making people feel bad.

In business, people want a coach or mentor who pushes them to reach their goals in the right way. The goals shouldn't be too easy—"it's just a game, so go have fun." Good coaches should train people well and encourage with positive feedback. Whether we are coaches, mentors, or managers, we all have the ability to make a difference. The way we use our words creates a positive "can-do" environment or a negative "can't-do" environment.

In this activity, the participants are looking at their choice of words and how they would handle situations in terms of giving advice and feedback, or just communicating in general. It's about letting people know they're doing well but not so much that we make them overconfident if they still have things to learn. Most coaches are not afraid to get tough when it's needed; they let people know if they're not doing their job.

If you close your eyes for a moment and think about telling someone, "You should," notice how your hands are. In our research most people agreed that their fingers were pointing in a directive way. Close your eyes and think about telling someone, "You could." In our research most people envisioned their hands with palms open. And finally, close your eyes and think about saying, "You would." In our research most people saw their hands as being open and strong.

Overview of Activity

Have participants break up into pairs. One person in each of the pairs will offer a challenge or problem he or she is having. The problem could be work or personal in nature, but it has to be something multifaceted enough to talk about for a while. The other person will respond by offering solutions first in the form of *should* statements and then, after a minute or two, in the form of *could* statements, and then finally *would* statements.

Time

Instructions—5 minutes
Each round—2 to 3 minutes
Debriefing—10 minutes
Total time—17 minutes

STEPS TO FOLLOW

Round 1

1. Have the participants partner up, preferably with someone they don't know.
2. In each pair, Person A will offer a problem or challenge she is facing. It could be something at work or at home. Tell Person A to make sure that the issue is multifaceted enough to talk about for a bit.
3. Person B will offer possible solutions in the form of *should* statements.

Round 2

1. Now have partners switch. Person B will offer a problem or challenge he is facing.
2. Person A will suggest possible solutions in the form of *could* statements.

Round 3

1. Have partners switch one last time. Person A will offer the same problem or a new challenge she is facing.
2. Person B will offer up possible solutions in the form of *would* statements.

Round 1 Example

Person A: "I'm having a problem getting my daughter to be motivated at school. The way she is headed she won't get into college, and it's affecting my other kids, and my husband and I argue about it all the time."

Person B: "You should get a coach for her. I did that for my son, and he ended up going to college—he's at med school now."

Person A: "We don't really have the money to get a coach. Plus, if I do that for her, then I have to do it for the other kids too, and my husband would never agree …"

Person B: "You should do what you think is necessary. Yes, listen to your husband, but at the end of the day, you should think about your daughter—this is her life and her education is at stake."

Round 2 Example

Person A: "I have 250,000 charts to scan into the system from the last five years, and I don't have the staff to do it. I am trying to find an outside vendor to do it, but their bids came in way too high."

Person B: "You could look at why you need to scan 250,000 charts into the system. We could just go back one year. Maybe you could just scan in the charts from the last year."

Person A: "We have to scan them in from the last five years. If a patient comes in looking for the chart, we are legally bound to have the chart for the last five years."

Person B: "You could do what we do. When a patient comes in asking for a chart, we scan it into the system at that time. Then we don't have to scan all the charts into the system at one time."

Round 3 Example

Person A: "We have a real problem with employees' being able to find space in the parking lot. We have to find new parking space. We are thinking of building a multilevel parking lot, or even shuttling people in, or giving them train tickets."

Person B: "Would a multilevel parking lot fit your budget?"

Person A: "We can put it forward as a plan. Something has to be done."

Person B: "Would the shuttle and train tickets work for the short term until you have a budget for the multilevel parking lot?"

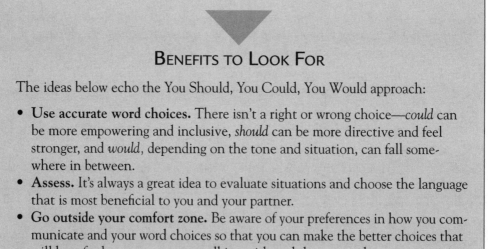

BENEFITS TO LOOK FOR

The ideas below echo the You Should, You Could, You Would approach:

- **Use accurate word choices.** There isn't a right or wrong choice—*could* can be more empowering and inclusive, *should* can be more directive and feel stronger, and *would*, depending on the tone and situation, can fall somewhere in between.
- **Assess.** It's always a great idea to evaluate situations and choose the language that is most beneficial to you and your partner.
- **Go outside your comfort zone.** Be aware of your preferences in how you communicate and your word choices so that you can make the better choices that will benefit the person you are talking with and thus expand your communication abilities. Going with what feels easiest or safest isn't always the best.

Discussion Points

- **Q: What is the difference between advice given in *should* versus *could* or *would* statements?** (Could *felt more unsure, casual, and constructive, and it built on ideas. Should felt more confident, directive, formal, and commanding. Would felt more like a suggestion than a directive.*)
- **Q: For those of you who gave advice, which was easier: *could*, *should*, or *would*?** (Would *and could felt more collaborate and inclusive. Should felt more like telling someone what to do.*)
- **Q: What body language goes along with *should* statements?** (*I noticed I was pointing my fingers.*)
- **Q: What body language goes along with *could* statements?** (*My palms were open.*)

Participant Action Plan

Provide all the participants with a copy of the following action plan. Ask them to complete it, and set up a time to review their results one week later. At that time, ask them what has worked and what has not worked. What do they need to do to improve?

You Should, You Could, You Would Actions

The actions I will take as a result of the You Should, You Could, You Would activity are:

_____

_____

_____

_____

ONE WEEK LATER: What results have I gained from the You Should, You Could, You Would activity?

_____

_____

_____

_____

Activity 13

Me, Me, Me Syndrome

When I let go of what I am, I become what I might be.

—Lao Tzu, mystic philosopher of ancient China and
author of the Tao Te Ching, sixth century BC

Level of Risk

Low

Background and Purpose

Everyone has been trapped in a conversation with someone who is oblivious to the fact that he has been rambling on about himself for far too long. All you want to do is find any reason to exit. It's the same for an improviser … except we have to stay and finish the scene. We stand there feeling useless and powerless as our scene partner steamrolls on. The way we combat this urge to talk incessantly about ourselves and our character is to focus on our scene partner. It's not that we don't talk about ourselves; it's just that we realize that communication is not a solo performance. We consciously turn our attention to the person beside us and look for opportunities to build upon her message whatever it may be. Since we are both focused on each other, we both create the scene together.

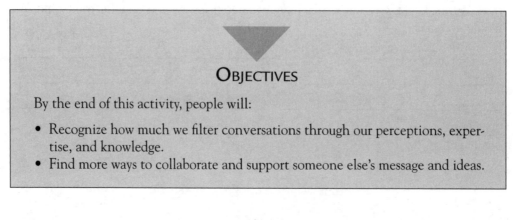

OBJECTIVES

By the end of this activity, people will:

- Recognize how much we filter conversations through our perceptions, expertise, and knowledge.
- Find more ways to collaborate and support someone else's message and ideas.

Mini Lecture

If we're being completely honest, most of us have the Me, Me, Me Syndrome. "What's in it for me?" is a very logical question to ask before we put our wholehearted effort into something. Most of us go to work to get paid money because we need to live—to survive—to experience a decent life. Most people volunteer because it gives them a deep and personal sense of satisfaction.

There is nothing wrong in thinking about ourselves and rewarding ourselves when we have done a good job. Entire marketing strategies are built on understanding and utilizing the "What's in it for me?" strategy. Whether it's about selling products and services, feeding the hungry, curing illness, cleaning up the environment, or even winning elections, most people are thinking about themselves first and foremost. Our customers want to know "What's in it for me?" If we don't address that, no amount of fireworks and freebies will do the job.

The problem with the Me, Me, Me Syndrome is that sometimes we don't know when or how to turn it off, and that can be a real problem in a work environment where we rely on the support of others. People who think only of themselves tend not to think about other people, and in a business environment where teamwork and collaboration are the cornerstones of success, the Me, Me, Me Syndrome can be destructive.

Coworkers, colleagues, and customers cannot rely on people who are in it just for themselves, because those types of people tend not to listen and not to create any "value added." People who are concerned only about "What's in it for me?" tend not to see the bigger picture. They take things personally because they are not able to see the other people's point of view and they do not understand that not everything is about them.

The antidote to the Me, Me, Me Syndrome basically boils down to "Do unto others as you'd have them do unto you." It is about actively listening and being curious about other people. It is the ability to see beyond our own limited needs and show a desire to serve. Being of service is a liberating activity because it allows people to make a real difference in the world. Change initiatives can be made for the betterment of all rather than the betterment of just a few. Ethics, truth, and honesty are highlighted as core values, which creates an environment of trust, integrity, and collaboration—the kind of environment that most people enjoy.

Overview of Activity

In groups, participants will have a conversation. The only condition is that no one can use the word "I." If a member of the group says "I," the others can "buzz" him. Participants are encouraged to look for ways to make others in their group use "I."

Time

Instructions—1 minute
Each round—2 to 3 minutes
Debriefing—5 to 10 minutes
Total time—10 minutes

STEPS TO FOLLOW

1. Have all of the participants team up and get into groups of from three to five people. Have the groups hold a conversation about a certain work-related event—for example, a corporate retreat, softball team meeting, office party, banquet, or picnic. The only stipulation is that no one can say the word "I." If someone in your group uses "I," the rest of the group buzzes them in a loud, obnoxious way.

2. Challenge the group members to see if they can get each other to say "I."

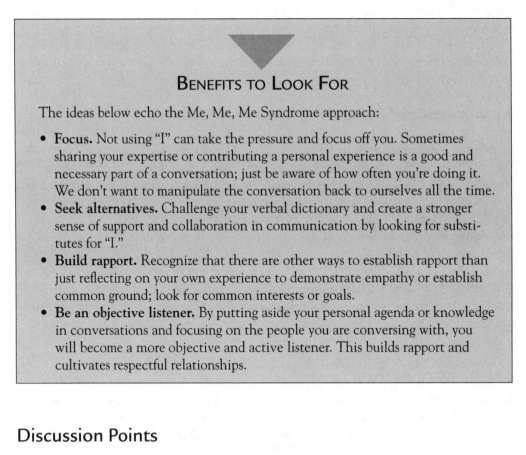

BENEFITS TO LOOK FOR

The ideas below echo the Me, Me, Me Syndrome approach:

- **Focus.** Not using "I" can take the pressure and focus off you. Sometimes sharing your expertise or contributing a personal experience is a good and necessary part of a conversation; just be aware of how often you're doing it. We don't want to manipulate the conversation back to ourselves all the time.
- **Seek alternatives.** Challenge your verbal dictionary and create a stronger sense of support and collaboration in communication by looking for substitutes for "I."
- **Build rapport.** Recognize that there are other ways to establish rapport than just reflecting on your own experience to demonstrate empathy or establish common ground; look for common interests or goals.
- **Be an objective listener.** By putting aside your personal agenda or knowledge in conversations and focusing on the people you are conversing with, you will become a more objective and active listener. This builds rapport and cultivates respectful relationships.

Discussion Points

- **Q: How did you verbally and nonverbally avoid saying "I"?** (*I used "we" instead and sometimes "one" like the queen. I spoke in third person. I didn't talk, or when I did, I kept my comments short or I made sounds like a caveman.*)
- **Q: How can saying "I" in some situations derail the conversation?** (*It puts the focus on me and away from the other message or the sender. It can make me appear bored or preoccupied or seem as if I don't care about what others are saying.*)

- **Q: How can eliminating "I" help a conversation?** (*It allows the listener to focus solely on the conversation and message. It facilitates solutions to challenges and supportive responses.*)

Participant Action Plan

Ask all the participants to find a partner and discuss what actions they will take as a result of this activity. Provide the participants with a copy of the following action plan. Ask them to complete it, and set up a time to review their results one week later. What has worked and what has not worked? What do they need to do to improve?

Me, Me, Me Syndrome Actions

The actions I will take as a result of the Me, Me, Me Syndrome activity are:

_____

_____

_____

_____

ONE WEEK LATER: What results have I gained from the Me, Me, Me Syndrome activity?

_____

_____

_____

_____

Activity 14

To the Point

I think people talk too much anyway. Sometimes people are talking to me and in my mind I'm just like, "shut up, shut up, shut up … blah blah blah blah blaaah."

—Ellen DeGeneres, American stand-up comedian,
television host, and actress

Level of Risk

Low

Background and Purpose

If you're ever onstage with people who are nervous, it is very apparent in their body language and delivery that they are worried and anxious. The biggest problem is that because silence makes them so uncomfortable, they start rambling. It's understandable—silence scares them so they keep talking to fill the seeming void. What happens with rambling improvisers is that they become so wordy, they miss all the opportunities their scene partner has to contribute, including their own creative opportunities.

People who are not okay with the absence of noise are so nervous onstage that they never get to experience the power of silence. They don't see the strength and influence that nonverbal communication and body language can bring to a scene.

There is a world of difference between a situation in which other improvisers can't get a word in edgewise and nothing makes sense and a situation in which the improvisers are connected with a brilliant stream of consciousness in which words create meaningful scenes and the other scene partners are wholeheartedly included in the creative process. When players ramble nervously, the first thing out of their mouth is not always the best. By holding their tongue, they can stop and come up with an idea that might not be as obvious but is more challenging and thought provoking. The only way to get there is by being more economical with words and allowing silence to take place.

▼

OBJECTIVES

By the end of this activity, people will:

- Understand the importance of clear and concise communication.
- End their statements and resist the urge to overtalk.

Mini Lecture

It's a curious thing, but public speaking is often listed as one of the worst of human fears—even scarier than death! And even though speaking in front of groups is for some people scarier than snakes, elevators, sickness, and heights, the truth is that no one has ever died (directly) from giving a talk. So why do otherwise accomplished businesspeople step in front of a podium and start every sentence with "Ummm" or whisper so quietly that no one in the front of the audience can hear them. Nervous speakers seem to experience other things too—their technology breaks down, they fumble questions, their mouth goes dry, or they forget everything they rehearsed.

Communicating our ideas to others is an important part of being in the workplace—it can be the difference between getting a promotion and being passed by. For example, in every workshop there is always a large number of people who don't want to speak out or speak up. When they are asked to introduce themselves, everyone has to lean forward to catch what they are saying—and when we ask people to volunteer and share an experience, they either don't talk at all, or they never shut up because they are so nervous. The problem is that they may have some of the best creative ideas in the group, but if people don't know, they are in real danger of being passed by for promotions, change initiatives, or new projects.

Part of the problem is that when we are onstage and looking out at an audience, we see a mass of humans staring back at us, and it triggers the primal fear response system—we are standing alone in open territory without a weapon! Once we understand that fear is a natural response, we can begin to train ourselves to set the fears aside and step onstage with a loud and powerful voice that uses silence as a powerful and bold ally.

Here are some tips to overcome nervous rambling:

- Arrive early and use the time to sit in one of the audience seats and visualize yourself onstage and being amazing.
- Get honest feedback from people after the talk.
- Practice. Rehearsing your material out loud isn't about memorization. It is about building confidence. By the time you present to your real audience, you will be able to improvise and respond to the unexpected things such as tough questions, bored audiences, and equipment failures.

- Be confident. If things like lighting, sound, or slides do go wrong, don't fumble. Just carry on confidently, as you would expect any professional speaker to do.
- Finally, be a bigger, louder, more assertive version of yourself. Be a passionate, interested, fully present version of you, because that's the person your audience wants to hear.
- Don't be afraid of silence. Take a breath, take a moment, collect yourself, and move on. A nice solid pause is an easy way to regain the attention of any audience. Silence has more power than people think.

Overview of Activity

In pairs, participants converse about any topic. The only requirement is that they must say "and that's all" at the end of their message.

Time

Instructions—1 minute
Each round—2 to 3 minutes
Debriefing—5 minutes
Total time—8 minutes

STEPS TO FOLLOW

1. Have everyone team up with a partner, preferably someone they are not familiar with.
2. In pairs, the participants will hold a conversation about any topic.
3. At the end of each part of the dialogue, the speaker will add the phrase "and that's all."

Example

Person A: "I am not drinking enough water. And that's all."

Person B: "Yeah, I have a habit of drinking too much coffee. But I have switched to decaf, which is good. And that's all.

Person A: "I never started drinking that because I don't know why but … and that's all."

Person B: "I come from a long line of coffee drinkers so I just picked up a mug early. And that's all."

▼

Benefits to Look For

The ideas below echo the To the Point approach:

- **Don't overtalk.** Recognize when you tend to overtalk and, instead, say only what you need to say. Paraphrasing is an excellent tool, but avoid restating when it is unnecessary to do so. When you have a start and an end point in mind, you will avoid talking "past the sell."
- **Keep it simple.** Communication can quickly go from simple to complicated in a matter of moments. Being precise and concise with your language will make your communication easier for your listeners to digest and understand.
- **The end.** When engaged in a conversation, it's essential to have both an objective and an end in sight. The urge to indulge and overtalk can be overcome by remembering to finish what you start.

Discussion Points

- **Q: How did hearing "and that's all" affect your conversation as the listener?** (*It was very clear when the conversation ended. It was a verbal period. I knew when the speaker was done.*)
- **Q: How did it affect you as a speaker?** (*It limited what I said. Focused my time and cleared my thinking.*)
- **Q: How can you signal that you're done without actually saying "and that's all"?** (*I can leave pauses and gaps in the conversation. I can be silent. I can ask questions.*)

Participant Action Plan

Have people partner up and share what they will do differently as a result of this activity. Provide all the participants with a copy of the following action plan. Ask them to complete it, and set up a time to review their results one week later. At that time, ask them what has worked and what has not worked. What do they need to do to improve?

To the Point Actions

The actions I will take as a result of the To the Point Activity are:

_____

_____

_____

_____

ONE WEEK LATER: What results have I gained from the To the Point activity?

_____

_____

_____

_____

Word Choice

The ill and unfit choice of words wonderfully obstruct the understanding.
—Francis Bacon, First Viscount Saint Alban, English philosopher,
statesman, scientist, lawyer, jurist, and author (1561 to 1626)

Level of Risk

Low

Background and Purpose

Going onstage with the adrenaline pumping can sometimes overpower every other faculty. But improvisers still have to be focused on the task at hand: to build a scene together brick by brick. You don't have to build the cathedral by yourself. You just have to bring the bricks. That's one of the differences between being a solo stand-up player and an improviser.

Improvisers work together by listening and "yes, anding." It's very easy to overcomplicate a scene with too many actions and too many words. There's an easy acronym that I use to remind myself of this concept: KISS, "Keep it simple, Stupid." It works.

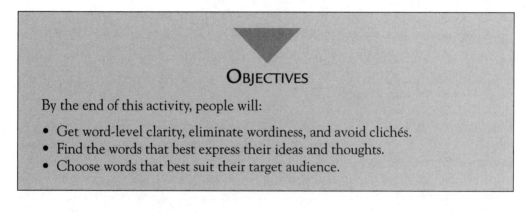

OBJECTIVES

By the end of this activity, people will:

- Get word-level clarity, eliminate wordiness, and avoid clichés.
- Find the words that best express their ideas and thoughts.
- Choose words that best suit their target audience.

Mini Lecture

The KISS acronym "Keep it simple, Stupid" was first coined by Clarence L. "Kelly" Johnson, a lead engineer at the Lockheed Skunk Works where a number of famous aircraft designs, including spy planes such as the F–22 Raptor, originated. Johnson's famed "down-to-brass-tacks" management style was summed up by his motto, "Be quick, be quiet, and be on time."

When Johnson used the KISS philosophy, he did not mean that an engineer was stupid—just the opposite! The story goes that Johnson gave a team of design engineers a handful of tools, with the challenge that the jet aircraft they were designing must be repairable by an average mechanic in the field under combat conditions with only those tools.

The idea of not adding what is not needed goes back even further to when a fourteenth-century Franciscan friar, William of Occam, wrote, "Entities must not be multiplied beyond necessity." Many others through the years have agreed, including Albert Einstein who said, "Everything should be made as simple as possible, but no simpler." Leonardo Da Vinci said, "Simplicity is the ultimate sophistication."

Disney's Nine Old Men—the core animators at Walt Disney Productions who created *Snow White*—had their own idea of the KISS principle. They said that inexperienced animators sometimes "overanimated"—that is, they made their character move too much and do too much, such as carrying every accent over into body language, facial expression, and lip sync. They urged animators to "KISS."

In the business world the KISS philosophy is an important aspect of all work. Take e-mails, for example. All of us should read our e-mails and edit words out before hitting Send. Don't forward long e-mails to everyone on the team just to create a paper trail—it's time wasting for everyone, and worse, you'll become known as the sender of long, boring e-mails that most people will delete without reading. If your job depends on your forwarding informational e-mails, do yourself and others a favor by highlighting the area that others need to read. Twenty people reading the same long e-mail to find one sentence that refers to them and their team is a huge waste of time.

Whether it's an e-mail, a presentation, or a training program ask yourself:

- What does the audience want to hear?
- What do they want to learn?
- What do they already know?
- How can I keep it simple?

If you match what you say or write with what your audience wants to hear, you tell a story, and if you are economical with your words, you will be communicating in a powerful and effective way. Your audience will pay attention, your efforts will be worthwhile, and, most important, your e-mails won't get deleted before people read them, and your presentations will not turn into text messaging sessions.

Overview of Activity

Participants are paired up and asked to have a conversation. In each exchange a participant may use no more than three words.

Time

Instructions—1 minute
Each round—2 to 3 minutes
Debriefing—5 minutes
Total time—8 minutes

STEPS TO FOLLOW

1. Have everyone team up with a partner. In pairs, the participants will hold a conversation about any topic.
2. The only rule is that each participant can say only three words when it is his or her turn to speak in each exchange.

Example

Person A: "Tired need coffee."
Person B: "Coffee provides energy."
Person A: "Energy I need."
Person B: "Need money now."

▼

BENEFITS TO LOOK FOR

The ideas below echo the Word Choice approach:

- **Be precise.** Remove vague and unclear dialogue that is not targeted specifically to your audience.
- **Eliminate space fillers.** Get rid of the "uhhm," "like," and "you know what I mean" phrases that you unconsciously say in conversations. And get more focused with your word choices.
- **Be aware that your word choices are critical to your audience's understanding.** Good speech and written word choices involve being able to select words that are active, powerful, and energetic. Choose just the right words that also sound natural. Word choice is what gives an exactness to details.

Discussion Points

- **Q: How did speaking only three words affect your conversation?** (*It was very awkward and unnatural. It took a long time for me to choose the correct words.*)
- **Q: What are some of the benefits to this activity? What are the takeaways?** (*I had to think before I spoke. I had to think about the people I was talking with and how to communicate with them.*)
- **Q: How will you change your e-mails as a result of this activity?** (*I will forward only relevant e-mails. I will highlight areas that the team needs to read. I will edit unnecessary words out of my e-mails.*)
- **Q: What will you do differently in terms of your audience needs?** (*I will consider what they already know and what they want to learn, and I will use that understanding to make my communication most effective.*)

Participant Action Plan

In groups of three to four people, ask the participants to discuss what changes they will make as a result of this activity. Provide all of them with a copy of the following action plan. Ask them to complete it, and set up a time to review their results one week later. At that time, ask them what has worked and what has not worked. What do they need to do to improve?

Word Choice Actions

The actions I will take as a result of the Word Choice activity are:

_____

_____

_____

_____

ONE WEEK LATER: What results have I gained from the Word Choice activity?

_____

_____

_____

_____

Activity 16

Paraphrase

Everyone can act. Everyone can improvise. Anyone who wishes to can play in the theater. . . . If the environment permits it, anyone can learn whatever they choose to learn, and if the individual permits it, the environment will teach them everything it has to teach. . . . "Talent" or "lack of talent" has very little to do with it.

—Viola Spolin, American drama teacher, author,
and founder of the Young Actors Company in
Hollywood (1906 to 1994)

Level of Risk

Low

Background and Purpose

Because they are too focused on the rules of improv or they are caught up in wanting to be funny, beginner improvisers are sometimes so in their head that they are not listening as well as they should. A perfect example would be when I was teaching. One improviser said, "Nurse, it's your turn to handle Mrs. Dores. Her Alzheimer's is kicking in again." The scene partner responded with, "Mrs. Dores is a smart young lady." Someone wasn't listening.

As improvisers advance with experience and coaching, they learn the importance of listening and responding to that last thing said, instead of replying to what they think they heard or pushing the scene in a direction they would prefer it to go. Paraphrasing is a great tool for forming great listening habits. Here's a visual for you: if my arm were a conversation, I would stop listening at the elbow. By paraphrasing, I have to listen to the end ... to the fingertips!

Obviously, paraphrasing in real life can get a little old or seem weird if we're just repeating everything like a parrot and restating things too much, but it's a great place to begin. If you think you are a bad listener, an interrupter, judgmental, or argumentative, then paraphrasing is a great place to help you go back to the basics of being a good listener. By giving speakers your complete attention, you are acknowledging them. When we paraphrase or repeat part of their message, it also allows us to get confirmation and understanding of the information.

OBJECTIVES

By the end of this activity, people will:

- Use paraphrasing as a way of effectively communicating.
- Diffuse emotional situations with calm and reassuring paraphrasing.
- Empathize by understanding the real meaning of what is being said.
- Clarify what speakers mean by summarizing and paraphrasing key words.

Mini Lecture

In both business and personal life, communication is one of the most important skills we can learn, yet the art of communication seems to often fall into the category of *information giving*. People think if they send the information in an e-mail, then everyone "got it." The reality, however, is very different. Wherever we travel and give talks and workshops about communication, we just have to mention the word "e-mail" and people scrunch up their faces and moan, "I get so many e-mails that it's impossible to read them all." People are e-mailing information thinking they are communicating with their team when in fact many people on teams tell us, "I am so busy that I just delete the e-mails without even reading them." This is not communication—this is information overload.

E-mails have almost become a way of "not communicating." If the communication is important, seek the people out, get eye contact, and talk to them. If you are at a distance or working from a virtual office, use the phone or one of the latest computer technologies with which you can actually see each other. If it is a larger group, use a webinar or a telephone conference with which the speakers can show a slide presentation while talking and the participants can type in questions to be discussed.

When people are communicating, one of the most effective and basic ways to ensure that you understand what they are saying is to paraphrase. When you actively listen to your coworkers and customers, it validates them and builds trust. Not only that, it helps you to align your ideas, services, and products with their needs and goals. When you understand other people, you experience a deeper satisfaction, an improved relationship, and an increased likelihood of collaboration.

When you use paraphrasing, you will get into the habit of listening to everything the speakers are saying and more fully understand their needs. One of the problems with paraphrasing, however, is remembering everything they just said; if they keep on talking and adding idea after idea, it is difficult to keep up. The solution is to artfully interrupt the speakers early on. Most people don't mind being interrupted if your purpose is to paraphrase for understanding. "Excuse me, I want to make sure I get this right. You believe that …"

Paraphrasing is not about parroting everything back to the people who are speaking; it is about using their key words and getting a real sense of what they mean and creating a deeper understanding within yourself. It's a way of building rapport and defusing conflict. When people feel they have been heard and understood, they are more open to hearing other points of view.

If you ever feel your mind drifting, paraphrase; it will bring you right back to what is being said and also allow you to summarize what people are saying—maybe they have drifted off point without realizing it.

When people have strong feelings about a subject, the skill of paraphrasing will help them understand that you "get" what they are talking about. If they are excited, show your own excitement. If they are angry, paraphrase their key words with a soft, calm tone and a confident manner that is both supportive and reassuring. If they express intense anger, paraphrase with intense concern or regret so as to reassure them that you understand how strongly they feel: "I very much want to help find a solution that works for you. What I think I heard you say is …"

Practice the paraphrasing technique at work with colleagues, in social situations, or at home with your family. Notice how people respond when they feel that you are really listening and understanding them. You will find yourself being more present, alert, and satisfied with your communication skills.

Overview of Activity

In pairs, the participants must paraphrase before adding new information, comments, or ideas in their response.

Time

Instructions—1 to 2 minutes
Each round—2 to 3 minutes
Debriefing—5 to 10 minutes
Total time—10 minutes

STEPS TO FOLLOW

Round 1
1. Ask the participants to pair up and then decide who will go first.
2. The participants in each pair will hold a conversation. The only requirement is that before adding new dialogue to the conversation, they must paraphrase what the other participant just said by replying first with "What you're saying is …"

Round 2
1. Still in those same pairs, they will repeat round 1 except without saying the phrase "What you're saying is …"
2. They must still paraphrase.
3. They must also limit questions. Instead, they will add statements.

Round 1 Example

Person A: "I'm very excited because my mom's birthday is coming up and I'm throwing a surprise party for her."

Person B: "What you're saying is you're celebrating your mom's birthday. Wow, surprise parties are so much fun. I had one on my fortieth birthday."

Person A: "What you're saying is that you had a surprise fortieth birthday party. It's so nice to have people you care about show up and have a good time and give you presents."

Person B: "What you're saying is that it's nice to have your family and friends around you to rejoice and bring gifts. Gifts are so much fun to open whether they cost $10 or $200."

Round 2 Example

Person A: "I watched the game last night, and it was awesome!"

Person B: "If I understand you right, you said you watched your team play last night. By the sound of your voice, they must have won. I don't get into sports."

Person A: "You don't enjoy sports? I am completely the opposite. I live, breathe, and sleep sports. It runs in my family."

Person B: "Sounds like you've got sports in your blood. I come from a long line of couch potatoes."

▼

BENEFITS TO LOOK FOR

The ideas below echo the Paraphrase approach:

- **Empathy.** When we actively listen and paraphrase others' key words back to them, they feel comfortable in hearing their own words being repeated. It's a confirmation that their message was received and understood.

- **Active listening.** The art of listening is about being engaged and understanding what the speakers really mean. When we paraphrase others' ideas and beliefs, we are helping ourselves to actively listen and understand exactly what is being said.
- **Safe environment.** Practicing the art of paraphrasing can help people create powerful relationships. Trust is built between the messengers and receivers. Communication thrives.

Discussion Points

- **Q: Did you feel you correctly paraphrased your partner's conversation points? Or when it was your turn to have your words paraphrased, did you feel that your partner added or missed important parts of what you said?** (*Sometimes I missed exact words, but I did pick up really well on the tone of voice and emotions.*)
- **Q: Why is paraphrasing so important in communication?** (*It helps us to actively listen and make sure that we understand what people mean and how they feel about it. It helps people pass along information effectively.*)

Participant Action Plan

Individuals pair up and talk about what they experienced during this activity and what they will do differently moving forward. Provide all the participants with a copy of the following action plan. Ask them to complete it, and set up a time to review their results one week later. At that time, ask them what has worked and what has not worked. What do they need to do to improve?

Paraphrase Actions

The actions I will take as a result of the Paraphrase activity are:

_____

_____

_____

_____

ONE WEEK LATER: What results have I gained from the Paraphrase activity?

_____

_____

_____

_____

Activity 17

Empathy

The great gift of human beings is that we have the power of empathy.

—Meryl Streep, American actress with 16 Academy Award nominations, winning 2, and 25 Golden Globe nominations, winning 7, more nominations than any other actor in the history of either award

Level of Risk

Low

Background and Purpose

Empathy literally translates as *feeling*, and it is the ability to share another being's emotions and feelings. Onstage that happened frequently. I used it as a technique to connect with my scene partners. It allowed us to get on the same page instantaneously.

It was so wonderful to step onstage and mirror my scene partners' emotions. If someone was onstage laughing and I shared that same emotion, it created a shared experience and understanding that allowed our characters and scene to soar. The same was true if someone was sad and I matched their energy. We would commiserate about the situation and build the scenes effortlessly. Whether it was winning the lotto or losing their cows, relating emotionally was gratifying and rewarding because it validated and supported my scene partners and acknowledged their choice, which in turn created trust.

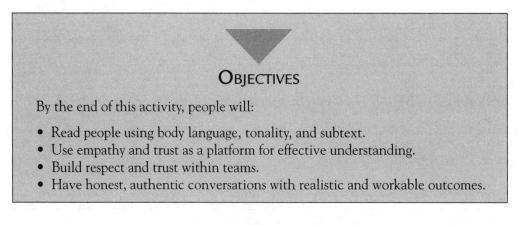

Objectives

By the end of this activity, people will:

- Read people using body language, tonality, and subtext.
- Use empathy and trust as a platform for effective understanding.
- Build respect and trust within teams.
- Have honest, authentic conversations with realistic and workable outcomes.

Mini Lecture

To build effective, constructive relationships requires empathy, which is being able to get in touch with other people's emotions and feelings and identifying with their situations. In today's world where so many people from different backgrounds and beliefs work together, it can seem difficult to have empathy because we don't have the same experience of a shared culture, religion, or political background. However, in the most basic way every person has the same feelings about life, and though it may sound corny and out of context in the business world, the reality is that every person on the planet wants to love and be loved.

We'll call it something different so that it's acceptable to talk about in a business environment; after all, we are not asking people to walk around the office saying, "I love you, man!" Let's call our shared experience of life as "wanting to be acknowledged, respected, and valued." If people feel unacknowledged, disrespected, or undervalued, they are not feeling good about themselves or the situation, and oftentimes they cannot move forward until they feel that someone understands what they are going through.

We can empathize with people (no matter what their background) when we look back in our own life and remember a time when we felt disrespected, undervalued, or unacknowledged. Empathy is about listening and understanding (but not necessarily agreeing with the other person), without judging. The best way to actively listen to other people is to uncover how they feel and discover what they want to achieve and help them to see ways they can achieve it.

Many times we forget that listening is not just about the content but also about the emotion. As leaders, listening and acknowledging both emotion and content can sometimes fall by the wayside in our busy daily lives. The reason for this could be:

- Preoccupation
- Past perceptions
- Impatience
- Open Ears/Closed Mind Syndrome
- Jumping to conclusions

Without the capacity to listen, we can't fully understand what is being said. Empathetic listeners listen for both emotion and content; however, acknowledging both emotion and content is easier said than done. Here are some active listening steps to follow:

1. Give the person your complete attention:
   a. Stop what you are doing.
   b. Make eye contact.
   c. Use nonverbal signals such as nodding, learning forward, or showing a facial expression of concern.
2. Acknowledge the emotion:
   a. "You seem angry about this." "Wow! You sound really excited."
   b. Get confirmation that you are correct.
   c. "No, I'm not angry. I'm just frustrated." "Yes, I'm very excited about this."

3. Paraphrase the emotion and message content:

"So you are frustrated because the customer wanted to talk to a supervisor."

"So you are excited that you were selected for the Accelerate program."

4. Check back for confirmation:

"Does that sound right?" "Am I understanding you correctly?" "Is that correct?"

Overview of Activity

In round 1, participants will talk at each other and not share the conversation. By round 4, they will engage in another conversation (same topic), but this time they will repeat the last line they heard and use it as the first sentence of their thought. This way the conversation will be connected and stay on topic, and the participants will listen (all elements of great scene work). This is one of those exercises that participants can take "onto the street" to make themselves better and more active listeners and to help them remember what they have been listening to.

Time

Instructions—1 to 2 minutes
Each round—2 to 3 minutes
Debriefing—10 minutes
Total time—15 minutes

STEPS TO FOLLOW

Round 1

1. Have all the participants team up with someone they don't normally work with, and decide on a simple topic to have a conversation about.

2. The only stipulation is that both people must talk at the same time. This is not a two-way conversation. This is a one–way, at-each-other conversation with zero sharing.

Round 2

With the same partner, ask both participants to close their eyes and listen to as many things in the room as they can in one minute.

Round 3

With the same partner, have participants resume talking at the same time but with an objective to now listen and respond to their partner while they are talking at each other.

Round 4

With the same partner, now have them engage in another conversation (different or the same topic), but this time they are to repeat the last line they heard and use it as the first sentence of their thought. This is a two-way conversation: pausing after each sentence and repeating what their scene partners have just said using a part of their sentence and incorporating it into their own.

BENEFITS TO LOOK FOR

The ideas below echo the Empathy approach:

- **Listen empathetically.** It's important for us to understand other people and to check the facts and feelings involved with their personal agenda.
- **Assess situations.** Making assumptions and jumping to conclusions lead to misunderstandings, bad feelings, conflicts, and poor morale. When we use empathy, we stand in the other person's shoes and gain a new perspective.
- **Be heard, feel love.** A radio program surveyed its listeners on how they knew when they were loved, and they responded that they knew they were loved when they felt heard. In surveys with employees on what makes a good manager, people have said they want to feel as though their manager listened to them.

Discussion Points

- Q: **What was it like to talk at each other?** (*I felt frustrated. I was unable to hear what the other person was saying. I experienced real life.*)
- Q: **What behaviors can you use to give the other person your complete attention?** (*I can stop what I'm doing, make eye contact, and use nonverbal signals such as nodding.*)
- Q: **When we hear the word** *empathy,* **we automatically think it applies only to people who are in pain. Is this true? If not, what other ways can we define** *empathy?* (*Empathy is about being in touch with other people's emotions whether they are in pain or are happy. When we feel what other people are feeling, we can communicate more effectively.*)

- **Q: How can you verbally acknowledge the speaker's emotion?** (*I can say, "You seem angry about this" or "Wow! You sound really excited."*)
- **Q: Why is it important to get verbal confirmation that you are correct?** (*It is important that I make sure I am on the same page as the speaker so that we can uncover the REAL problem or situation.*)
- **Q: What is an example of paraphrasing the emotion and message content?** (*I can say, "Are you frustrated because the customer wanted to talk to a supervisor?" or "So you are excited that you were selected for the Accelerate program?"*)
- **Q: What would checking back for confirmation sound like?** (*I can say, "Does that sound right?" or "Am I understanding you correctly?" or "Is that correct?"*)

Participant Action Plan

Have participants form teams of three to four people to discuss their experiences in this activity. How did it feel? What worked? What did not work? What will they do differently as a result of this exercise? Provide all the participants with a copy of the following action plan. Ask them to complete it, and set up a time to review their results one week later. At that time, ask them what has worked and what has not worked. What do they need to do to improve?

Empathy Actions

The actions I will take as a result of the Empathy activity are:

_____

_____

_____

_____

ONE WEEK LATER: What results have I gained from the Empathy activity?

_____

_____

_____

_____

Activity 18

Observe

I think you learn from watching other people. I don't really hang out in my trailer so much, unless it's going to be a really, really, really long day. But, I'm one of those people that like to sit on the set and watch. Watch other actors work and how they work. I love to see how directors work. I watch from take to take to take—how the actors change a little bit, or how they keep it the same, or how they get into it, or the playfulness of how engaging two people can be. And how a director works and the ideas that come from that because sometimes, somebody will create something in a moment and then the director is like, "Great! Oh my God. Do that. Do that again!" Or, "Why don't we try it this way?" So, I think that you learn from other people, . . . from how they do the shots and how they create that.

—Mindy Sterling, American actress, played
Frau Farbissina in the *Austin Powers* movies

Level of Risk

Low

Background and Purpose

This activity is about observing and paying attention to the details and behavior of others for the purpose of learning and being on top of your game. Being observant means being on the ball, alert, watchful, attentive, and sharp-eyed—in other words, all the things necessary to improvise.

In a scene anything can happen at any moment and it usually does. Improvisers must always be on the alert because everything in a scene is fodder—from a mistaken word, a sneeze, a cough, or an audience heckle, although heckling rarely happens. I do remember one night a scene was being played in a kitchen. The two improvisers were talking about their marriage and some of the problems they were having. An audience member must have related to the situation and without thinking said out loud, "That's what she said!" Well, the audience cracked up and so did the improvisers waiting in the wings. But the two improvisers onstage didn't miss a beat and responded by saying, "Wow, we've really got to start closing our windows, honey. Our poor neighbor can hear everything. Sorry,

Mr. Johnson!" He then pretended to close the window. This of course made the audience cheer with delight and applaud enthusiastically. If those improvisers had not been on their toes and awake, they would have missed that wonderful opportunity. Everything can be used to enhance and move the scene forward, so we must be observant.

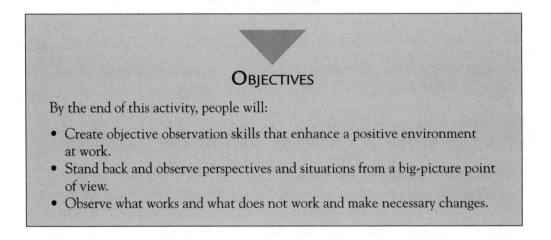

OBJECTIVES

By the end of this activity, people will:

- Create objective observation skills that enhance a positive environment at work.
- Stand back and observe perspectives and situations from a big-picture point of view.
- Observe what works and what does not work and make necessary changes.

Mini Lecture

In business we need to be discerning and know what constitutes a good decision versus a bad one. Whether you are managing a team or part of a team, you have to know your colleagues and what they are capable of. Who is doing what? How do these people deal with responsibility? Do they take appropriate action and provide follow-through? I recently had a conversation with a personal assistant to a CEO who said, "I can't trust my employees to follow through so I just do most things myself." Sometimes this may be justified and the employees really can't be trusted to follow through; other times it is the manager who is not willing to let go of the projects.

I was recently teaching a class called "Creating a Culture of Change and Innovation," and it was lunchtime, and I noticed one of the managers was not going to lunch with the rest of the group. She was someone who had earlier complained about working 10-hour days, so I asked her where she was going for lunch, and she said, "I'm going back to work. It's just a couple of blocks from the hotel." I asked her why she had to go back to work; all her colleagues were taking a well-deserved lunch break. She said, "I have these reports to send out." But something about the way she said it made me ask her if she was the one who had to send out the reports, and she replied, "No, my employees are sending them out, but I need to make sure they do it properly."

I gave her the opportunity to make a decision and let her people send out the reports while she went to lunch. She came back after lunch glowing. She had not gone back to work, and she had called in to check on whether the reports had gone out correctly and they had. Sometimes we need to step back and see the big picture: *Am I working 10-hour days because I don't trust my people and I am not delegating?* Observe your team members and play to their strengths and weaknesses; that is being discerning, and it requires observation.

Overview of Activity

Participants will first mingle, and then they'll stand in a circle and observe the space around them. They will mirror the actions from each other, having the opportunity to observe and follow each other's movements.

Time

Instructions—5 minutes
Each round—2 to 3 minutes
Debriefing—10 minutes
Total time—20 minutes

STEPS TO FOLLOW

Round 1

The beauty of this exercise lies in its simplicity. First, as a quick warm-up, have the participants walk around the group saying "hi," giving and receiving eye contact.

Round 2

1. Have the participants stand in a circle so that they can see everyone. They are in a neutral position with their arms down by their sides. Tell them this is a silent exercise. It's okay to laugh if they need to, but for the most part, they should try to be silent.

2. Tell them to watch each other's movements (everyone's movements—don't focus in on one person) and match or mirror exactly what they see. They are not to miss any movement by their fellow players.

   Note: In round 2 people are usually big and bold, moving their arms and making large movements. Sometimes there will be two different things happening at the same time because some people are not paying attention and they do not know whom to follow.

Round 3

1. Have them repeat the mirror process with an added stipulation: participants cannot make a move that they did not see from someone else. No "inorganic" movements—that is, they are to just follow the follower—there is no leader.

---

2. Side coach and encourage them to mirror the details. Mirror the look in people's eyes, each other's facial expressions, how people's hands are positioned, their posture, the rhythm of their breathing.
3. Be sure to have the students follow the follower's smallest movements. Don't miss a single hair movement, a cough, or giggle.
4. Encourage participants to stay "in" the activity as opposed to where they think the activity should go or where they want the activity to go because it would be more fun or challenging.

   Note: It's okay if this feels a little awkward. Participants find the movements together—there is no specific leader.

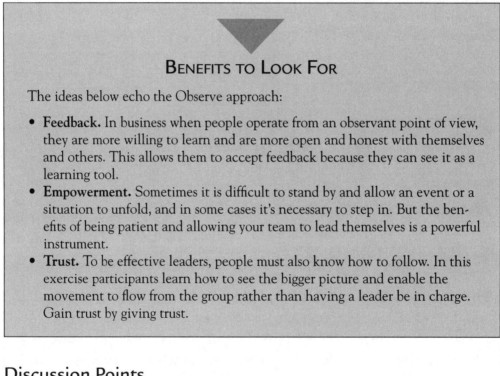

BENEFITS TO LOOK FOR

The ideas below echo the Observe approach:

- **Feedback.** In business when people operate from an observant point of view, they are more willing to learn and are more open and honest with themselves and others. This allows them to accept feedback because they can see it as a learning tool.
- **Empowerment.** Sometimes it is difficult to stand by and allow an event or a situation to unfold, and in some cases it's necessary to step in. But the benefits of being patient and allowing your team to lead themselves is a powerful instrument.
- **Trust.** To be effective leaders, people must also know how to follow. In this exercise participants learn how to see the bigger picture and enable the movement to flow from the group rather than having a leader be in charge. Gain trust by giving trust.

Discussion Points

- **Q: What did you notice?** (*I found it really difficult to not make a big and bold movement. It felt like someone had to be the leader, and it was difficult to follow without being given specific instructions to follow.*)
- **Q: How did it feel to watch the whole group instead of focusing on one person?** (*I wasn't able to see what everyone in the group was doing at first, but when I let go of being in control, I realized that there was an organic movement taking place.*)

- **Q: What did you learn?** *(I learned that the group had a definite thought, that it wasn't necessary for one person specifically to be the leader, and that we can all lead together if we observe each other.)*
- **Q: How important is it to observe in the workplace?** *(If I don't observe what is going on, I can make some big mistakes. It's a learning tool. When I observe how people are feeling and reacting, I can time my communication better—maybe I don't need to say what I was going to say at that exact moment, or maybe I can observe when it is the best time to act and when it is the best time to be silent.)*

Participant Action Plan

Ask participants to find a partner they have not normally worked with and discuss what they learned from this activity and what they will do differently as a result. Give all the participants a copy of the following action plan. Ask them to complete it, and set up a time to review their results one week later. At that time, ask them what has worked and what has not worked. What do they need to do to improve?

Observe Actions

The actions I will take as a result of the Observe activity are:

_____

_____

_____

_____

ONE WEEK LATER: What results have I gained from the Observe activity?

_____

_____

_____

Activity 19

Building Rapport

We still have that same burn, to get that same kind of laughs. So whether the studio wants us to or not, we're going to do it. The money is just a by-product of coming out with good stuff. Our whole thing is building that rapport with the audience.

—Shawn Wayans, American actor, producer, writer, and comedian

Level of Risk

Low

Background and Purpose

Having been onstage a long time, I had the honor of performing with legends Eric Idle (*Monty Python*) and Harry Shearer (*The Simpsons*) at iO West in Los Angeles. I hadn't met them before. I had only seen them on TV, and I had only 15 minutes or so to build a solid relationship before performing onstage with them! I had to use this time in the green room backstage to get to know each of them. And here's how we built rapport quickly. Of course, my fellow improvisers were over the moon to be improvising with such legends so we were smiling like idiots, and we greeted Eric and Harry with sincere eye contact and hearty handshakes. The feeling was reciprocated, and Eric and Harry were genuinely thrilled to be performing with us so we all started laughing and joking about what was to come.

We found a commonality right away; the commonality was, "We're going to be onstage, and we're going to make each other look good." We all respected each other's abilities, and because we were all standing in this green room together, there was a mutual respect … otherwise, we wouldn't be standing there! And that's what building rapport is about.

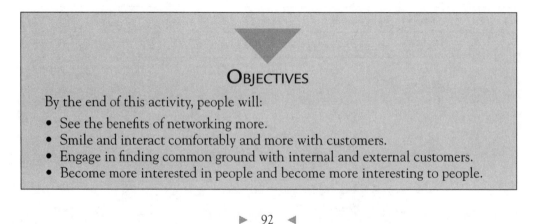

OBJECTIVES

By the end of this activity, people will:

- See the benefits of networking more.
- Smile and interact comfortably and more with customers.
- Engage in finding common ground with internal and external customers.
- Become more interested in people and become more interesting to people.

Mini Lecture

Building rapport is such an important skill that many corporations teach it as a basic course in communication skills. To some people, building rapport comes naturally, and for others it is more difficult. For example, people in sales often build rapport without even knowing they are doing it. Customer service representatives also find that rapport building helps them create loyalty in their customers and handle difficult people.

The way we think about people and what "label" we put on them happens instantly. In seconds we judge people by the way they dress, stand, and talk, and we put them in a box. The problem with instant judgment, however, is that we miss a lot of important information and exceptional opportunities. At the beginning of our workshops, we often ask people to tell us something about themselves that we don't know. People are amazed to find that they are working alongside a skydiver, a cake decorator, a toast master, a skier, a swimmer, or a person who collects ducks. And you may think, "What does this have to do with building rapport?" The answer is, "Everything!" When you know what your coworkers enjoy, you have a broad perspective on them, and when you have a broad perspective on people, it opens your mind and gives you a big picture and a wide scope for collaboration and teamwork.

From a customer service perspective, building rapport sometimes means the difference between a company representative creating a new market and losing a customer. Consider this true story: Thomas worked in the retail store of a large telecommunications company. One day a young man walked in with a competitive product that he was having problems with. Instead of sending him on his way, Thomas discovered that the customer was deaf and that his phone did not have the vibrating alert—clearly a vital feature for deaf users. By the end of their meeting, Thomas had converted the man to a new vibrating phone with his company, and he decided to teach himself sign language. The word soon spread among the local deaf community and finally reached the regional deaf association who decided to officially recommend the store to their members—new customers, new market, new opportunity—all from building rapport!

Overview of Activity

Participants will find different ways to discover as many things as possible that they have in common with other people.

Time

Instructions—2 minutes
Each round—2 to 3 minutes
Debriefing—6 minutes
Total time—9 minutes

STEPS TO FOLLOW

Round 1
1. Tell participants to find a partner they don't know so well.
2. Have them discover five different things that they have in common with each other without talking, for example miming, charades, lip reading, writing on a note pad, texting, painting or drawing pictures.

Round 2
1. Have partners find and join another pair. They will now be a group of four.
2. Tell them to find one thing in common without talking.

Round 3
1. Have the group split, with each member pairing with their original partner to find one more thing they have in common.
2. Tell them they can talk.

BENEFITS TO LOOK FOR

The ideas below echo the Building Rapport approach:

- **Know the power of a smile.** A smile is the fastest way to build rapport with another human being. In an instant you are telling someone, "I am harmless. I am on your side. I am easy to get to know. I want to collaborate."
- **Be curious.** We never know what is going on with a person unless we ask, and to ask is to be curious. What, why, where, when, and how are open-ended questions. You will soon find out if a person does not want to answer your questions, but most people love to talk about themselves.
- **Use the person's name.** When someone calls us by our name, we feel an immediate connection; on some level, it is as if we're already friends. Remember the names of your colleagues, coworkers, and customers. You may have noticed that many customer service representatives supply their first name; if you use it, you may even get better service yourself.
- **Make eye contact.** It seems too simple to be mentioned, and it is one of the first things that people look for: people who do not make eye contact seem as if they have something to hide. So always make eye contact in a friendly way without getting into a "staring contest."

Discussion Points

- **Q: What was it like to explore commonalities without using words?** *(I kept working on communicating with my eyes and sign language. There are more ways to communicate than just talking.)*
- **Q: Was it more difficult in the group of four?** *(I kept thinking "I can do this," and I focused on not giving up and, instead, finding different ways to communicate without talking. I also watched how other people did it, and I copied the more successful ones.)*
- **Q: What are some of the ways you communicated?** *(I used mime and charades. We had a great time texting. I pulled out my wallet with my kids' pictures. I showed some Facebook pictures of me skydiving. It was great and a relief to be finally able to talk.)*

Participant Action Plan

Provide all the participants with a copy of the following action plan. Ask them to complete it, and set up a time to review their results one week later. At that time, ask them what has worked and what has not worked. What do they need to do to improve?

Building Rapport Actions

The actions I will take as a result of the Building Rapport activity are:

_____

_____

_____

_____

ONE WEEK LATER: What results have I gained from the Building Rapport activity?

_____

_____

_____

_____

Activity 20

Listen Up ... Listen!

If A equals success, then the formula is A equals X plus Y and Z, with X being work, Y play, and Z keeping your mouth shut.

—Albert Einstein, German-born American physicist
who developed the special and general theories of
relativity and was awarded the Nobel Prize for
Physics in 1921 (1879 to 1955)

Level of Risk

Low

Background and Purpose

Improv can be scary and intimidating, and that's why listening is such a good tool to use to get out of your head and become fearless onstage. When performers focus on the scene, on the characters, and, more important, on their partners, it takes the pressure off "performing for a laugh." Humor will appear naturally and organically.

On my first team, I had the honor of being coached by Liz Allen, coauthor of *Improvising Better: A Guide to the Working Improviser.* She taught me a lot. In the beginning, she basically told me I talked too much and hardly listened. Not a good combination for improvisation. Literally, before every show she would single me out and pin me against the wall and say, "Support whomever you are onstage with, and don't be funny, Sarah." At first I thought, "What, me? Don't be funny? No way. Impossible." It was a big blow to my ego because I thought I was hilarious and brilliant! But here I was being told I wasn't as funny as I thought I was. Fortunately, my love for improv and desire to grow and learn kicked in, and I decided to follow her advice. That meant I had to listen. Thank the Lord I did because that's how I became one of the best female improvisers in Chicago.

▼

OBJECTIVES

By the end of this activity, people will:

- Understand personal negative listening patterns.
- Have the ability to correct the patterns.
- Recognize the negative patterns in others.
- Cultivate patience in communication.
- Become a better listener.

Mini Lecture

The ability to listen attentively, and without judgment, advice, or logic, is one of the most difficult and most prized skills for leaders to master. Emotionally intelligent leaders know that listening to employees is critical to forming strong bonds and developing an open, friendly environment conducive to creativity, productivity, and high quality. They also know that listening reduces conflict and encourages more creative problem solving.

However, negative listening habits can erode our abilities as leaders and diminish our abilities to build high trust bonds with employees. Five negative listening habits are often at the root of our inability to listen. The purpose of this exercise is to identify which, if any, of these listening habits may be interfering with our abilities to be effective leaders and to heighten our awareness of these negative listening habits in our interactions with other people.

The five negative listening patterns are as follows:

1. **The phonies.** It seems like these people are listening because they're making all the right signs: nodding, making eye contact, and occasionally making soothing sounds like "uh-huh." However, the phonies aren't concentrating on the speaker—their mind is elsewhere.
2. **The butt-ins.** The butt-ins, or interrupters, don't allow the speakers to finish and they don't ask clarifying questions or seek more information. They're so anxious to speak their own words that they show little concern for what is being said. When the speakers say something, the butt-ins steal the focus and then change it to their own point of view. Favorite butt-in lines are "Oh, that's nothing. Here's what happened to me ..." "I remember when I was ..."
3. **The brains.** These people are always trying to interpret what the speakers are saying and why. They are judging the speakers' words and trying to fit them into their own logic box. They rarely ask about the underlying feelings or emotions attached to the messages.

4. **The stroppies.** These listeners listen only long enough to form a denial. Their point is to use the speakers' words against them. At worst, the stroppies are argumentative and want to prove other people wrong. At best, they always want to make the speakers see their point of view.

5. **The counsels.** Giving advice is sometimes helpful. However, this behavior interferes with good listening because it does not allow the speakers to fully articulate their feelings or thoughts. Giving advice doesn't help the speakers solve their own problems; it prohibits venting; it could also belittle the speakers by minimizing their concerns by providing quick solutions. Well-placed advice is an important function of leadership, especially when asked for. However, advice given too quickly and at the wrong time is a turn-off.

Overview of Activity

In pairs, the participants discuss the negative listening habits and decide which one they are most likely to use. Participants then use that negative habit in an exercise to bring awareness and create the possibility for change.

Time

Instructions—2 minutes
Each round—3 to 4 minutes (two rounds in total)
Debriefing—8 minutes
Total time—18 minutes

STEPS TO FOLLOW

Round 1

1. Participants each find a partner and sit opposite each other. The one closest to the front of the room will be Partner A.
2. They discuss and decide which of the five negative listening patterns they most often use in their daily lives:
   - Phony
   - Butt-in
   - Brain
   - Stroppy
   - Counsel
3. The (A)s will be the speakers. They can pick any topic to talk about. If they are paired with a counsel, they must come up with a problem.
4. The (B)s will practice their personal negative listening pattern.
5. They have three to four minutes to talk.

Round 2

1. Participants will switch, and repeat the steps of round 1.
2. Remind the participants to have fun.

   Note: If you have time, ask the participants to repeat rounds 1 and 2 with a different partner and this time use positive listening skills such as paraphrasing, repeating the last word said, and/or listening without any interruptions.

▼

BENEFITS TO LOOK FOR

The ideas below echo the Listen Up … Listen! approach:

- **Uncover negative listening habits.** Sometimes we aren't even aware of what we are doing when we listen to people. We are so used to our own habits that we don't realize that we are using negative listening skills. Fortunately, awareness is the key to unlearning a negative habit. Once we are aware of what we are doing, then we can make a choice to change our patterns.
- **Create positive listening skills.** Listening is all about paying attention to what speakers are saying. People have different ways of paying attention such as repeating the last word the speaker said, paraphrasing, or just being silent until the speaker has finished. Whatever listening skills are used, active listening is about wanting to listen rather than be heard.

Discussion Points

- **Q: What was it like to discuss negative listening patterns?** (*It was uncomfortable to be aware of my negative listening habits, but I now realize that I have the opportunity to change.*)
- **Q: How did it feel to use your negative listening habits?** (*I realized that I do that a lot, and it's not good for listening and understanding what other people are saying.*)
- **Q: What kind of listening habits will you adopt after this exercise?** (*I will pay more attention to listening to what others are saying without interrupting. I will pay attention to my listening habits and make sure that I have total understanding before I put my own point of view forward.*)

Participant Action Plan

Provide all the participants with a copy of the following action plan. Ask them to discuss with their partner what changes they will make. Ask them to complete the action plan, and set up a time one week later to review their results. At that time, ask them what has worked and what has not worked. What do they need to do to improve?

Listen Up ... Listen! Actions

The actions I will take as a result of the Listen Up ... Listen! activity are:

_____

_____

_____

_____

ONE WEEK LATER: What results have I gained from the Listen Up ... Listen! activity?

_____

_____

_____

_____

Activity 21

Nonverbal Communication

Behavior in the human being is sometimes a defense, a way of concealing motives and thoughts, as language can be a way of hiding your thoughts and preventing communication.

—Abraham Maslow, American professor of psychology at
Brandeis University who founded humanistic psychology and
created Maslow's hierarchy of needs (1908 to 1970)

Level of Risk

Low

Background and Purpose

You just have to be watching. When you're creating an organic game onstage in front of an audience with every team member involved yet you cannot speak, the only tool you have is your eyes.

In a couple of shows I did with a house team called Valhalla at iO in Chicago, we performed silent games within our performance. We would filter onstage, and without an idea in our head we'd experiment with quiet. Could we create a game without speaking that was inspiring to us and watchable to the audience? It was possible. A tool we used to accomplish this was to intensely *look* at each other and notice anything and everything the other person did. For example, someone might not *blink*, then we would not blink. This would turn into all of us *staring eerily*, which would turn into all of us realizing we were wearing *a pair of goggles*, which would turn into all of us *scuba diving in the ocean*, which would turn into all of us noticing *a killer shark*, which would turn into all of us *frantically swimming away in slow motion*.

Literally we had to have eyes in the back of our head. The stage was big, and there were many players, and every participant had to be involved. The only way to accomplish that was through deep nonverbal connection.

OBJECTIVES

By the end of this activity, people will:

- Portray confidence and expertise when they communicate.
- Learn how to interpret others' body language and vocal tones.
- Take responsibility for giving and receiving nonverbal cues.
- Recognize how nonverbal cues can be misinterpreted in other cultures.

Mini Lecture

The first scientific study of nonverbal communication was Charles Darwin's book *The Expression of the Emotions in Man and Animals* (1872). He argued that all mammals show emotion reliably in their faces. Studies now range across a number of fields, including linguistics, semiotics, and social psychology. It's not *what* you say but *how* you say it.

Modern research has shown that the majority of our communication is nonverbal. Nonverbal communication, or *body language*, includes our facial expressions, gestures, eye contact, posture, and even tone of voice. Someone can say the words, "I love you," which would seem to say that the person is in love. However, the tone of voice, pitch, facial expression, and body language provide a variety of possible meanings from "You are the love of my life" to "I hate you!"

Nonverbal communication is a powerful tool that helps people to connect with others, express what they really mean, navigate challenging situations, and build better relationships at home and work. Every time we speak or listen to other people, it seems our attention is focused on the spoken words rather than the body language; however, our judgment includes both. An audience processes both verbal and nonverbal cues at the same time. When leading a meeting or speaking to a group, recognize the nonverbal cues and what they can tell you:

- **Facial expressions.** Facial expressions are universal. The human face expresses countless emotions without saying a word; happiness, sadness, anger, surprise, fear, and disgust are the same across all cultures.
- **Postures.** The way we stand, walk, sit, or hold our head communicates a wealth of information to our audience. We may think we are hiding our thoughts and feelings, but our posture, bearing, stance, and subtle movements say it all.
- **Gestures.** We use our hands to wave, beckon, point, argue, and speak. Unlike facial expressions, gestures can vary across cultures, so it's important to know your audience and avoid misinterpretation.
- **Eye contact.** Eye contact is a critical part of nonverbal communication. The way we look at someone communicates interest, attraction, affection, or hostility.

Eye contact helps us maintain the flow of conversation and gauge our audience's response.

- **Touch.** Next time you shop, notice how much you need to touch the fabric and products. Touch is a big part of communication; a firm handshake is reassuring whereas, a too strong handshake is intimidating and a timid tap on the shoulder may show uncertainty and even fear. A warm bear hug or a reassuring pat on the back sends a different message from a patronizing pat on the head or a controlling grip on your arm.
- **Space.** Some people stand close and others stand far away. Our physical space differs depending on the situation, culture, and the closeness of the relationship. Physical space can communicate nonverbal messages that include signals of intimacy, aggression, dominance, or affection.
- **Voice.** Even without words our voice is a powerful communication tool: tone, pitch, volume, inflection, rhythm, and rate are all expressions of how we feel. Nonverbal speech sounds provide subtle and powerful clues into our true feelings and what we really mean, including feelings of sarcasm, anger, affection, or confidence.

Overview of Activity

As a group, participants will practice verbal and nonverbal communications in a cocktail party setting. Multiple rounds will be played to highlight different competencies.

Time

Instructions—5 minutes
Each round—2 to 3 minutes
Debriefing—10 minutes
Total time—18 minutes

STEPS TO FOLLOW

Round 1

Ask the participants to walk around the space as if they were at a cocktail party, and have them say a quick "hi" to as many people as they can.

Note: They should mingle with as many people as they can in all rounds.

Round 2

Now ask them to repeat the last round, only this time they have to say "hi" in gibberish (a made-up language).

Round 3

Now they must greet, again using gibberish, as many people as they can as if they were their long-lost best friend.

Round 4

1. Now they must greet as many people as they can as if they were people they don't like. For whatever reason, they wish they could avoid these particular people, but they can't and they just have to put up with them.
2. Again this round is in gibberish.

Round 5

Now they must greet as many people they can as if they were their boss or their boss's boss … in gibberish.

▼

BENEFITS TO LOOK FOR

The ideas below echo the Nonverbal Communication approach:

- **Listen with your eyes.** People communicate in many different ways and levels. They use facial expressions, eye contact, posture, hand and feet movements, body movement and placement, and their appearance and passage as they walk toward you. Every movement is communicating something. Increase your ability to read nonverbal communication by listening with your eyes.
- **Read past the words.** If a person's words say one thing and their nonverbal communication says another, you are more likely to listen to the nonverbal communication—and that is usually the correct decision.
- **See the whole person.** The nonverbal communication during an interaction should also highlight the skills, strengths, weaknesses, and concerns of the person you are speaking with. Again, the nonverbal cues may reveal more than the person's spoken words.

Discussion Points

- **Q: How did speaking gibberish affect your interactions?** (*It was funny. Even though we didn't understand the words, we understood each other.*)

- **Q: How did you treat your partner differently as your best friend versus someone you would prefer *not* to be around?** *(We were so LOUD when we were greeting each other as best friends! Everyone was smiling and had open body language. When I greeted the person I didn't like, we were both closed off and suspicious.)*
- **Q: What changed when you were asked to greet your boss or your boss's boss?** *(I noticed everyone started bowing! Everyone's facial expressions and gestures totally changed and became more respectful.)*

Participant Action Plan

Provide all the participants with a copy of the following action plan. Ask them to complete it, and set up a time to review their results one week later. At that time, ask them what has worked and what has not worked. What do they need to do to improve?

Nonverbal Communication Actions

The actions I will take as a result of the Nonverbal Communication activity are:

_____

_____

_____

_____

ONE WEEK LATER: What results have I gained from the Nonverbal Communication activity?

_____

_____

_____

_____

Listen to Learn

I like to listen. I have learned a great deal from listening carefully. Most people never listen.

—Ernest Hemingway, American author and journalist (1899 to 1961), whose distinctive writing style was characterized by economy and understatement

Level of Risk

Medium

Background and Purpose

You can learn a lot from people just by listening. In the movie *Waiting for Guffman*, there's a funny part where Eugene Levy playing the role of Dr. Pearl says, "People say, 'You must have been the class clown.' And I say, 'No, I wasn't. But I sat next to the class clown, and I studied him.'"

I can relate to this statement in improvisation. Listening was a tool I used to become a great improviser because, even though my family and friends thought I was funny, it was a different story onstage. I had to work for many years to make a name for myself. There are some improvisers—for example, John Lutz (*Saturday Night Live* writer, *30 Rock*)—who are naturally funny. The moment I started performing with him, I realized he was brilliant. There are very few naturally brilliant improvisers. The rest of us have to practice. And one way to practice is to "shut up and listen." You can learn so much from watching.

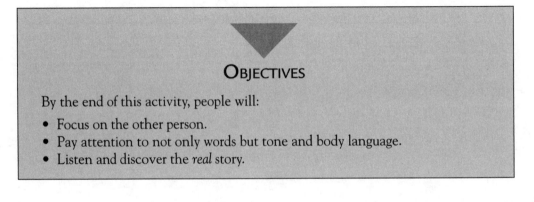

OBJECTIVES

By the end of this activity, people will:

- Focus on the other person.
- Pay attention to not only words but tone and body language.
- Listen and discover the *real* story.

Mini Lecture

For most people a good listener is someone who listens to other people and gets an understanding of their needs. Once they understand their audience, they can then tailor their own message to better fit the needs of their audience. They are not listening to learn but rather listening to sell, or listening to present or market their own ideas to that audience.

When we listen to learn, we are taking listening to a different level. We are observing what others do and learning from our observation and study. When we have been consulting in large corporations or associations, one of the things we often hear is the disconnection between new employees and older more experienced employees who say, "These new employees may have the educational qualifications, but they don't know the business—they don't have the experience."

In order for any business to be successful, we need to listen and learn from each other. It's not just older employees who have all the experience and don't need to learn; they too have a lot to learn from the new intakes. As one lady said, "I get a lot of help from the younger employees. They teach me how to use different software programs—I don't know what I would do without them."

In order to listen to learn, we have three main tools at our disposal:

- **Focus on the speaker.** When you listen to learn, you are focused not just on the speakers' words but also on their body language, facial expressions, and tone of voice. What are they saying behind their words? What are they enthusiastic about? What can you learn?

  In addition, although you don't want to seem weird and overly focused by not averting your eyes, you do want to get into the habit of maintaining natural eye contact so that you feel comfortable with people in any situation.

- **It's not all about you.** Here's a great quote from Ed Howe, a noted Massachusetts ornithologist and prolific writer: "No man would listen to you talk if he didn't know it was his turn next." If you think about it, how often would you listen to someone speak if you didn't know that your own turn to say something was coming? In listening to learn, however, it is mostly about observing other people, those who have experience in something that you want to learn.

  If you want to learn something, don't be overly eager to dazzle the person with your own knowledge; instead, observe, study, and learn. Don't be afraid of silence; in fact, practice enjoying the silence.

- **Listen to the music.** It may sound a little strange to talk about the music in spoken words; however, if you listen to learn, you will notice music in other people's tone of voice. Does their smile light up their face and make their eyes sparkle, or do just the corners of their mouth turn up? Listen to your own tone of voice. Notice the difference when you hear yourself or others say, "Okay, I'll take care of it," as opposed to, "Okay, *I'll* take care of it!" or, "OKAY, I'll take care of it!" What is the real message being sent?

You've most likely heard the quote, "We have two ears and one mouth so we can listen twice as much as we speak." It's good advice for anyone who wants to listen to learn.

Overview of Activity

This is a closed-eye activity. Participants get to experience communicating with their partner without talking.

Time

Instructions—2 to 5 minutes
Each round—5 minutes
Debriefing—10 minutes
Total time—20 minutes

STEPS TO FOLLOW

Round 1

1. Tell participants to close their eyes. They are not to speak, sneeze, cough, or make any kind of sound … if possible.

   Note: You will pair them up with their eyes closed so that they will not know who their partner is.

2. Move the participants one at a time (with their eyes still closed) to different areas of the room, and pair them up with someone unexpected. Guide their hands so that they are holding each other's hands:
   - Ask participants to communicate with their *hands only*.
   - Ask them to tell each other about their day or week. They have about two minutes each to communicate.

Round 2

Still with their eyes closed and holding their partner's hands, ask them to communicate silently with their hands about a problem they have at work.

Round 3

Still with their eyes closed and holding their partner's hands, ask them to communicate silently with their hands a fear.

Round 4

Still with their eyes closed and holding their partner's hands, ask them to communicate silently with their hands something that works well at work—something they are thankful for or proud of.

Round 5

Have the participants open their eyes. Give them a few minutes to discuss this exercise with each other.

BENEFITS TO LOOK FOR

The ideas below echo the Listen to Learn approach:

- **Communicate without talking.** The focus of this exercise is to appreciate that we can communicate so much without talking.
- **Make assumptions.** It's okay to make assumptions about what people tell you because assumptions can lead to great things and there really aren't any right or wrong assumptions as long as they are not preventing solutions and communication from moving forward.
- **Have patience.** Patience is a great virtue. "One moment of patience may ward off great disaster. One moment of impatience may ruin a whole life."
  —Chinese proverb

Discussion Points

- **Q: How many of you figured out who your partner was, and were you surprised?** (*I had no idea. I thought I knew, but when I opened my eyes I was surprised.*)
- **Q: How was it to communicate with just your hands?** (*It was a sensation I'd never had before. I realized how much can be said without talking. I felt really connected to this person. I trusted my partner.*)
- **Q: When communicating face-to-face, is body language important?** (*Very. Body language tells us what people are really feeling.*)

Participant Action Plan

Provide all the participants with a copy of the following action plan. Ask them to complete it, and set up a time to review their results one week later. At that time, ask them what has worked and what has not worked. What do they need to do to improve?

Listen to Learn Actions

The actions I will take as a result of the Listen to Learn activity are:

_____

_____

_____

_____

ONE WEEK LATER: What results have I gained from the Listen to Learn activity?

_____

_____

_____

_____

Activity 23

Trust

The key is to get to know people and trust them to be who they are. Instead, we trust people to be who we want them to be—and when they're not, we cry.

—Unknown

Level of Risk

Medium to high

Background and Purpose

I was invited to do a two-person show with Scott Adsit (*30 Rock*, *Moral Orel*, and *Mary Shelley's Frankenhole*). He was a role model for me and the reason I became an improviser. I saw him on the main stage at Second City and said, "This is what I want to do with my life." So when I had the honor of performing with him, I had to trust that I was good enough to be onstage with him.

We had a great run of shows. I noticed that some performances were marginally better than others. When I had 100 percent trust in myself and my abilities, the shows rocked. Adversely, when I was off by even 10 percent, the shows were not as satisfying. And this was all created and was happening within my own head. Trust comes from within, and in order to trust someone else, you have to trust yourself first. Scott trusted himself and was able to trust me. The lesson I learned there was to continue believing in myself.

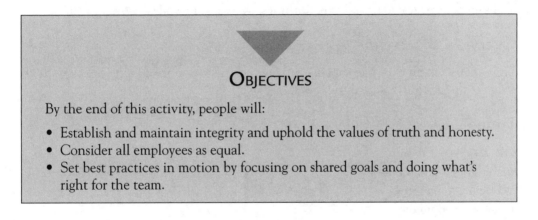

OBJECTIVES

By the end of this activity, people will:

- Establish and maintain integrity and uphold the values of truth and honesty.
- Consider all employees as equal.
- Set best practices in motion by focusing on shared goals and doing what's right for the team.

Mini Lecture

Trust is a two-way relationship—one person trusts, and the other person is trusted. But they are not the same thing. The person who trusts may sometimes trust someone or something that isn't necessarily trustworthy. If people who trust are let down, they may never trust again. The problem with not trusting, however, is that we are operating at less than 100 percent. We may become worried, anxious, and nervous: "I just can't trust it to work." Relationships with potentially trustworthy people and situations may be harmed by just one "bad" experience with trust.

When people work in an atmosphere of nontrust, it creates more work and less productivity. For example, I asked a group of employees why they forwarded so many e-mails to their coworkers, and they all agreed, "We need to create a paper trail—if we don't have one, then people won't trust that we've done the work." In this scenario, many people do not trust each other to get the job done. Long e-mails with even longer attachments are being forwarded just to create documentation. From a big picture point of view, it's like forwarding an entire filing cabinet of information from person to person.

It's a good thing to keep records, but at some point we have to use common sense and forward just the relevant documentation. For example, if you feel you need to document and keep a paper trail, maintain your own e-mail filing system. You don't have to forward everything to everybody—it just wastes time and energy, both your own and other people's.

Trust cannot be reduced to pure behavior, and it cannot be bottled as a competency model. However, there are specific principles that govern trustworthy behavior. They include:

- **Transparency.** Being open and honest about all dealings
- **Collaboration.** Working together to create joint goals and approaches
- **Focus.** Seeing others' points of view instead of just focusing on your own
- **Long-term relationships.** Creating multiple transactions that over time build trust

Trust allows you to be open and honest. It allows you to give and receive feedback, knowing you're in a safe environment where people aren't going to be bringing lots of politics into the mix or creeping around doing things behind other people's backs. Trust opens up the way for you to talk about things, to discuss new ideas without fear.

Overview of Activity

This is called Blind Car! Participants will pair up and take turns driving the car (which is one of the partners) around the room.

Time

Instructions—1 minute
Each round—2 to 3 minutes
Debriefing—5 minutes
Total time—8 minutes

STEPS TO FOLLOW

Round 1

1. Have everyone pair up with a partner.
2. Ask one person to raise her hand—she is Partner A, the car. The other person is Partner B, the driver.
3. Follow the Blind Car Driving Instructions on how to drive the car: Blind Car Driving Instructions:
   - This is a brand new car so treat it with the utmost respect.
   - Go forward: One hand on the upper back
   - Go right: One hand on the right shoulder blade
   - Go left: One hand on the left shoulder blade
   - Reverse: One hand tapping the back with "beep, beep, beep" sound
   - Stop: Both hands off
   - Emergency brakes: Both hands on the shoulders
   - Honking: Tapping on the top of the head (the car makes honking sound)
4. Partner B's job is to ensure that the car does not get into an accident.
5. Partner A will now close her eyes. Partner B will *drive* her around the room.

Round 2

1. Switch! Now it's B's turn!
2. A drives B around the room.

▼

BENEFITS TO LOOK FOR

The ideas below echo the Trust approach:

- **Give up control.** It's difficult for most people to give up control of their actions, especially when they don't know the person who is taking over. In the business world, we have to trust that other people are doing their job. That doesn't mean we don't observe and put on the "emergency brakes" when we see something going badly—but we do give people the opportunity to take charge.
- **Share values and vision.** Communication is important because it provides the artery for information and truth. By communicating the organization's vision, management defines where it's going. By communicating its values, it establishes the methods for getting there.
- **Tell the truth.** It's not always easy to tell the truth, but it is important in building and maintaining integrity. It's the overarching standard for any organization, and it starts at the top. If the organization has integrity, it will be believed.

- **Treat people with equality.** It's hard to see the rookie as an equal, especially if you've been at your job for a few years. However, trust is established when even the part-timer or the lowest-paid employee feel important and part of the team. This begins with management's not being aloof but instead, getting out and meeting the troops.
- **Acknowledge people and give credit.** Leaders should always seek the opinions and ideas of their employees, and they should always know their employees by name and know something about their employees' family. Leaders should treat one and all with genuine respect.

Discussion Points

- **Q: How did you feel about your partner after the exercise?** (*I had trust in myself and my partner. I trusted that my partner was going to take care of me and not run me into a wall.*)
- **Q: How can we build trust in the workplace and/or avoid losing it?** (*Keeping promises and being honest. Sharing and building core values. Being not afraid to apologize. Always showing appreciation. Not playing favorites. Treating everyone as equals.*)
- **Q: Why is trust important in the workplace?** (*Trust builds openness and honesty—the ability to give and receive feedback. It creates an environment in which people can bring new ideas to the table without fear.*)

Participant Action Plan

Have all the participants share their experience with their partner. Ask them to choose one thing they learned that they will continue to work on. Provide all the participants with a copy of the following action plan. Ask them to complete it, and set up a time to review their results one week later. At that time, ask them what has worked and what has not worked. What do they need to do to improve?

Trust Actions

The actions I will take as a result of the Trust activity are:

_____

_____

_____

_____

ONE WEEK LATER: What results have I gained from the Trust activity?

_____

_____

_____

_____

Activity 24

Let Go

Man is free the moment he wishes to be.

—Voltaire, a French Enlightenment writer, historian, and
philosopher famous for his wit and for his advocacy of
civil liberties, including freedom of religion and
free trade (1694 to 1778)

Level of Risk

High

Background and Purpose

Some people would rather join the Polar Bear Club and jump into a frozen lake than stand onstage and improvise. It can be such a frightening experience—feeling awkward, being judged by the audience, performing next to strangers without a script or written jokes.

One negative coping mechanism to use with these overwhelming feelings is to control the scene by declaring everything: tell your scene partners what to do, when to do it, and how to do it. By controlling the scene, you feel in charge, grounded, and certain. The problem with controlling everything is that you don't learn how to collaborate, and you kill the relationship with your scene partners because they will never feel empowered or a part of the creative process.

The only solution is to let go! Stop being the director and start being a participant.

OBJECTIVES

By the end of this activity, people will:

- Distinguish between the judgments that hinder them and those that help them.
- Build trust.
- Collaborate for mutual success.
- Reward and recognize individuals' strengths.

Mini Lecture

By letting go of the uncontrollable and unchangeable things in life, we have more strength and energy to be creative and solve problems innovatively at home and work. Sometimes, however, we get confused about what we can let go, and we hang on to things that we should not be hanging on to.

One manager we were coaching had developed a habit of going into her office and closing the door for most of the day. Her team could talk to her only if it was an emergency. When we talked to her, we discovered that she had recently gotten divorced and couldn't cope with the ensuing situation. When she realized how much her personal life was affecting her team and jeopardizing her work, she was able to step back and let go of the things she could not change. She could not change the divorce, and she could not change her ex-husband. But she could change her attitude to the situation. She could take charge of her thoughts and feelings.

Why, then, do people have such a hard time letting go? After talking with many people from different industries worldwide, here's just a partial list of what people say:

- "I'm the only one who can solve the problem."
- "If they fail, it will reflect badly on me."
- "It's quicker to do it myself than explain it to others."
- "If I do it, then I know it's being done properly."

The problem with not letting go is that we never allow others to be responsible for their own work. If people are not given responsibility for projects, if they are micromanaged, they will come to expect others to do it for them and begin to do less and less.

Once we do let go, we are free of the tremendous burden of "being the only one who can do things." Here are some ways to let go:

- **Acknowledge what you can and cannot do.** Be realistic about what is and what is not your obligation or duty to correct, change, or control.

- **Release being perfect.** Free yourself from the sense of obligation, duty, or requirement to make everything perfect in your life and the life of others.
- **Let go of over-responsibility.** You are not responsible for the whole world. You cannot correct a problem that is beyond your competency, power, or authority.
- **Say "no."** Allow yourself to say "no" or "I can't" when faced with an insurmountable problem that is out of your reach.

Overview of Activity

In this activity you need at least eight participants—four on each side holding their legs, arms, torso, and head. One by one, each participant will be supported and held up in the air and "flown" around the room.

Time

Instructions—3 minutes
Each round—2 to 3 minutes per participant
Debriefing—5 minutes
Total time—32 minutes for eight participants

STEPS TO FOLLOW

Round 1

1. Ask participants if any of them have any physical reasons (injury or pregnancy) to not take part in this activity. If they do, have them sit this one out and observe. *You do need at least eight participants for this activity.*

2. Have participants form a tight circle, and inform them that they will **one by one** fly around the room.

3. Ask for a volunteer, *someone who is willing to be flown first,* to stand in the middle of the circle. Tell him to cross his arms over his chest for protection.

4. Instruct the rest of the group to be ready to catch the volunteer and fly him around the room *safely!*

5. This is not a competitive, rushed exercise. This is about trust. So make sure the person's entire body is supported from toes to head.

6. Tell the volunteer to fall back—the rest of the circle will pick him up and fly him around the room.

Round 2

After you have safely grounded the volunteer, ask for the next person to fly. Each round someone else will be flown around the room until everyone has gone. (If they are very confident, participants can fall forward instead of backward.)

Note: Make sure the participants holding the volunteers being flown switch roles—that is, if they always hold the flyer's toes, tell them to switch to the torso. This is a group effort, and it should not fall on one person to carry each person.

▼

BENEFITS TO LOOK FOR

The ideas below echo the Let Go approach:

- **Be open-minded.** When we hold on to something, we are removing the space for creativity. If we hold on to certain ideas, we are closing our mind to new thoughts, and when we close our mind to new concepts, we may be missing the best ideas ever.
- **Avoid seeking perfection.** No one likes to make a mistake or, worse, be responsible for a mistake that someone else has made! But the problems with seeking perfection are that you never delegate, your workload increases, and your stress level goes up—not to mention that you lose faith in your team members, which affects their creativity and productivity. Let go. Don't rob your team of the opportunity to *learn*.
- **Let others share responsibility.** We all have certain responsibilities at work, and sometimes we have standard operating procedures by which we can perform and measure the results. But that doesn't mean we are responsible for everything that happens. Collaboration, teamwork, and leadership require that we let others take responsibility for their part in the process. If we don't empower others, then we fall into the trap of micromanaging, and that reduces the power and energy of the workforce.

Discussion Points

- **Q: What did you think when you first heard the instructions for this activity?** (*I felt really scared, but I also felt willing to let go and go for it. I thought I would be too big and heavy to be supported by the group—but I found out that I could be supported, and it felt really good.*)

- **Q: How did it feel to be flown around the room?** (*It felt like nothing I had ever felt before; it was liberating. Once I got over the fact that I was flying round the room supported by my coworkers, I was able to let go and just experience the exhilaration.*)
- **Q: How does letting go empower people?** (*It removes the responsibility from being completely on one person's shoulders, and it allows everyone to take part in the process.*)
- **Q: What will you do in the future to let go?** (*I will remember this activity and just allow myself to let go. Once I've experienced this, I think I can always re-create it in my mind and allow myself to be supported by my coworkers.*)

Participant Action Plan

Ask all the participants to shout out what they will do or change as a result of this activity. Provide all the participants with a copy of the following action plan. Ask them to complete it, and set up a time to review their results one week later. At that time, ask them what has worked and what has not worked. What do they need to do to improve?

Let Go Actions

The actions I will take as a result of the Let Go activity are:

_____

_____

_____

_____

ONE WEEK LATER: What results have I gained from the Let Go activity?

_____

_____

_____

_____

Activity 25

Team Confidence

Coming together is the beginning. Keeping together is progress. Working together is success.

—Henry Ford, American industrialist, founder of the Ford Motor Company, and sponsor of the assembly line method of mass production (1863 to 1947)

Level of Risk

High

Background and Purpose

Gaining confidence in your team and teammates doesn't happen overnight. It usually takes time, energy, and practice. After I had earned a name in the Chicago improv community, Charna Halpern (owner of iO) invited me to join a cast of my colleagues to invent a new form of improvisation. It was very exciting and nerve-racking at the same time. I had the utmost confidence in the members of our team, but I wasn't quite sure how we would do it. Invent a new improv form? How? I felt like everything had been done before by my predecessors. But after three months of rehearsals and late night rapport, we invented a new form that we called JTS Brown, which is still being performed to this day by young fresh improv groups.

How did we accomplish this task? First, we had to communicate and get on the same page as to what improvisation meant to each of us, how we wanted to improvise as a team, and where we wanted to push improv to moving forward. Then we had to build confidence in each other and ourselves by practicing our vision.

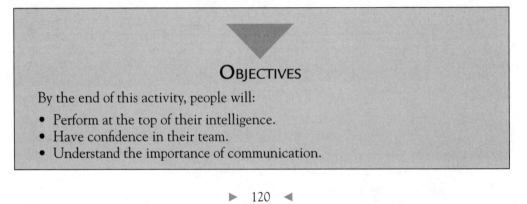

OBJECTIVES

By the end of this activity, people will:

- Perform at the top of their intelligence.
- Have confidence in their team.
- Understand the importance of communication.

Mini Lecture

If we believe a project will be successful, we put ourselves behind it 100 percent. We look for solutions and eliminate obstacles that might cause failure. A team full of people looking for solutions has a much higher success rate than a team of people looking for excuses to use in case of failure later on. The idea then, is to build team confidence, and here are some easy steps:

1. Have confidence in the team. Play to their strengths, and expect good results.
2. Have confidence in yourself as a supervisor, manager, or team leader. You have been given the job because someone had confidence in you—now you just need to share it with your team.
3. If possible, create simple projects for the team to work on together. When a team works on an easy project that the members believe will be successful, it has a very good chance of success. Think of any game show: the beginning questions are always easy, and the participants build their confidence.
4. Create something in memory of the success. Historically, nations build monuments in memory of their success. When Yahoo! completed a groundbreaking version of its Web mail system, the company hired an artist to create a sculpture celebrating the success. The statue is on display at the Yahoo! headquarters. Create a trophy that reminds the team of their wins.
5. Turn failures into positive learning experiences. Remember Edison when asked about the thousands of experiments he had gone through to invent the electric light bulb? He replied, "I have not failed, not once. I've discovered 10,000 ways how not to invent the electric light bulb."

Overview of Activity

This is all about physics. The participants stand in a perfect circle and then sit down directly on the lap of the person behind them. If they all sit down together at the same time, it is weightless and nobody falls. *Before this activity you must check that everyone is free of injury and that the space is completely clear of any objects such as chairs or tables.*

Time

Instructions—4 minutes

Each round—2 to 3 minutes

Debriefing—8 minutes

Total time—15 minutes (more if the team completes a second or third round)

STEPS TO FOLLOW

1. The space must be completely free of objects such as chairs and tables.
2. Every participant must be free of injury.
3. Have all the participants stand in a tight circle.
4. If all the participants stand in a perfect circle and sit down at the same time, directly in the lap of the person behind them, this activity works. They can actually move the circle!
5. Explain that to become a cohesive team, they must work together:
   - If you don't work as a unit and sit at the exact same time, the circle will collapse.
   - By taking care of the person in front of you, each person is taken care of.
   - If someone is not paying attention and allows the person in front of her to fall, the rest of the circle will tumble.
   - Trust is imperative in this exercise because your team is only as strong as its weakest link.
   - You must all talk to each other and agree on actions.
6. Explain why some groups fail:
   - One person stands up before the rest of the group stands up.
   - One person sits too early.
   - The circle is a rectangle.
   - Someone is not sitting directly behind someone else in the circle.
7. Tell the participants to turn to their left so their right shoulder is inside the circle and their left shoulder is outside and they are staring directly at the back of the head of the person in front of them.
8. Tell them to simultaneously sit down on the lap of the person behind them.

   Note: The first time you do this, people may fall. The participants may want to accomplish it and have another go, or they may find it too difficult to try it a second or third time. Either way, the discussion is the place to bring out the objectives of building team confidence.

BENEFITS TO LOOK FOR

The ideas below echo the Team Confidence approach:

- **Communicate your actions.** If someone is going to take a certain action that will affect other members of the team negatively, it is important that he communicate it beforehand so he can get input, hear concerns, and listen to improvements. Open and assertive communication is one way people can accomplish their mission.

- **Pull your weight.** You've heard it before: "You are only as strong as your weakest link." It is impossible for any team to move forward if one of its members is dragging an anchor and sabotaging the team's collective efforts. Imagine it like this: there is a huge rowing boat, and all the crew members are working well, rowing together and pulling on the oars. Unbeknownst to the rowers, however, one person has stopped rowing and is drilling holes in the bottom of the boat. Eventually the boat will sink, and the entire crew will go down—including the person who is drilling holes!

Discussion Points

- **Q: What did you feel when you learned what you were about to do?** *(I felt like I wanted to leave because I was so scared. But it was really a fun idea. It was good to get out of our comfort zone and do something completely different.)*
- **Q: How did you feel after the activity?** *(It was much easier than I thought. We all communicated our actions and worked well together. It was great.)*
- **Q: Did you expect what happened to happen?** *(I was surprised at the outcome; and I think we did a good job.)*
- **Q: What would you do differently?** *(I would encourage everyone to communicate every action no matter how small.)*

Participant Action Plan

Ask participants to shout out what actions they will take to build team confidence. Provide all the participants with a copy of the following action plan. Ask them to complete it, and set up a time to review their results one week later. At that time, ask them what has worked and what has not worked. What do they need to do to improve?

Team Confidence Actions

The actions I will take as a result of the Team Confidence activity are:

_____

_____

_____

_____

ONE WEEK LATER: What results have I gained from the Team Confidence activity?

_____

_____

_____

_____

Activity 26

Advance Jointly

Some men storm imaginary Alps all their lives, and die in the foothills cursing difficulties that do not exist.

—Edgar ("Ed") Watson Howe, American author and editor,
wrote realistic regional and romantic novels
(1853 to 1937)

Level of Risk

Medium

Background and Purpose

The key to this exercise is the word *jointly*, which means that everyone is involved. No one is carrying the burden on her shoulders alone. Together we advance. For example, one time when I was performing with Valhalla, a house team of eight players at the iO in Chicago, we were performing the Harold—a long-form improvisation—and the audience gave us the word *couch* as the suggestion. Together we created three different scenes, but each scene had a couch involved. One scene was about an older couple who was sitting on a couch and fighting over the remote. Another scene was about a wife waking her husband who had passed out on the couch the night before. And the third scene was about two homeless people discussing the relevancy of wisdom teeth while sitting on a couch in a junk yard. Now no one knew we were going to do all of that. But we embraced each other's ideas and said "yes, and" to each other. Everyone was utilized. Whether someone was a TV repairer or a kid asking why Daddy was on the couch, we jointly advanced the scenes.

OBJECTIVES

By the end of this activity, people will:

- Rely on innovation from within a group or team.
- Work together to organize themselves in a short amount of time.
- Become a cheerleader of others' ideas.

Mini Lecture

Frank Wells joined Disney in 1984 as its president and COO, and within 10 years, the company's annual revenues went from $1.5 billion to $8.5 billion. To have that kind of success requires advancing jointly with other people, and that's what Frank did. When an idea was thrown out, Frank would instantly become the idea's biggest cheerleader. When someone had a concept for an animated movie, Frank would decide it was a winner. When someone asked, "Should we build more hotels at Disney World in Florida?" Frank's immediate response was, "Let's build a dozen."

Advancing jointly in business or in your personal life requires seeing the bigger picture, setting goals, providing project management, ongoing development, and job performance appraisals. However, before these systems are put into place, the first and foremost requirement is being a cheerleader of other people's ideas—deciding that something is a winner and saying "yes!"

Advancing jointly is about being an optimist and a glass-half-full kind of person instead of a glass-half-empty kind of person. It's not about looking for winning ideas. It's about deciding that an idea is a winner!

Overview of Activity

Participants are given two tasks that they must complete in a short amount of time without speaking. They can communicate with each other in any way they want, but it must be done in silence. To accomplish these two tasks, they must work as a team and leverage the resources in the room such as letter-sized paper, flip charts, or markers.

Time

Instructions—2 minutes
Each round—5 to 10 minutes
Debriefing—8 minutes
Total time—20 minutes

STEPS TO FOLLOW

Round 1

1. Give the participants the task of building the tallest tower. Tell them they must complete the task within five minutes without speaking. They can communicate with each other in any way they want except speaking. It must be done in silence.
2. Suggest they work as a team and leverage the resources in the room to accomplish the task.

Round 2

Give the participants the task of selling themselves as a team on how they worked together to build the tallest tower. In this round they can speak. How did they apply their strengths? What worked really well? Give them two minutes to strategize and three minutes to present.

BENEFITS TO LOOK FOR

The ideas below echo the Advance Jointly approach:

- **Nonverbal communication.** Body language, eye contact, and facial expressions are all part of jointly advancing a project. Never underestimate the power of nonverbal communication. People who roll their eyes at an idea could be killing the best idea that was ever thought of.
- **Participation.** It goes without saying that participation is the most important part of any joint adventure. If people are shy and do not contribute, they may be holding back a powerful observation that could make something work more effectively. So participate and don't hold back.
- **Cheerleading.** When people cheer other people on, it creates a powerful "can-do" environment. The opposite of cheerleading is being a naysayer, and that is the fastest way to kill ideas and stop forward movement.

Discussion Points

- **Q: How did working together without speaking help advance a project?**
  (*It was fun to communicate without speaking. We had to pay attention and make sure we included everyone.*)

- **Q: What is the purpose of being a cheerleader?** *(Cheerleaders make people feel they can do things. Cheerleaders create an environment in which people feel they can do better and achieve more.)*
- **Q: How does advancing jointly help in the workplace?** *(When people are pulling together and working to advance projects, it creates an atmosphere of optimism that in turn creates productivity and positive communication.)*

Participant Action Plan

Provide all the participants with a copy of the following action plan. Ask them to complete it, and set up a time to review their results one week later. At that time, ask them what has worked and what has not worked. What do they need to do to improve?

Advance Jointly Actions

The actions I will take as a result of the Advance Jointly activity are:

_____

_____

_____

_____

ONE WEEK LATER: What results have I gained from the Advance Jointly activity?

_____

_____

_____

_____

Activity 27

Support

The focus of improv leads to conversers being present, meaning they exist in the here and now. The acceptance in improv leads to the speaker's connection, meaning each becomes part of a co-creation team. The distance between the communicators is thereby no longer a gap to be closed. It becomes a connector, filling the space between bodies like a seesaw connects the two riders on either end. Each is dependent on the other for flow and movement. This synchronicity of focus and acceptance is what results in full body listening.

—Izzy Gesell, author, humor and creativity coach

Level of Risk

Low

Background and Purpose

This competency is one of the founding tools of improvisation, and it is ingrained in improvisers at the very beginning. This tool is my favorite, and it actually made me fall in love with improvisation. In essence, what you are doing is making your scene partners look good. And in turn they do the same for you. This mindset and philosophy create an amazing environment on and off stage. I felt so confident and empowered. It allowed me to get really good because I knew I had support whether I was terrible one night or just okay. This tool was also great for me because it enabled me to see the value in being a giver rather than a taker.

In business and life, it's sometimes quite the opposite. In survival mode, it's often necessary, easy, or profitable to be competitive and self-seeking. Putting yourself first can get you ahead and make you very successful. But for me, the problem is that it leaves me empty. The joy and pride I have felt over the years creating moving or hysterical shows comes from the support I received and the support I gave to the incredible people around me.

P.S. When I was teaching this activity at Duke University with the executive MBA students, I found that many adults thought this activity was horrifying—for them, to pretend to be a machine was embarrassing. I noticed, however, that as soon as they actually started to perform the activity and build a machine, they soon got into it. By the end, they were starting to say, "Can we do this again?" or "I want to be the inventor."

Just as it is with many activities in life, it's always toughest for the first person to start. But after one person fearlessly begins, it's amazing how everyone jumps in to support the performance. Sometimes the performers need encouragement from the facilitator, which sounds like, "Okay guys, don't leave them out there too long." Or, "Don't leave them hanging." The amazing thing about improv, however, is that people always do want to support each other, and that's what builds fantastic camaraderie.

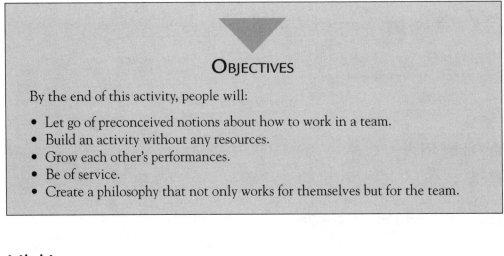

Objectives

By the end of this activity, people will:

- Let go of preconceived notions about how to work in a team.
- Build an activity without any resources.
- Grow each other's performances.
- Be of service.
- Create a philosophy that not only works for themselves but for the team.

Mini Lecture

Support is about finding ways to increase interaction between coworkers so that they work effectively together even on tough projects. It is the willingness to connect, collaborate, and cooperate with coworkers that builds lasting support. Here are some tools and tips on how to effectively create a supportive work environment:

1. Acknowledge that we need the support of coworkers to get things done; whether it is delegation, follow-through, or handing off a telephone call, we need to be supportive and supportable.
2. Provide assistance as needed. When people need help, be the one they go to and you are more likely to become a leader.
3. Invite opinions and viewpoints from coworkers, and be open to change.
4. Maintain an open-door policy especially if you are a manager, supervisor, or team leader.
5. Admit mistakes and be willing to say, "I don't know."
6. Publicly acknowledge and reward team members' exemplary work.

7. Become a mentor or provide coaching in areas where your skills excel.
8. Build a network and connect with key people who are critical to your goals.

In some workshops we deliver, we ask the group, "Who would be honored to have someone call you up for support?" Everyone answers with a resounding "Yes!" We do want to support other people, and it doesn't have to be a long-winded difficult thing to do. Being a support doesn't mean you have to take on other people's jobs or spend hours talking to them. It simply means providing a motivational pep talk or pointing them in the right direction. Suggesting a book, Web site, or group can often be the exact support that someone needs.

Overview of Activity

Participants will stand in a circle and one by one they will create a human machine.

Time

Instructions—3 minutes
Each round—2 to 3 minutes
Debriefing—6 minutes
Total time—18 minutes

STEPS TO FOLLOW

Round 1
1. In a loose circle, tell the participants they will create a human machine.
2. A brave volunteer will begin by going into the middle and start making a motion.
3. After a couple of seconds, another participant will join the volunteer and add a movement related to the last one.
4. This will continue until everyone is a part of the machine.

Round 2
   To make it funnier, repeat with sound.

Round 3
1. To challenge participants, have two people not join.
2. At the end, as the machine is still functioning, have the two be the inventors of this machine.
3. They should tell you exactly what parts of the machine do what, when and how they got the idea for the invention, what it will cost, and what they hope to achieve with this invention.

Round 3 Example

Person A: "This is a cheese dispenser."

Person B: "Yes, it is. It has all types of cheeses from Gouda to Stilton, and all you do is stand here with your hand out and wait for the cheese."

Person A: "Over there is the button you push to select your cheese."

Person B: "And this part here is what melts the cheese in case you want to make a cheese fondue."

▼

BENEFITS TO LOOK FOR

The ideas below echo the Support approach:

- **Build on each other's ideas.** When we are willing to build on another's idea, we can create projects that move far beyond our expectations. We expand the opportunities and open up doors that we never knew existed.
- **Be supportive.** Being supportive is not just about learning tools and skills and using them to build relationships. Being supportive is about having a mindset that is built on cooperation rather than competition. When we cooperate with others, we are creating a culture of support.
- **Participate.** Everyone at one point or another has been shy. If you ask the most expressive people, they will tell you that underneath their gregarious actions they are quite shy. Shyness is just par for the course—a given, if you will. When people participate, their shyness disappears and their true selves come forth. When you are in a team, participation is an important part of the creative process. If you have an idea but don't tell anyone, it is like knowing the directions to a gold mine but withholding the map.

Discussion Points

- **Q: What made you participate more fully?** (*I could see when my coworkers needed help. They were up there, and if I didn't move forward, they would feel embarrassed, and I didn't want that.*)
- **Q: How did it feel to be part of a human machine?** (*It was a lot of fun. I enjoyed it. The more I got into the part, the more I felt that I was helping my coworkers.*)
- **Q: What were some things that stopped you from participating fully?** (*I didn't want to be too big and take the spotlight. I wanted to make it easier for everyone else so they could fit in. I didn't understand the activity at first. I judged it.*)

- **Q: Now that you have completed the exercise, what benefits do you see?**
  (*I feel more support. I see a little more willingness from the group. It was nice to see us be creative once in a while.*)

Participant Action Plan

Ask participants to form groups of three to four people and discuss what they will do differently as a result of this activity. Provide all the participants with a copy of the following action plan. Ask them to complete it, and set up a time to review their results one week later. At that time, ask them what has worked and what has not worked. What do they need to do to improve?

Support Actions

The actions I will take as a result of the Support activity are:

_____

_____

_____

_____

ONE WEEK LATER: What results have I gained from the Support activity?

_____

_____

_____

_____

Activity 28

Problem Solving

Life just serves it up sometimes, doesn't it? And life doesn't care what you're doing when it does.

—Robin Quivers, American radio personality most notable for being the news anchor and cohost of *The Howard Stern Show*

Level of Risk

Low

Background and Purpose

Unless a show is going down the tubes and it's a creative issue, the only real problems that arise in improv are problems with the venues. For example, when I performed at the twenty-fifth celebration of iO at the Chicago Theater downtown, I was onstage with performers such as Mike Meyers, Tim Meadows, Amy Poehler, and Tina Fey. The rehearsals had all gone really well, except that come nightfall when everyone in the audience was seated and ready to watch the performance, we suddenly realized that all our microphones were dead.

It happened because the sound engineers had checked only one mic at a time and assumed everything was working. But when eight players stood onstage all with their microphones, the mics went dead. So we had to be creative! We started joking with the audience, doing an impromptu dance, roasting each other until finally five standing microphones where placed at the front of the stage … not exactly appropriate for improv, but still the show must go on, and go on it did!

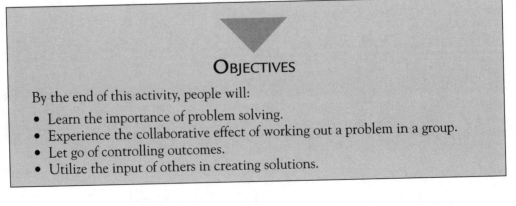

OBJECTIVES

By the end of this activity, people will:

- Learn the importance of problem solving.
- Experience the collaborative effect of working out a problem in a group.
- Let go of controlling outcomes.
- Utilize the input of others in creating solutions.

Mini Lecture

There are many ways to solve a problem, but one of the most important steps is to understand the source of the problem. Why is it happening in the first place? One of the simplest problem solving techniques to help people discover the root cause of an issue is to ask a series of "why" questions. Asking why sets off a chain reaction of questions and answers that lead back to the source of the issue.

Asking why gets to the root cause very quickly, and it doesn't require forms or writing. If there are several root causes, it can also help people determine the connections and relationships between causes. It's also a very flexible tool that adjusts to the complexity of the issue. Sometimes it may take only two or three why questions to reveal a root cause, and other times it may take more than five or six. Here is an example of how this works:

1. Why do customer waiting times peak between 2 and 3 p.m.?
   All time zones access the same dial-in number at that time.
2. Why are the western time zones using the same dial-in as the eastern time zones?
   We're staffed to cover only the eastern time zones.
3. Why can't senior staff cover the western time zones?
   Senior staff members are busy coaching new reps.
4. Why do senior staff members coach new reps during peak business hours?
   The senior staff members are not available to coach the new reps at any other time.
5. Why are senior staff members unavailable to coach the new reps at any other times?
   They are covering for staff members on breaks, or they are handling escalated calls.

Asking the why questions targets the central issue: Why is X occurring? Or why are we experiencing X? The second why question is based on the last answer: "Okay, but why did this happen?" Continuing to drill down by asking questions and challenging the responses with new questions can help reveal the logical root cause. In the above example, the root cause provides the solution: we need to resolve the staff issue.

Overview of Activity

This activity is about people standing in a circle, holding the hands of two different people and thus creating a "people knot." The next step is to unravel the people knot.

Time

Instructions—2 minutes
Each round—2 to 3 minutes
Debriefing—7 minutes
Total time—18 minutes

STEPS TO FOLLOW

Round 1

1. Have participants get into groups of no fewer than five people and no greater than nine.
2. Have all the participants put their hands into the center of the circle and grab two hands from two different people. *Tell them not to hold both hands of just one person.*
3. Now have them pass "a squeeze" around the circle to make sure the group is all joined. One person will gently squeeze her right hand. Say, "If your hand gets squeezed, pass it on until the original person's left hand is squeezed. If the squeeze does not come back to the original person, let go of your hands and start over again."
4. Say, "Now disentangle the 'people knot' so that you are standing in a perfect circle *without* letting go of any of the hands you are holding. You can adjust the position of your hands for comfort, but the idea is to solve the problem of the people tangle."

Round 2

Have participants repeat the activity—this time, without talking.

Round 3

Have them repeat the activity. This time they can talk, but they must close their eyes.

BENEFITS TO LOOK FOR

The ideas below echo the Problem Solving approach:

- **Be flexible in mind and body.** When we get out of our mind and go with the flow, we can achieve more, especially with problem solving activities. Oftentimes our biggest challenge is to overcome any negative thoughts such as, "I can't do this." When we are optimistic about the outcome, we have more fun and are more likely to find solutions.
- **Have a vision.** When we visualize finding a solution and seeing the problem solved, we are more likely to solve the problem.
- **Work together.** Whether we enjoy working with people or not, we often have no choice—we are required to solve problems that involve other people. It makes sense then to work at solving problems in an environment of collaboration, communication, and cooperation. When we do, we experience positive outcomes.

Discussion Points

- **Q: How did you feel in this activity?** (*It was uncomfortable at times, but I really tried hard to relax and help others work out the solution.*)
- **Q: What happened when people tried to force the solution?** (*It didn't work. When people used force, it just made the "people knot" get tighter and more uncomfortable. But when we relaxed and worked together, we were able to unravel ourselves.*)
- **Q: When did you think it would succeed or fail?** (*I felt that some people were giving up and that others wanted to succeed. I decided to work on untangling ourselves.*)
- **Q: What can you take away from this exercise?** (*Patience. Support. There's always a solution—I just have to keep trying.*)

Participant Action Plan

Work as a whole group and shout out what you will do differently as a result of this activity. Provide all the participants with a copy of the following action plan. Ask them to complete it, and set up a time to review their results one week later. At that time, ask them what has worked and what has not worked. What do they need to do to improve?

Problem Solving Actions

The actions I will take as a result of the Problem Solving activity are:

_____

_____

_____

_____

ONE WEEK LATER: What results have I gained from the Problem Solving activity?

_____

_____

_____

_____

Activity 29

Collaboration

Being in a band is always a compromise. Provided that the balance is good, what you lose in compromise, you gain by collaboration.

—Mike Rutherford, English musician and a
founding member of Genesis

Level of Risk

High

Background and Purpose

There are many different ways to produce a written sketch show. And let me tell you, it's not always an easy, joyful process. But there are definitely ways to help the process go smoothly, one of them being collaboration.

One way to create a sketch show is to *pitch* your idea and have the rest of the group throw out suggestions to flesh it out or make it better or give it a point of view. Another way is to actually write a scene, bring it to the group, have a read-through, and get suggestions. It may sound like this: "How about if you do this ... ?" or "What if you do that ... ?" or "Maybe do this ... ?"

Whatever the method, you literally take a germ of an idea and, through the process of collaboration, turn it into a scene that kills. No one ever says in the process, "That sucks." We might be thinking it for a split second, but we know better. Negative judgments can kill the energy in the group and possibly the idea. There are thousands of reasons why a scene will not work, even when we have challenged ourselves to make it work or be brilliant. With collaboration, it's not that everyone's suggestion in the collaboration process will be utilized or is even good, but it's helpful to my mental health and to my productivity to have coworkers around me supporting my idea. If we all pitch and collaborate, then everybody wins and ultimately the audience does too.

OBJECTIVES

By the end of this activity, people will:

- Support each other for mutually beneficial outcomes.
- Create supportive relationships.
- Proactively handle issues with a sense of urgency.
- Work in partnership with cross-functional teams.

Mini Lecture

Collaboration is about working together on a common task and taking action with respect to the needs and contributions of others. In the workplace, collaboration creates a successful environment in which people feel free to ask questions, gain support, and accept consensus—all of which will help people achieve the objectives and goals of the team. Here are some skills that will turn lone wolves into team players:

- **Compromise.** It's impossible for everyone to get his or her own way when working in a team. Be prepared to give and take.
- **Don't take things personally.** There's always a chance your feelings will be hurt by insensitive team members when the group makes decisions. Remember that decision making is not personal. It's just part of the process.
- **Focus on the success of the project.** Remove the urge to get your own way by keeping your eye on the task and working toward a successful outcome.
- **Be kind, necessary, and wise.** Problems pop up when you work with people—it's the nature of being human. Before you say anything, think, "Is it kind, necessary, and wise?"
- **Pinpoint the hurdles.** If you have difficulty collaborating with others, take a moment to reflect: "What is causing my discomfort, and how can I map out ways to overcome it?"
- **Ask for help.** Lone wolves don't ask for help—collaborators do. If you have a problem, seek help.
- **Check for agreement.** Instead of forging ahead, gain commitment to shared goals.
- **Notify others.** Don't keep information to yourself. Tell others of changes or problems, and don't keep people in the dark.

- **Make practical suggestions.** If you know a way to get something done that will bring success to the project, don't keep it under your hat. Let others in on the secret.

Overview of Activity

Participants will form four groups. Each group will prepare and create a movie trailer that they will pitch (perform) to the other groups.

Time

Instructions—2 minutes
Each round—5 minutes
Performances—10 minutes
Debriefing—6 minutes
Total time—23 minutes

STEPS TO FOLLOW

Round 1

1. Divide participants into four groups.
2. Have each group give a movie genre to another group:
   - Drama
   - Horror
   - Disney
   - Special effects/science fiction
   - Action
   - Western
   - Comedy
3. Give the groups five minutes to prepare a movie trailer keeping in mind:
   - Main characters: heroes, sidekicks, villains
   - Plot or conflict
   - Beginning, middle, and end
   - Voice-over person
   - Length: The trailer can be no longer than 60 seconds.
4. Everyone must have a role in the trailer.

Round 2
   Each group will perform their trailer in front of the other groups.

BENEFITS TO LOOK FOR

The ideas below echo the Collaboration approach:

- **Work toward a goal together.** Collaboration is about keeping your eye on the goal and working with other people to achieve it. This means not taking things personally, focusing on success, pinpointing the hurdles, and mapping a way to achieve the best outcome for all.
- **Avoid the lone-wolf mentality and collaborate instead.** Some people by necessity work alone. Writers, some IT people, and researchers often have to close the door so they can create, solve problems, and write code or presentations. But even these people who work alone the majority of time need to work with other people at some point in the process. Collaboration therefore is a necessary skill to ensure the best results at the start and end of any project.

Discussion Points

- **Q: How did it feel to work together on a process?** (*It was fun and at the same time frustrating; sometimes one person had an idea that he or she wouldn't drop. In the end though, we all collaborated.*)
- **Q: What energy did you create? How will you create this back at your desk?** (*Good energy. More verbal support. More appreciation and acceptance.*)
- **Q: Did a leader emerge in this process?** (*Some people naturally take the lead, and one or two people did make certain idea choices. If we hadn't had a leader, we wouldn't have gotten the job finished.*)
- **Q: Was everyone's voice heard? If yes, how did you make sure?** (*We tried to include everyone, but some people are quiet, and in the short amount of time we had to work with, we just had to get on with it. It's probably up to the leader to make sure we all get heard.*)

Participant Action Plan

Have each team discuss what they learned and what action they will take as a result of this activity. Provide all the participants with a copy of the following action plan. Ask them to complete it, and set up a time to review their results one week later. At that time, ask them what has worked and what has not worked. What do they need to do to improve?

Collaboration Actions

The actions I will take as a result of the Collaboration activity are:

_____

_____

_____

_____

ONE WEEK LATER: What results have I gained from the Collaboration activity?

_____

_____

_____

_____

Activity 30

Adapting to Ambiguous Information

I look for ambiguity when I'm writing because life is ambiguous.
—Keith Richards, English guitarist, singer-songwriter, Rolling Stones

Neurosis is the inability to tolerate ambiguity.
—Sigmund Freud, Austrian neurologist and founder of the psychoanalytic school of psychiatry

Level of Risk

Medium

Background and Purpose

It's the worst feeling to be standing onstage lost. Obviously, I'm not talking about physically being lost. I'm talking about being lost in the scene. And to make matters worse, there's an audience watching you, and you're trapped onstage until you can find some sort of ending. It can happen in the blink of an eye. All it takes is one person not listening, being uncertain in his or her choices, being vague, or thinking that osmosis really works. All of it is bad communication. However, in life, as onstage, we sometimes find ourselves in situations exactly like this, and when that happens, we have to adapt.

When I am onstage with "ambiguous man," we'll probably end up staring at each other like two deer in the headlights. It's a terrible feeling. In those types of situations, my partner and I have to get clear and get on the same page as quickly as possible. It sometimes means that I have to take the lead and take charge of the scene by being very direct in my talk or actions. It may mean I need to support my scene partner to get clarity. I might even actually have to say, "I'm totally lost. What is going on?" The audience will appreciate the reality check because they were probably just as lost as we were. Hopefully, my scene partner and I can then retrace our steps and clear up any misinformation that happened. Then we can figure out where the scene needs to go or how to end the scene.

▼

OBJECTIVES

By the end of this activity, people will:

- Gain confidence.
- Have clear communication.
- Assess adaptation strategies and deal with margins of error.
- Effectively deal with uncertainty and change.

Mini Lecture

Ambiguity is a condition in which information can be understood or interpreted in more than one way. People don't usually like it because it means uncertainty, doubt, and change. Yet in life, many things are ambiguous. For example, a long-standing, profitable customer is about to take her business to the competition, and you have to act quickly—usually without the proper instructions and without knowing how your decision is going to impact others. Or senior executives implement budget cuts, but they expect the work to still be completed on time and at the same high quality. In either scenario, it's how we deal with it that makes us succeed or not.

When we deal with ambiguity, we must find ways to live with a margin of error. If we wait for everything to be perfect, we lose our window of opportunity. Here are some tips on how to adapt and deal with ambiguity:

- Prioritize, and focus on the few critical items that will generate success.
- Minimize distractions that are "nice to do" but don't add value.
- Be willing to not be able to complete one task before starting another.
- Be comfortable not tying up loose ends.
- Manage your stress level. Anxiety can increase with ambiguity.
- Anticipate the impact of future change on your profession or company.
- Read and research what is happening in your field continuously.

If you lead others, resist the urge to micromanage in a misplaced effort to regain control. Ambiguity means a loss of control, so redirect your efforts to understanding and managing any changes affecting your business.

Overview of Activity

Participants stand in a circle, and someone poses a problem the company may be facing. The second person provides a solution that makes no sense, and the third person links the two together.

Time

Instructions—3 minutes
Each round— 1 to 2 minutes
Debriefing—5 minutes
Total time—10 minutes

STEPS TO FOLLOW

1. Participants stand in a circle, and someone in the group must pose a random problem the company is facing.
2. The person standing next to the first person must propose a solution that makes no sense.
3. The third person, that is, the participant next in line, must link the first two.
4. Keep repeating this pattern until everyone has had a chance to do all phases of the activity.

Example

Person A: "Tardiness."

Person B: "Require everyone to wear purple."

Person C: "When people wear purple, it gets them excited and makes them drive faster to work!"

BENEFITS TO LOOK FOR

The ideas below echo the Adapting to Ambiguous Information approach:

- **Consider unexpected solutions.** Sometimes the solution may be something we would never have thought possible. When we open our minds to different ideas, we allow creative solutions to unfold and unexpected answers to develop.
- **Accept something less than perfection.** Be willing to live with a margin of error, and focus on the thoughts and actions that will create success.
- **Take the lead.** If action is required and there are no clear instructions, take the lead and do the next best thing. Use common sense, and take the action that is within your capability and within the scope of your knowledge and authority.

Discussion Points

- **Q: Which of the problems were most surprising?** (*I didn't expect there to be so much anxiety around the current changes. I thought everyone was on board, but now I realize we are not all on the same page. We can work together to create more cross-functional teams.*)
- **Q: Which were some of the best solutions?** (*The shadowing idea was great. Spending a few hours with my contacts in accounting will allow me to see how my job affects theirs and how we can work together more effectively.*)
- **Q: If the solutions weren't viable, did they spark any other ideas to come forth?** (*Yes, I actually have some different ideas of what I can do because of this exercise.*)
- **Q: How did it feel to link the solutions to the problems?** (*At first it seemed impossible to link the two ideas because they seemed so random. But as we went on with the activity, it began to make sense—every idea has a seed of truth that can be used.*)

Participant Action Plan

In the large group, choose one issue that is relevant to their work environment, and determine an action they can take that will improve the situation. For example, "Employees who achieve their sales goal for the week go home early on Friday." Provide all the participants with a copy of the following action plan. Ask them to complete it, and set up a time to review their results one week later. At that time, ask them what has worked and what has not worked. What do they need to do to improve?

Adapting to Ambiguous Information Actions

The actions I will take as a result of the Adapting to Ambiguous Information activity are:

_____

_____

_____

_____

ONE WEEK LATER: What results have I gained from the Adapting to Ambiguous Information activity?

_____

_____

_____

_____

Activity 31

Managing Change

When you're finished changing, you're finished.

—Benjamin Franklin, founding father of the United States,
author, printer, satirist, political theorist, politician, postmaster,
scientist, inventor, civic activist, statesman, and diplomat

Level of Risk

Low

Background and Purpose

In any improv cast you are very lucky if the ensemble stays the same. At iO there hundreds of students chomping at the bit to get onstage. If you're not showing talent in the first couple of months, you're kicked off the team and replaced with a "rising star." This has an effect on any team because there's a loss of friendship and confidence. To make matters worse, whoever was kicked off is then replaced with a stranger. Teams now have to deal with a different personality, which can throw the whole energy of the team out of whack.

I was on a team called Valhalla where at least five people left and five people joined in the span of five years. Even our coaches rotated. Any time this happened, whether it was a performer or a coach who left, we had to put aside our emotions and get on board with the new dynamic.

For example, one of our coaches, Liz Allen (a nurturing, caring mother figure), had gotten us to be an amazing group. We were all functioning well, everyone was happy, and we felt productive and empowered. So when she left, it was scary, and we had quite a lot of uncertainty. Not without reason! The next coach (a grumpy, over-it, know-it-all) had a totally different way of communicating. I was lucky enough to have a really great team whose members supported each other through this difficult transition. We could talk about our feelings and create positive attitudes in each other by saying things like, "This coach will be amazing. He's going to take us to the next level." By managing change, we learned a new style and a new philosophy of improvisation that ultimately made us even better.

Objectives

By the end of this activity, people will:

- Experience communication as storytellers.
- Utilize cooperation and contribute to the action to move change forward.
- Actively listen and respond positively without judgment.
- See change as a normal function of life.

Mini Lecture

Most businesses experience change. If managed right, change is an amazing and powerful dynamic that increases success on all levels. If not managed right, change can cause failure, loss of production, and falling quality. Managing change is really about managing fear. Even though experts tell us that change is natural and good, when faced with the reality of change, our reaction can be unpredictable and even irrational.

We usually resist change because we fear the unknown, so the most important step in managing change is to tell people why it's happening and what to expect. In our own experiences in talking to many employees going through change, we have found that when senior executives and managers keep employees in the dark, people make things up. They get disgruntled, they gossip, they talk about it endlessly, and they lose faith and trust. The bottom line is that it lowers morale and productivity, which in turn affects earnings. In other words, the things people make up can be much more disruptive to business than what is actually going to happen.

We hear people talk about it all the time in large and small organizations: "If they would just let us know what's happening and why we are going through this change, we'd be able to handle it. It's the not knowing that we hate." We even hear it from employees who are actually going through change management training, "Why are we changing? Things were great just the way they were." Knowledge is power, and when people don't have the knowledge, they feel powerless, and that makes people resist.

If you move an employee's desk four inches, he probably won't care. But if those four inches are to accommodate the desk of a new hire, it will most likely create resistance. If the new hire brings much needed assistance, there will be less resistance, but if the new hire is a threat to someone's job or if no one knows the what or why, there will be high resistance.

A promotion would seem to be a good change, but it might not be if the employee doubts she can handle the work. A layoff for an employee who has savings and investments may not seem to be such a big deal, but it might be if that employee feels overextended and worried about a long and complicated job search. Any kind of bulldozing to resistance will fail. Trying to rationalize things will also fail. The only way to manage change effectively is to focus on opening and maintaining clear channels of communication so people understand what is coming and what it means to them. As early as possible tell the employees as much as you can about the change and provide updates so that the employees are clear about what is happening: "Our sales have increased by 30 percent, and we're hiring people to meet the demand. We're moving things around to make room for them. If you have any ideas on how we can rearrange the space, please let us know." You don't have to accept their suggestions, but it does open a two-way flow of communication.

If resistance persists, find out the reasons behind it: "What is it about the promotion that is worrying you?" Sometimes the truth is hard to uncover. A doctor once said, "Patients come into my office and explain what is wrong with them. But it's often when they have their hand on the door handle on their way out that they tell me the real reason for their visit."

Understanding is a two-way street—you want people to understand what is changing and why, and you also need to understand their reluctance. It's also important to let people know what is not changing. This provides them with something to hold on to as they face change.

Overview of Activity

Participants will work together to create a story using one word at a time.

Time

Instructions—1 minute
Each round—2 to 4 minutes
Debriefing—8 minutes
Total time—12 minutes

STEPS TO FOLLOW

Round 1
1. In pairs, have a conversation. The only rule is that each person can say only one word at a time.
2. The topic to discuss is "unusual occupations."

Round 2
1. Now have pairs join up to become four-person groups.
2. Again, tell them to have a conversation one word at a time.
3. The topic is "vacations gone wrong."

Round 3

1. Now have everyone join into one big circle. Again, participants will speak one word at a time, but this time they will tell a story as if they were one author.
2. The topic is "Betty's bad hair day."

Round 1 Example

Person A: "Goat …"

Person B: "… herders …"

Person A: "… are …"

Person B: "… obsolete."

Round 2 Example

Person A: "Swimming …"

Person B: "… in …"

Person C: "… Michigan …"

Person D: "… is …"

Person A: "… not …"

Person B: "… a …"

Person C: "… vacation."

Person D: "Hawaii …"

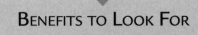

BENEFITS TO LOOK FOR

The ideas below echo the Managing Change approach:

- **Communicate what you know.** We all say that we acknowledge that change must happen in order to grow, and yet many people fear change and resist it. One of the most important aspects of managing change is to communicate what is actually happening. Just don't communicate your fear because that creates more fear and resistance.

- **Share the vision.** If you know the goal or long-term vision of what or why the change will hopefully bring … share it. People need knowledge. If they don't get it, they start gossiping and making it up, which creates denial, anger, and indifference. Tell people what's going on so they feel in commune, empowered, and a part of the change.
- **Ask questions.** Whether you are a manager or frontline employee, always ask questions about change. Why is it happening, and how will it affect the workplace? Even if you don't get an immediate answer, you are letting others know that you are interested in the whole story.
- **Be an advocate of change.** In order for things to survive and grow, change must happen. People who resist change don't stop change from happening; they just stop themselves from growing. Be an advocate of change, and allow yourself to grow to your full potential. Take advantage of the opportunities. Even if they do not seem like opportunities today, when you look back, you will view them as some of the most important changes you made.

Discussion Points

- **Q: What did you have to do in order to make this work?** (*I had to respond just to the last thing said. No judgments! I had to think about the simplicity of the story so I would say an easy word in order for the story to make sense.*)
- **Q: What did actively listening and responding positively, without judgment, do to the story?** (*The story was natural and easy flowing. It felt like the story had already been written.*)
- **Q: Did you have to change your word at the last minute because of what the person before you said? And how does this apply to the workplace?** (*Well, yes, I had to adapt quickly! And it happens all the time.*)
- **Q: What are some techniques you can use when you are faced with an unexpected or expected change?** (*Listen before responding. See the bigger picture, the story behind the change. Take a breath and let go of resistance. Ask questions and seek understanding.*)

Participant Action Plan

In pairs discuss one action participants will take to improve change processes in the workplace. Provide participants with a copy of the following action plan. Ask them to complete it, and set up a time to review their results one week later. At that time, ask them what has worked and what has not worked. What do they need to do to improve?

Managing Change Actions

The actions I will take as a result of the Managing Change activity are:

_____

_____

_____

_____

ONE WEEK LATER: What results have I gained from the Managing Change activity?

_____

_____

_____

_____

Activity 32

Flexibility

Empty your mind, be formless, shapeless—like water. Now put water into a cup, it becomes the cup, you put water into a bottle, it becomes the bottle, you put it in a teapot, it becomes the teapot. Now water can flow or it can crash. Be water, my friend.

—Bruce Lee, Chinese American and Hong Kong actor, martial arts instructor, philosopher, film director, film producer (1940 to 1973)

Level of Risk

Low

Background and Purpose

I learned the most about flexibility with the Second City Touring Company going from city to city in a big blue van. Although it was all fresh, exciting, and new, touring can be demanding and chaotic, and you must be flexible. For example, each new location we traveled to had completely different stages, equipment, and systems. At some venues there were no spotlights so we'd have to pull out a scene that needed a spotlight and replace it with another on one on the fly. In some places we had to be politically correct and couldn't say any inappropriate words because the audience was more sensitive. I would have to be very careful in our improv sets not to offend anyone. In some venues the sound systems were old and in others they didn't work so we'd have to figure out a way to dance to a piano. Improv is just like life—flexibility is a major key to success.

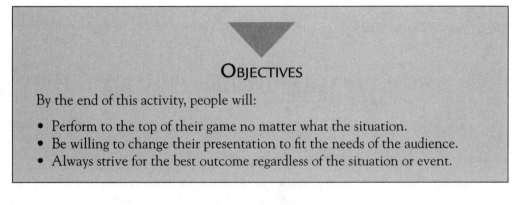

OBJECTIVES

By the end of this activity, people will:

- Perform to the top of their game no matter what the situation.
- Be willing to change their presentation to fit the needs of the audience.
- Always strive for the best outcome regardless of the situation or event.

Mini Lecture

Being flexible means getting along well with others, being open to new ideas, and adjusting to the quick-paced work environment in which we operate. Difficult people who are not able to play well with others rarely get promoted—it doesn't matter how much knowledge they have or how well they do their job. People who want to develop their career need to accept others, and they need to be willing to work with all kinds of people, including the more difficult ones.

The goal therefore is to get branded as being flexible and easy to work with. This is best done by utilizing the following steps:

- Recognize other people's needs and priorities, and be willing to put them before your own when necessary.
- Have the perspective of "this can work!" even while considering others' challenges in meeting it.
- Make compromises to ensure that goals are met, and pick your battles wisely.
- Think with an open mind—a flexible person does not always have to be right.
- Keep silent— even when you are more right than not.
- Seek first to understand—and then be understood.
- Listen in meetings, stay open to ideas, and don't interrupt.
- Choose your words carefully when reacting to new ideas.

With the advancement of technologies and constantly changing processes, people are pushing for more efficiency, and managers expect more with less. To thrive in this world, you must let go of the old ways of doing things, embrace the new, and be ready to react quickly. If you are used to doing things one way and don't like to be told you have to do it another way, welcome to planet earth.

Overview of Activity

Participants are sports announcers and flies on a wall.

Time

Instructions—5 minutes
Each round—2 to 3 minutes
Debriefing—8 minutes
Total time—22 minutes

STEPS TO FOLLOW

Round 1
1. Divide participants into groups of three, and tell them they are professional commentators at a sporting event.
2. Have one of the groups volunteer to come up to the front of the room and go first. Their job is to talk as if they were live on the radio commentating play by play and giving background information on the sport, location, and

players. They can speak in any particular order just as long as everyone is contributing and one person is not doing all the work. Support each other. "Yes, and" each other, and suspend judgment of themselves and each other.

3. Now that you have given the rules, ask the audience for a sporting event. To make it more interesting, you can ask them for a winter sport or an obscure sport. Or, better still, ask them to make up an obscure sport, for example, toe racing!

Round 2

Switch groups and have another group come up to the front of the room and repeat.

Round 3

1. Shake it up and tell the next group they are flies on a wall gossiping about what is happening.
2. Ask the audience for a wall that the flies could land on. (The wall could be personal or professional: business meeting, awards banquet, break room, IT department, wedding, Thanksgiving dinner.)

Round 1 Example

Person A: "Here we are at the Mouse Lakes annual Shovel Race."

Person B: "Yep, it's cold up here."

Person C: "Sure is. But the competitors are bundled up in their snow jumpsuits."

Person B: "And there goes John Bacalar. He won last year."

Person C: "Yep, his time to beat is five minutes and two seconds."

Person A: "Yeah, these driveways are not very large so it doesn't take that long."

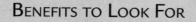

BENEFITS TO LOOK FOR

The ideas below echo the Flexibility approach:

- **Be open-minded.** One of the keys to being flexible is the ability to get along well with other people, and this means that you don't sulk and take your ball home if someone disagrees with you or has a different point of view. Stay open-minded, and expect others to be different. In fact, celebrate the differences, and look for ways in which to collaborate instead of getting upset.
- **Don't take things personally.** This is a key rule for anyone who wants to build flexibility and get along well with other people. If someone says something that you don't agree with, it's not personal—it's just a different point of view. Being flexible is about allowing others to think differently.

- **Listen without interruption.** This is one of the hardest things to do, especially when listening to new ideas. Usually we want to jump in and either agree or disagree. In building flexibility, know that listening to other people makes them feel respected and important, which are keys to getting along well with other people.

Discussion Points

- **Q: What worked best?** (*When we listened to each other and let people talk, it worked really well. Larry was really funny. At one point, we all started talking at the same time, and no one gave up the space. It was really difficult to understand what was being said, and we couldn't build on it.*)
- **Q: How did it feel listening to the other groups?** (*I really got to see what worked and what did not work. It was like getting a big picture of the activity. When we acted like real sports commentators on TV and we listened to each other, it worked really well.*)
- **Q: What did you notice about your own flexibility?** (*I always thought I got along well with people, and now I see that it's easy to interrupt and want to get my own point across. I also see it doesn't help to build flexibility.*)
- **Q: How can you practice being more flexible at work?** (*Listen more. Not be so scared. Join in and participate. Be the solution, not the problem. Be more open-minded. Don't gossip.*)

Participant Action Plan

Working in the same groups, have participants decide on one action they will take to improve their flexibility. Provide all the participants with a copy of the following action plan. Ask them to complete it, and set up a time to review their results one week later. At that time, ask them what has worked and what has not worked. What do they need to do to improve?

Flexibility Actions

The actions I will take as a result of the Flexibility activity are:

_____

_____

_____

_____

ONE WEEK LATER: What results have I gained from the Flexibility activity?

_____

_____

_____

Activity 33

100 Percent Commitment

When you want something, all the universe conspires in helping you to achieve it.
—Paulo Coelho, a Brazilian lyricist and author
of *The Alchemist*

Level of Risk

High

Background and Purpose

Many scripted shows are developed through improvisation. These shows are performed night after night and must be delivered the exact same way in order to elicit the laughs at the desired times. However, for a variety of reasons, the laughs are not always as loud or they don't come at the same spots. For example, the audience's responses might differ depending on whether it's a full house or half empty, or whether it's a matinee versus a Friday night audience.

But no matter what, every performance, no matter what the size of the house, the players must stimulate laughter from the audience and enjoy every show. Otherwise, the players are not doing their job. In order for every show to succeed, the players cannot "phone it in" or become bored with the material. The audience has paid good money and is expecting an amazing show. Whether you are in front of 15 people in a small theater in Muskogee or performing to a sold-out show in LA, you've got to give it your all. From the audience, to your teammates, to the stage manager, everyone deserves your best. Every show must be performed as though it is the very first time you've ever done it.

Objectives

By the end of this activity, people will:

- Understand the difference between setting goals and giving 100 percent commitment.
- Know the importance of giving relationships 100 percent commitment.
- Guarantee productive, positive results.
- Create the habit of setting high standards.

Mini Lecture

What does it really mean to go for it 100 percent? How do we measure our effort, and how do we know when we've achieved it? Mostly we measure our commitment by setting goals and prioritizing tasks, but even if we achieve a goal and complete our tasks, how do we know we gave it our all? And if we do use goal setting as a way to measure our commitment, how do we stop ourselves from just being an achiever of goals and not knowing or caring how we got there? How do we know if, with a bit more commitment, we could have gotten our goals achieved much faster and be well on our way to achieving a third, fifth, or sixth goal?

One way to measure our commitment to something is to actually take out the usual "What's in it for me?" question and replace it with "What can I do for you?" It may be the most effective way to create and sustain great relationships with other people—taking full responsibility to commit 100 percent and expect nothing in return! Try it for a week and see how you feel at the end of the week. Examine how other people are reacting toward you, and look at the unexpected gains of knowing that you have committed 100 percent to creating long-lasting relationships. Here are the steps:

1. Choose a couple of key people in your life, and make a 100 percent commitment to show respect and kindness to them for one week.
2. Expect nothing in return——nada, zip, zero.
3. Allow nothing (no annoying habits) to affect your 100 percent commitment to showing them respect and kindness.
4. Be persistent.

Expect to feel a shift in energy by the end of the week. Even if you chose to work on a difficult relationship, you will find that by committing to treat that person with respect and kindness, the other person often chooses to take responsibility as well. When that happens, the individuals involved and their team, their organization, and their family all experience the breakthrough.

Overview of Activity

Stand in a circle and sing. No one has to have a great voice—the point of this activity is to go for it with 100 percent commitment and not leave any team member hanging.

Time

Instructions—5 minutes

Each round—Depends on the size of the group

Debriefing—5 minutes

Total time—15 to 30 minutes

STEPS TO FOLLOW

Have participants stand in a circle, and explain to them that in the center of this circle is a spotlight, a very hot spotlight. Someone must always be standing in it, and whoever is standing in the hot spot must *sing!*

Rules

- At any time, someone can replace the singer in the hot spot.
- Whenever participants enter the hot spot, the song must change. The person entering the hot spot just taps the other person on the shoulder, replaces the person in the hot spot, and starts singing a different song.
- This is an exercise of perpetual motion so someone must always be singing in the hot spot.
- All of the participants must stand in the hot spot and sing at least once. They can go in as many times as they want, but all participants must sing. Ask them, "Why is it important for everyone to participate?"
- Tell participants not to leave each other out to dry, explaining that this exercise is also about providing support. Tell them to think about the other person first.

Explain

- Tell participants that it's okay if individuals don't have a good voice. They are not looking for the next American Idol.
- Tell them that this is a go-for-it exercise and that it doesn't matter if they don't know any songs. They can always sing "Happy Birthday" or a nursery rhyme, for the point of this exercise is to practice committing 100 percent, suspending judgment, and supporting team members.

Challenge

Tell participants to sing a song that is somehow related to the previous song. It can be a thematic or word association, or it can be in the artist's repertoire or it can be related in some other way. Have them suppose that (A) is singing a nursery rhyme, "Jack and Jill went up the hill to fetch a pail of water, Jack fell down … " Then (B) could step in and sing: "Humpty Dumpty sat on a wall, Humpty Dumpty had a great fall …"

BENEFITS TO LOOK FOR

The ideas below echo the 100 Percent Commitment approach:

- **Go for it.** Obviously, sometimes it's necessary and wise to think critically before acting. But on the other hand, sometimes it's necessary and wise to leave your fear behind you and step into the unknown.
- **Take full responsibility.** When we choose to give 100 percent commitment to our relationships and expect nothing in return, we allow ourselves the experience of being fully committed.
- **Don't have expectations.** Normally, when we set goals and prioritize tasks, we expect something in return. But when we give 100 percent commitment to something without expectations, then we are really committing ourselves to the process of commitment.
- **You need nothing but commitment.** With most tasks and goals, people need resources to see them through. The benefit of making a 100 percent commitment to showing respect and kindness to other human beings (with no expectations of return) is that there is no measure except the feelings that you get. Whether the other person is experiencing a benefit is not important. The important result is that you are experiencing giving 100 percent commitment.

Discussion Points

- **Q: Was it harder to think about doing this activity than it was to just do it?** *(I found that if I jumped in and just sang, even though I don't have a good voice, it felt good to do it, and it was easier than standing there thinking about it.)*
- **Q: What is the rip-off or consequence of thinking about something in a negative way?** *(I don't get things done. I don't move forward. I'm stuck. I'm in my comfort zone, and sometimes that's limiting.)*

- Q: **What are the benefits of participating and action?** *(When I participate, I feel good that I have pushed through a barrier—I've gone outside my comfort zone and I've done something different, something that I wouldn't normally do. So it gives me confidence to do other things.)*
- Q: **What would the effect be if one person didn't go?** *(It would feel like being hung out to dry. If we all do it, then it feels like a team activity. But if one person doesn't do it, then it gets embarrassing and awkward.)*
- Q: **How was it to commit?** *(I really enjoy committing to things, but it's usually things that I want to do. In this activity I was committing to something I would never have thought of doing in a million years, but I realized that it's like that sometimes at work. I don't always want to commit, but when I do, it just feels better.)*

Participant Action Plan

Have the whole group shout out the actions they will take as a result of this activity. Then provide all the participants with a copy of the following action plan. Ask them to complete it, and set up a time to review their results one week later. At that time, ask them what has worked and what has not worked. What do they need to do to improve?

100 Percent Commitment Actions

The actions I will take as a result of the 100 Percent Commitment activity are:

_____

_____

_____

_____

ONE WEEK LATER: What results have I gained from the 100 Percent Commitment activity?

_____

_____

_____

_____

Activity 34

Concentration

When you write down your ideas, you automatically focus your attention on them. Few if any of us can write one thought and think another at the same time. Thus a pencil and paper make excellent concentration tools.

—Michael Leboeuf, American business author
and former management professor at the
University of New Orleans

Level of Risk

High

Background and Purpose

Repetition and discovering patterns are major success factors and important aspects of comedy, and it requires concentration to know what's going on so that you don't miss opportunities to discover patterns. The long-form improvised comedy called Harold is a perfect example of an improv situation in which the players have to concentrate. It was developed by Del Close and brought to fruition through his collaboration with Charna Halpern, cofounder of the iO Chicago. The Harold is still being used today and performed by improvisational theater troupes and teams across the world. Performers have to remember characters, scenes, themes, and suggestions and weave them all into a half-hour performance.

Without getting into too much detail about the Harold, if the performers check out for one split second and lose focus on what is going on, they can miss important information that other performers might pick up and use throughout the show. I guess you could compare it to driving a racecar: you have to focus hard on the task at hand because if you lose focus, you'll crash the car—that's exactly what it's like in improv, except the crash isn't physical. In improv the crash is a mental confusion of not-funny, weird scenes that seem to drag on to eternity. No one wants that. We must concentrate and focus on the piece at hand so that the end result is a masterpiece.

▼

Objectives

By the end of this activity, people will:

- Engage the brain in intense concentration.
- Demonstrate how patience supports teamwork.
- Multitask verbally and nonverbally.
- Maintain eye contact and observe people's communication needs.
- Learn that the message's success is on the shoulders of the sender, not the receiver.

Mini Lecture

Concentration is easy when you enjoy what you are doing, but when you are doing something that you don't particularly want to do, it becomes more difficult. And that is the challenge: to concentrate on doing a great job regardless of whether you want to do it or not. Deadlines help provide focus, but they can also create a feeling of being overwhelmed. Don't allow being overwhelmed to stop you from concentrating. Instead, concentrate on completing the job, and the feeling of being overwhelmed will naturally lessen.

Give yourself rewards and breaks. For example, I write in time spans of two-hour periods. After two hours, I need a break. If I don't take a break at that point, then I get tired and unfocused, and the work suffers as a result. I also give myself rewards like a cup of coffee or 10 minutes to read an article or to take a short walk. It is not good to sit tied to a desk working, working, working—we are after all human beings and as such we need breaks and rewards to keep us satisfied.

Another key concept to improve concentration is to create a space to work. Not all work requires total concentration, but if it does, then you need to seal off your cubicle (even if it is only in your mind) from outside distractions. I do that when there are a lot of people around. I mentally seal myself in my space and get on with the job. People soon realize that I'm serious about the project I am working on.

If you can't do that, find an empty meeting room where you can complete the work in relative silence. If that is not possible, let your coworkers kindly know that you are "off limits" until your project is complete. If your boss is seeking attention, let him or her know that you need some time to concentrate if the work is to be finished on time. Concentrate on doing it in a great way so that you don't ruffle any feathers.

A couple of other tips to help concentration: keep the lights bright, and don't eat large portions of fatty foods that will make you sleepy. Maybe drink a glass of lemon or lime juice to keep you awake.

Finally, learn how to deal with random thoughts and/or actions. Our brains are like noisy machines wanting our attention. We can be working on a project when suddenly we start thinking about laundry or a shopping list or our kid's school calendar. Whatever pops into your head, if you cannot let it go, write down the message and then continue concentrating on the work. Your list will still be waiting for you at the end of the day, but if you have concentrated on your work and finished your task, you will feel satisfied and ready to take care of other things in your life.

Overview of Activity

This activity has two debriefings, one between rounds 2 and 3, and one after round 3. Standing in a circle, participants will in turn raise their right hand and point to another participant and say, "You." Rounds 2 and 3 add other names.

Time

Instructions—4 minutes
Each round—2 to 3 minutes
Debriefing—4 minutes and 4 minutes (two debriefings)
Total time—20 minutes

Note: You will be participating in this activity and starting each round.

STEPS TO FOLLOW

Round 1

1. Have participants form a circle so that everyone can see each other. Inform the participants that they will create a simple pattern. Instruct the participants to raise their right hand.

    Note: You, the instructor, will play a large role in this activity. You are the conductor, and you start and stop the game.

2. Gain eye contact with one of the participants in the circle, and point to her with your right hand and say "you." Tell her to point to someone else who has his hand up. Keep pointing to this person.

3. They in turn point with their right hand to someone else and say, "You." They also keep pointing to that person.

4. This pattern continues until there are no more right hands up and all of the participants are pointing to someone else in the circle. The last person to be pointed at must point back to you, completing the pattern.

5. Repeat that exact pattern. Point to the exact same person and say, "You." Repeat this as many times as you feel are necessary to make sure the pattern is solidified. Then move onto round 2.

Round 2

1. Now instruct all the participants to raise their right hand again. Tell them they will start a second pattern. This pattern will be different from the first,

and therefore, they must point to a different person in the circle. This time they will say the name of the person they are pointing to. Repeat steps 2 through 5, but instead of saying "you," they will say the name of the person they are pointing to.

2. After this new pattern is complete and you have practiced it a couple of times, tell them they will now do the "you" pattern and the "person's name" pattern together.

Note: You will start both patterns one after the other. Be sure to gain eye contact. When both of the patterns have come back to you, stop. If one of the patterns does not reach you, go back and repeat that pattern alone to fix problems.

Round 2 Debriefing

- **Q: Ask, "What do you have to do to be successful?"** (*Eye contact. Look at the person who is giving you the pattern.*)
- **Q: How many times did you have to call out the person's name or say "you"?** (*Three to six times. At one point I started waving my hands to get the person's attention!*)
- **Q: If we could only say "you" or the person's name once, what would we have to do to accomplish that?** (*Slow down. More eye contact. Don't say anything until the person is looking at you. Only look at the sender—the person who is passing "you" or the person's name.*)

Note: Do not say "you" or the person's name until you have that person's eye contact. The responsibility is on the sender. If no one is looking at you, don't pass the information. This ensures that the message is sent.

Round 3

1. Now surprise the participants, and instruct them to raise their right hand a third time! Tell them they will start a third pattern. Again, they must point to a different person in the circle. This time they will say their own name. Repeat steps 2 through 5 from round 1, but instead of saying "you," participants will say their own name.

2. After this new pattern is complete and you have practiced it a couple of times, tell them they will now do the "you" pattern, plus the "person's name" pattern, plus their "own name" pattern all together!

3. Tell them they can say "you," the "person's name," and "your own name" *only once.*

4. You will start all three patterns one after the other to ensure the success of each pattern.

Note: Participants will drop a pattern. You will notice because it will not come back to you. Just wait for the other patterns to come back, then stop the activity. Ask what happened and how can we improve. Again, you may have to revisit a pattern on its own to find out where the problem lies.

▼

BENEFITS TO LOOK FOR

The ideas below echo the Concentration approach:

- **Be aware that concentration is not always planned.** Deadlines, projects, and tasks don't always happen at the most convenient times. Sometimes we are brought into a meeting and have to concentrate fully on the present moment. When this happens, let go of everything except the process of concentration. Take notes to help you focus on the speakers, the project, and the most relevant points.
- **Take breaks and reward yourself.** Most people cannot concentrate for an entire eight-hour workday. As human beings, we need to take breaks. Keep the breaks short, and reward yourself with a cup of coffee, a glass of water, or a short walk outside.
- **Concentrate on the work.** People working at home can easily become distracted by household chores. It is fine to take breaks to put the laundry in the machine or vacuum or even start dinner. The problems start when the breaks take over from the work. Be sure to concentrate on the project, and allow yourself a break only when you feel you have completed a certain amount of work.

Discussion Points

- **Q: What happened if just one person dropped one of the patterns?** (*The whole exercise stopped.*)
- **Q: What can you do in the workplace to achieve concentration?** (*I can let coworkers know that I am working to a deadline. I can create a mental barrier, or even place a plant at the entrance to my cube to let people know that I am concentrating on a project. Of course, I'd check with my boss first before doing this. I could go to a quiet meeting room and concentrate on my task, again, letting my boss know.*)
- **Q: In what ways does repetition help concentration?** (*When I make a habit of concentrating on finishing a project, following through, or making deadlines, I am building on my strengths and my ability to focus and concentrate.*)
- **Q: How can you deal with interrupting thoughts?** (*I can write them down. They will be waiting after I have concentrated on my project and completed the tasks.*)

Participant Action Plan

Provide all the participants with a copy of the following action plan. Ask them to complete it, and set up a time to review their results one week later. At that time, ask them what has worked and what has not worked. What do they need to do to improve?

Concentration Actions

The actions I will take as a result of the Concentration activity are:

_____

_____

_____

_____

ONE WEEK LATER: What results have I gained from the Concentration activity?

_____

_____

_____

_____

Activity 35

The Right Attitude

Switch is not about changing the people or events in your life. It is about you changing your reaction to them. It is about living your life from love instead of fear—from power instead of weakness—from acceptance instead of anger.

—Val and Jeff Gee, coauthors of *The Winner's Attitude*

Level of Risk

Low

Background and Purpose

In the beginning when we were first forming the group Valhalla (one of the most successful and most tenured house teams at iO Chicago, having had 75 percent of its final cast as original members who performed from the first show until its last, exactly six years later), we weren't that good, and we didn't trust each other, and we didn't know if we could ever become as good as our role models. But Liz Allen, our coach who had won the Del Close Coach of the Year award five years in a row, would always make sure we had a positive attitude. She would say, "We're just going to do what we do and hit 'em like pirates." I loved this vision. She didn't mean we would rape and pillage the audience. She meant that if we practiced hard enough and trusted the process, we would be amazing. I pictured us in Viking hats rowing across the Atlantic and getting to shore victorious. This little quote she said to us often instilled a feeling of "we can do it."

She didn't stop there. She always complimented us and empowered us to believe in ourselves. Now some people don't need the "fluffy" motivational talk. Some people actually get motivated by competitiveness or by the word *no*. But that atmosphere doesn't create support or teamwork.

We had one guy in our group who was really negative. He was never happy or positive, and always pessimistic. Fortunately he was outnumbered by positive happy people. We accepted him for who he was. We understood that he would never change and that we were stuck with him. We challenged ourselves to create a positive attitude around him, and he became our lovable Eeyore. When we'd had too much, we ignored him or removed ourselves. We were just determined to keep our attitudes positive despite the people or situation around us.

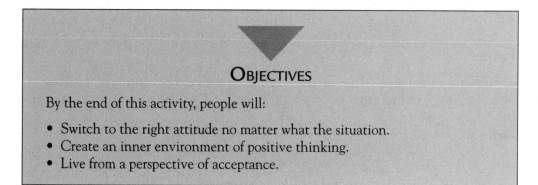

OBJECTIVES

By the end of this activity, people will:

- Switch to the right attitude no matter what the situation.
- Create an inner environment of positive thinking.
- Live from a perspective of acceptance.

Mini Lecture

Most people believe that our attitude creates our thoughts, but actually it is our thoughts that create our attitude. For example, if people wake up feeling depressed, anxious, or worried about the day ahead, those negative thoughts will create a bad attitude that will result in a bad day. If in that moment of waking, they remember that thoughts create attitude, they can choose to think a better feeling thought and change the entire day as a result. A better feeling thought does not mean that we go from depressed to outstandingly happy in one moment. But it does mean that we can go from depressed to not feeling too bad, and from not feeling too bad to feeling quite good, and so on.

A better feeling thought is like this: "I am grateful that I have ..." It could be something as simple as having food, a roof over your head, a family, a job, the ability to walk. A better feeling thought is one that is a level up from the bad thought that is creating the bad attitude.

At work it is important to have the right attitude because we spend so much time there—at least eight hours a day, and maybe more! If we don't choose to think good thoughts and create the right attitude, then we are spending much of our life with the wrong attitude—one in which we feel miserable about our job, our coworkers, our boss, and even our customers. When we feel unhappy about these things, we usually take our attitude home with us, and we "infect" our family with our bad attitude. "I'm having a bad day" means, "I am thinking bad thoughts, and I am giving them power so that they become a bad attitude."

Creating the right attitude is about creating the right habit of thinking good thoughts. Whenever you start to think negative thoughts, *stop*! Know that you have the choice in that moment to switch your thoughts and turn yourself in a different direction. Thinking a better feeling thought is just a small movement in the right direction that will change your attitude and eventually your life—it is that powerful.

Overview of Activity

Participants are given a simple topic to discuss with the added instruction that they will communicate with better feeling thoughts.

Time

Instructions—4 minutes
Each round—2 to 3 minutes
Debriefing—8 minutes
Total time—15 minutes

STEPS TO FOLLOW

Round 1

1. In groups of three, ask one person to raise her hand; she is Partner A. Ask a second person to raise his hand; he is Partner B. The third person is Partner C.
2. Say, "Partner A, your job is to have a bad attitude and play a character that is argumentative and enjoys conflict. You can use someone in real life that you know, or use a character from a movie or a book. You are also going to pick a topic to be negative about: a political viewpoint, an environmental issue, or a business issue."
3. Say, "Partner B, your job is to have a good attitude and play a character that is happy and enjoys good things. Whatever Partner A says, your job is to provide a better feeling thought."
4. Say, "Partner C, your job is to be the idea person who keeps generating ideas to keep the conversation moving along. Partner C, you can either support Partner A, the bad attitude, or Partner B, the good attitude."

Rounds 2 and 3

If there is time, switch the partners around so that everyone has a chance to play the different roles.

Round 1 Example

Partner A: "I think the parking situation at work is a disaster. I can never find a place to park, and if I don't bring my car, it takes me over an hour to get to work, plus it costs me a lot of money."

Partner B: "Maybe you could ride in with a coworker and find a space?"

Partner C: "That would work. It would save on gas too."

Partner A: "I don't know anyone who lives in my area, and I don't like people riding in my car."

Partner B: "What if you got a bus pass—they're very cost effective."

Partner A: "I hate buses."

▼

BENEFITS TO LOOK FOR

The ideas below echo the Right Attitude approach:

- **Everything begins with a thought.** Switch your thoughts. If people are having negative thoughts, they will create a negative attitude. By switching to better feelings and thoughts, they will create a better attitude that will lead them in the direction of the right attitude.
- **The right attitude feels better.** If people make a habit of thinking positive thoughts and creating a mindset of being in the right attitude, it gets easier and easier to stay with that attitude. When it becomes a habit, they become leaders who are able to facilitate a space that is uplifting no matter what the situation appears to be.
- **The right attitude makes sense.** Some people think that having the right attitude in a difficult situation is by default condoning the situation, but it is not about that. Having the right attitude no matter what is happening provides a happier, more joyful life. If we are waiting for the right situation to come along before we have the right attitude, we will be waiting forever.

Discussion Points

- **Q: How did it feel to play the different characters?** (*I had to force myself into the character; it's not one I usually like to play.*)
- **Q: How did it feel to play Partner C?** (*I realized at the end of the activity that I was choosing just one side. It made me think about my choices in life and how I can choose to be on any side I want.*)
- **Q: What did you learn most from this activity?** (*I learned that thoughts do come before attitude, and if I choose to have negative thoughts, then I will develop a negative attitude. If I choose to have positive thoughts, then I will develop the right attitude. It's all a choice.*)

Participant Action Plan

Provide all the participants with a copy of the following action plan. Ask them to complete it, and set up a time to review their results one week later. At that time, ask them what has worked and what has not worked. What do they need to do to improve?

The Right Attitude Actions

The actions I will take as a result of The Right Attitude activity are:

_____

_____

_____

_____

ONE WEEK LATER: What results have I gained from The Right Attitude activity?

_____

_____

_____

_____

Activity 36

Conflict Resolution

ID badges are long overdue. Security in this office park is a joke. Last year, I came to work with my spud gun in a duffel bag. I sat at my desk all day with a rifle that shoots potatoes at 60 pounds per square inch. Can you imagine if I was deranged?

—Dwight Schrute, a character on NBC's
The Office portrayed by Rainn Wilson

Level of Risk

Low

Background and Purpose

Conflict naturally arises in most great stories. Whether it's an internal or external conflict, it serves a purpose. In life, however, most human beings would like to avoid it at all costs.

Sometimes conflict does arise in improvisation either in the writing process or because of differing personalities. When you have to conceive of a show and must work and collaborate with others, mini disputes may happen. It could be because someone is too heavy in a show, or a director and producer might have disagreements about what scenes should go in the show. Don't get me started on personalities. There could be a more aggressive player or a too passive player or a talky player or an egomaniac or whatever. Somewhere down the line, heads will butt.

For our shows, the directors or our fellow improvisers are always there to sort it out. The general rule is to leave judgments about ourselves and each other at the door. In the forefront of our mind is that improvisation is a joint effort and everyone will shine, and in order for that to happen, we have to trust the process. It's okay if conflicts happen as long as they don't stop the productivity and deadline for the opening of the show. Sometimes you have to have a little pressure to make a diamond.

Objectives

By the end of this activity, people will:

- Learn how to manage their own emotions.
- Build a cooperative problem solving perspective.
- Actively listen and find out what the customers need and the solutions that can be achieved.

Mini Lecture

People are responsible for creating their work environment. However, some people think it is up to their coworkers, their managers, or the senior executives to create a conflict-free work environment. The truth is that turf wars, disagreements, and differences of opinion result from people not being willing to take responsibility for their thoughts and actions. Watching interpersonal conflicts evolve is like watching children fight in the schoolyard; they have forgotten where they are, and they don't care who is watching or who has to get involved. They don't care about the consequences of their actions because they expect someone else will work it out—even if it brings them disastrous results.

By the time a manager has to intervene in conflict resolution, the problem has already escalated to a point of being virtually unmanageable. All of the coworkers in the office are involved. Even if they are not actively part of the situation, they feel as if they are walking on eggshells whenever the people involved in the conflict come into view. In worst-case scenarios, coworkers take sides, which creates an even more dangerously volatile work environment and ultimately a divided business.

Trying to avoid conflict doesn't work either. Even if the conflict seems to have cleared up, it will rear its ugly head the moment a new issue arises. Unresolved conflict festers like an untreated wound. Sooner or later it will surface, usually at the worst possible moment when stress is high, deadlines are imminent, and customers are present.

Managers can use the following steps if they feel conflict is present within their team:

- Meet together with the people involved, and let them know that you will not choose sides and that you expect them to resolve the conflicts proactively as adults. If they are unwilling to do so, you will be forced to take disciplinary action that could lead to dismissal for both parties.
- Ask them to briefly summarize their point of view, without comment or interruption from the other person. Intervene if the discussion becomes attacking in nature—this is not acceptable
- Ask them to identify what they would like the other party to do more of, less of, stop, and start.

- Ask them to describe specific actions they want the other party to take that would resolve the differences.
- Ask them to discuss and commit to making the necessary changes to resolve the conflict.
- Ask them to notice when the other person has made a change, no matter how small, and to commit to treating each other with dignity and respect.
- Explain that it is okay to have reasonable disagreements but it is never okay to have personality conflicts that affect the workplace.
- Finally, let them know you have every faith in their ability to resolve their differences and to participate in the success of a shared organization. Set a time to review progress.

It's never easy to mediate conflict; however, the willingness of each person to take responsibility to resolve conflict sets the stage for success.

Overview of Activity

With a partner, the participants get a chance to practice diffusing emotions.

Time

Instructions—4 minutes
Each round—2 to 3 minutes
Debriefing—8 minutes
Total time—15 minutes

STEPS TO FOLLOW

Round 1
1. Have the participants team up with a partner and decide who is Partner (A) and who is Partner (B). In this exercise, participants in groups of two will role play with each taking a turn as the irate client.
2. If possible, have the (A)s pick a situation that actually happened to them in which they were the customers and lost control of their emotions. If they can't think of an actual situation, they can choose one they have seen; a good example would be that of an angry passenger yelling at an airport customer service agent.
3. The (B)s will use the "yes, and" technique, active listening skills, and conflict resolution tools to solve the issue.

Round 2
Have the partners switch roles.

Round 1 Example

Person A: "I booked this flight over a month ago! I need to get on that plane."

Person B: "Yes, and I appreciate that, sir. However, the gate is closed, and I have no way to open it."

Person A: "Unbelievable! I can see the plane! It's still here at the gate. I have a ticket, and I need to get on NOW!"

Person B: "Yes, and I can see that it looks as if you would be able to board the flight, but the gate closes 10 minutes before the flight takes off, and you got here just 5 minutes ago after the gate was closed."

Person A: "I don't care about your rules. I want to get on that plane now, so just please open the gate … the door. I know you have the code."

Person B: "Yes, and the best way I can help you is to look up the next available flight for you."

▼

BENEFITS TO LOOK FOR

The ideas below echo the Conflict Resolution approach:

- **Take responsibility for finding a resolution.** If everyone took responsibility for ending conflict, there would be no conflict. Sometimes people need others to mediate a situation. But mediation is not always the best answer. It would often be better for people to have the opportunity to resolve their own conflicts because in doing so, they will be empowered to be successful in all areas of their lives.
- **Don't take sides.** When onlookers take sides in a conflict, they are unconsciously creating a problem within the workplace. Gossip, intrigue, and a loss of faith occur, and work suffers as a result. If people are having a conflict that is affecting the work environment, it should be brought to the attention of management so that the conflict can be resolved quickly to avoid its affecting the entire staff.
- **Share your feelings.** People who are involved in a conflict should talk honestly about their feelings. Sharing their feelings openly will lessen the likelihood that they will point their finger at other people. Feelings are honest, whereas making other people wrong usually comes from our own judgments that may not be accurate and our own beliefs that may not be true.

Discussion Points

- **Q: What did you notice when you played the role of irate customer?** *(I really got into the part, but I appreciated the "yes, and." It's so easy to get angry.)*
- **Q: What was it like to be with an irate customer?** *(Using the "yes, and" tool helped me to remember that I was not there to defend anything, but to help the customer find a solution. Saying "yes, and," put me in the right frame of mind to help resolve the conflict.)*
- **Q: Did "yes, and" always work? If not, what else can you say?** *(No, sometimes it felt very contrived. But at other times it did seem to get the customers to calm down or at least to realize I was not against them. I can say, "I understand" or "You've been through a lot" or "I appreciate your honest feedback.")*

Participant Action Plan

Provide all the participants with a copy of the following action plan. Ask them to complete it, and set up a time to review their results one week later. At that time, ask them what has worked and what has not worked. What do they need to do to improve?

Conflict Resolution Actions

The actions I will take as a result of the Conflict Resolution activity are:

_____

_____

_____

_____

ONE WEEK LATER: What results have I gained from the Conflict Resolution activity?

_____

_____

_____

_____

Activity 37

Feedback

Ask permission to give another improviser a note. Don't give other improvisers notes. If you must give a note, don't, don't, don't do it during the show.

—Mick Napier, actor, director, teacher, author, founder and
artistic director of the Annoyance Theatre, and an
award-winning director at the Second City, Chicago

Level of Risk

Low

Background and Purpose

When we teach improv classes, we always give notes at the end of the session or the scene. The notes were written in real-time based on our observations of what was taking place on stage. The students expect feedback and are disappointed if they don't receive any because they all want to improve their performance. At work we don't have that same environment.

I was working with an inexperienced facilitator whom I shall call Chris, teaching business improv to a group of senior executives at a large corporation. At the end of one of the sessions, Chris was rambling on and on, but I didn't say anything because we were in the middle of the workshop and it would have been very unprofessional. But when it was my turn to deliver information, Chris kept saying, "We have to think about the time. We're talking too much. We need to move on!" In my head I was thinking that I was being amazing, and he was telling me that I was not. It didn't help my performance and it didn't help the participants—it was a potential disaster. At one of the breaks I told him to stop giving me feedback in the middle of a session and in front of our clients—he got the message, and the workshop continued with a much better atmosphere.

It's very easy to give feedback, but if it's not given at the right time or in the right way, it can be very destructive. Everyone has an opinion for every situation and a perception of what will work or not work. It's easy to forget that there is another person involved who also has opinions and emotional reactions. When we're not considering the situation and the people involved, we can give feedback in a way that is unproductive. I'm sure we've all given and received great feedback and terrible feedback in our lifetime. The key is to remember to give feedback at the right time and in the right way, and always focus on behavior that can be changed.

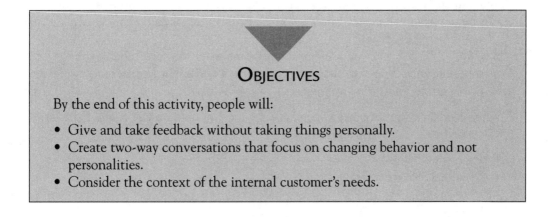

OBJECTIVES

By the end of this activity, people will:

- Give and take feedback without taking things personally.
- Create two-way conversations that focus on changing behavior and not personalities.
- Consider the context of the internal customer's needs.

Mini Lecture

Most people don't enjoy getting feedback, and few bosses or coworkers relish giving it. Except for professional athletes' receiving pointers from their coach on how to enhance their performance, most people take feedback in a negative way. Maybe one of the reasons that the coach-to-athlete feedback system works is that the coach doesn't wait all year for an annual review to give feedback in one big information dump. Effective coaches provide feedback based on the observations they make in real time, and their observations are relevant to performance improvement rather than performance shortcomings. Good coaches want their athletes to win, and they understand that providing feedback is a necessary part of the process. Feedback doesn't mean a terrible performance. It just means that the outcome could be better!

Most managers want their people to win, but often they give all of their feedback in one annual review, which is like cramming a year's worth of study into one day and expecting people to pass the exam—it just doesn't work. Coworkers often give feedback when a situation has escalated and gotten so bad that they just *must* say something, but by that time, they are so tense that their tone is harsh and sometimes even angry—not good for giving feedback. Feedback given regularly acknowledges real performance. Employees are told when they are doing the job right more than when they are "caught" doing it wrong.

Feedback provided in real time as close to the moment when something happens remains fresh and relative to job performance. Also, when the feedback is "sandwiched" in a two-for-one way—two pieces of affirmative feedback and one constructive piece of feedback—it is easier to swallow. For example:

"Taylor, I've observed your telephone techniques, and I like the way you answer the phone and say, 'May I help you?' It shows good customer service skills." (*Affirmative feedback*)

"I recommend that you also smile when you say it so that people can hear a sincere tone of voice. I've noticed that if you are not smiling, it can sound harsh." (*Constructive feedback*)

"I've also observed that you use brand marketing when you say, 'Thank you for shopping with Blue-sky," and I appreciate that because it affirms our brand with the customer." (*Affirmative feedback*)

When feedback is information specific, issue focused, and based on observations, it is a way of bringing people's attention to:

- What is working
- What is no longer working
- What is changing
- What is staying the same

If managers or coworkers have ideas and information that will help people to perform better, it's imperative to share it with them. Here are some feedback suggestions:

- Be clear about what you want to say.
- Emphasize the positive (two for one).
- Be specific.
- Focus on the behavior rather than the person.
- Refer to behavior that can be changed.
- Use "I" statements.

Finally, don't give advice. Feedback is about helping people understand their issue—how it developed and how they can identify actions to address it more effectively.

Overview of Activity

Participants begin in pairs conducting a conversation one word at a time. Participants then form groups and construct a correspondence letter one word at a time.

Time

Instructions—5 minutes
Each round—2 to 3 minutes
Debriefing—8 minutes
Total time—22 minutes

STEPS TO FOLLOW

Round 1

Participants pair up and have a conversation one word at a time. The conversation can be about anything (see example).

Round 2

Materials Needed

Pad of paper and pen for each group

1. Ask pairs to join up with another pair so there are four people in a group, and have them sit in a tight circle.
2. Hand each group one pad of paper and a pen.
3. Tell them that each group will write a letter giving feedback to someone. However, they must write this feedback letter one word at a time.
4. Appoint one person per group to be the designated writer. The letter writer will also contribute one word to the letter.
5. Assign each group a specific type of letter to write from the following:
   - Jilted lover giving feedback to an ex
   - Teacher giving feedback to parents about their child
   - Camper giving feedback to his or her parents
   - Coach giving feedback to a player
   - Child giving feedback to Santa Claus
6. Depending on the time available, give the groups 5 to 10 minutes to create their letters. Explain they cannot go back and reread the letters until you call time.

Round 3

When the groups have completed their letters, the designated writers will take turns reading the letters to the entire group.

Round 1 Example

Person A:	"This …"
Person B:	"… is …"
Person A:	"… a …"
Person B:	"… great …"
Person A:	"… day."

Round 2 Example

Person A: "Dear ..."

Person B: "... Chris,"

Person C: "You ...

Person D: "... stink!

▼

BENEFITS TO LOOK FOR

The ideas below echo the Feedback approach:

- **Give feedback in real time.** The best time to give feedback is as it happens. Sometimes, however, you may be so angry or frustrated at what you have observed that you may need a few hours to get yourself together. If you need to sleep on it, then by all means do so. Just don't let there be too long of a gap between what happened and your feedback; otherwise, the feedback could become your interpretation of the situation instead of your observation.
- **Identify the topic in your first sentence.** Begin each key point with an "I" statement. "I have noticed." "I have observed." "I have seen." Or if it is feedback that you are passing along, "I have been told."
- **Be direct.** Don't beat around the bush. Give your feedback in a straightforward manner without the emotional attachment, and focus on the person's behavior, not his or her personality.
- **Express concern.** A tone of concern will communicate caring and a sense of importance. A tone of anger, frustration, disappointment, or sarcasm will turn constructive feedback into negative criticism, and the content of the message will be lost.

Discussion Points

- **Q: What did you notice about giving one word?** (*It was interesting because I wasn't in control of where the conversation went. I was sometimes surprised at what came out of my mouth. It was fun to see what happened.*)
- **Q: How was writing the letter?** (*Being given a certain type of letter or correspondence led us down a specific pathway. We all started out going along a specific premise until one of us changed a word and took it down a completely different path.*)

- **Q: How did this activity relate to feedback?** (*Words make up a story, and feedback can be interpreted by a point of view—it could be right or wrong. Feedback is all about observation, and it's important to concentrate on what actually happened. It's important for me to control my tone of voice when giving feedback because it can affect the communication in a positive or negative way.*)
- **Q: How do you give and receive great feedback?** (*Use "I" statements and be clear about what you want to say. Focus on behavior that can be changed.*)

Participant Action Plan

Have the whole group shout out what actions they will take to improve their feedback skills. Provide all the participants with a copy of the following action plan. Ask them to complete it, and set up a time to review their results one week later. At that time, ask them what has worked and what has not worked. What do they need to do to improve?

Feedback Actions

The actions I will take as a result of the Feedback activity are:

_____

_____

_____

_____

ONE WEEK LATER: What results have I gained from the Feedback activity?

_____

_____

_____

_____

Activity 38

Be Specific

All my life, I always wanted to be somebody. Now I see that I should have been more specific.

—Lily Tomlin, American actress and comedian,
recipient of the Mark Twain Prize for American Humor

Level of Risk

Low

Background and Purpose

In comedy, the funny is always in the specific. It's the difference between saying "He's no good" and "He's as useless as a chocolate fire screen." The improvisers who utilize details get more laughs than improvisers who generalize. I have not studied the reasons why, but my intuition tells me that specificity brings a clear picture to mind that the whole audience can see and relate to.

And of course it's great as an improviser to be onstage with someone who is specific because the communication is easy, clear, and efficient. I will know exactly where I am and who I am and what is going on in the scene. If I were onstage and my partner walked in and said, "Nice room," it wouldn't give me much to work with. It could be any room in any location in the universe. My partner and I would waste a lot of time trying to figure it out. But if my scene partner came in and said, "This is the largest, most complete walk-in closet I've ever been in," that would be a different story.

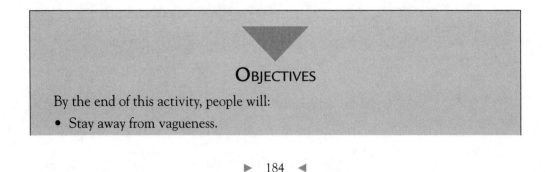

OBJECTIVES

By the end of this activity, people will:
• Stay away from vagueness.

- Take uncertainty out of communication to get specific results.
- Get and give clear and concise information.
- Give clear instructions.

Mini Lecture

"Hey, let's be careful out there." Sergeant Phil Esterhaus, a fictional character on the 1980s TV hit series *Hill Street Blues* always sent his force out with those words ringing in their ears. In real life when police are dealing with deadly gangs involved in all kinds of life-threatening criminal activity, does saying "be careful" really help? It may be motivational, but it's not specific enough. If, on the other hand, a sergeant has reports of increased gang activity and says, "Don't patrol that area alone … and, hey, be careful out there," the specific warning could make the difference between life and death.

Being specific helps people know exactly what to do and provides them with clear direction. Nonspecific instructions make an assumption that people know what to do. If, for example, a driving instructor tells new drivers, "Be careful at stop signs," it means entirely different things to different people. One driver might think, "I need to come to a complete stop at every stop sign." Another driver might think, "If no pedestrians or cars are present, I will just come to a rolling stop." Another might think, "If the coast is clear, I'm just going to slow down."

In business where different styles of leadership can mean the difference between people losing their jobs or gaining new employment or doing a good job, it's very important to be specific. Many years ago, I worked for Pitney Bowes as a salesperson. Every Monday morning our sales manager gave us a specific sales quota: this is how much you need to sell this week! When we had our next meeting four days later on Friday afternoon, we had either reached or exceeded our sales quota, and if we hadn't, we were in trouble. Being specific is a discipline that works; having that sales quota was the main reason I made the President's Club and went to Palm Springs with the other top salespeople. I knew the specifics of my job—no doubts and no excuses.

If you catch yourself delivering a "feel good" message with no specific direction to your team, stop for a moment and be specific. Being clear and concise could be the difference between having a winning team or a losing team.

Overview of Activity

Participants stand in a circle and "pick out" an imaginary object from the middle. The activity continues by having players mingle and exchange their objects.

Time

Instructions—5 minutes
Each round—5 minutes
Debriefing—8 minutes
Total time—18 minutes

STEPS TO FOLLOW

Round 1

1. Have the participants form a circle. Instruct them that this is a silent exercise. Ask the participants to grab an object from the center of the group. Instruct them to literally stick their hand into the middle of the circle and pull out an imaginary object. Tell them not to judge the object they pull out. Whatever it is, it is perfect.
2. Instruct them to solidify what it is in their mind by using it. See the color and shape, and feel the weight of it. Again they should do this in silence.

Round 2

Now that the participants have chosen their imaginary object, instruct them to take their object and find a partner and silently exchange objects. They can use any method except talking to show their partner what object they have. Again this is a silent exercise.

Round 3

1. With this new object in their hands, instruct them to find another partner and exchange this new object. Again in silence.
2. You can repeat this exchange up to six times.

Round 4

1. Have the participants one by one reveal what object they are now holding.
2. Ask the original owners to raise their hand. If the original owners do not recognize their object and therefore do not raise their hand, trace the object back to the original owner and have fun discovering how the object turned into something else. For example, what could have started out as a dog collar may now have turned into a blind person's walking stick.

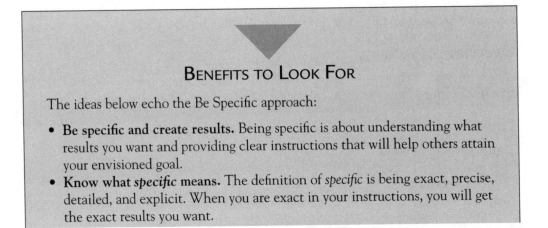

BENEFITS TO LOOK FOR

The ideas below echo the Be Specific approach:

- **Be specific and create results.** Being specific is about understanding what results you want and providing clear instructions that will help others attain your envisioned goal.
- **Know what *specific* means.** The definition of *specific* is being exact, precise, detailed, and explicit. When you are exact in your instructions, you will get the exact results you want.

> • **Be specific to sharpen your focus.** When you write down your specific short- and long-term goals, you can focus on following through and taking the right actions. Being specific will help you look at the puzzle one specific piece at a time, which will enable you to identify where the piece fits.

Discussion Points

- **Q: What could you have done to be more specific?** *(I could have focused more on the object. I could have envisioned the object better. I could have used body language to enhance the object.)*
- **Q: How difficult or easy did you find the activity?** *(It was a bit frustrating. Sometimes I didn't understand what object was being handed to me. I had to concentrate on the object as I was handing it over. Some objects I got instantly, and others I couldn't get.)*
- **Q: What are the benefits of being specific?** *(Being specific can help me avoid miscommunication and wasted time and resources.)*
- **Q: What can you do in the future to be specific?** *(I can make sure I know the results I want and be specific about what needs to be done. I can practice at home with friends and family. I can be specific in identifying my goals and what action I need to take.)*

Participant Action Plan

Provide all the participants with a copy of the following action plan. Ask them to complete it, and set up a time to review their results one week later. At that time, ask them what has worked and what has not worked. What do they need to do to improve?

Be Specific Actions

The actions I will take as a result of the Be Specific activity are:

_____

_____

_____

_____

ONE WEEK LATER: What results have I gained from the Be Specific activity?

_____

_____

_____

_____

Activity 39

Leadership

I have yet to find a man, however exalted his station, who did not do better work and put forth greater effort under a spirit of approval than under a spirit of criticism.

—Charles Schwab, founder and chairman
of the Charles Schwab Corporation

Level of Risk

Low

Background and Purpose

In improv there are no stars and there are no lead actors within the ensemble. But obviously natural leaders emerge. These natural leaders look at the big picture: they know when to edit and how to tie themes together, and they look for ways to connect characters to the suggestion throughout the show.

Leaders in improv are usually the ones who are the most confident on and off stage. They don't exclude people but instead operate in an inclusive way. They give the ensemble a feeling of "This is easy, and we can do this." And "Follow me. It will all work out, and it will be amazing."

We trust this person too—and this is all unspoken.

The natural leader in the group is the person people ask advice from. It is the person that other people generally just want to be around, hoping to learn from them. They're great with the audience and with their teammates, and they take feedback really well from the coach. I'm thinking of John Lutz, a writer for *30 Rock*. He was our leader without a doubt, and it was great because if he didn't know something, he would be the first one to say, "I don't know." He was always 100 percent supportive of everyone's idea, and he provided committed, positive energy. To me that's the hallmark of a true leader.

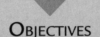

OBJECTIVES

By the end of this activity, people will:

- Know the difference between being a boss and a leader.
- Understand that there are different leadership styles.
- Understand that there are different types of personalities, each with different strengths and weaknesses.
- Be able to identify the type of leadership style that is closest to theirs.

Mini Lecture

I recently asked a manager who had just come back from a two-week training course on leadership, "What did you learn?" He mentioned that there were many steps and tools and strategies that he had learned, but he couldn't exactly remember the specifics of any one of them. Leadership is like that: We can learn about it, but putting it into practice is a whole different experience.

A leader is a person who influences a group of people toward the achievement of a goal. There are three basic ways to become a leader:

- Personality traits lead some people to naturally become a leader.
- A crisis or an important event causes some people to rise to the occasion, and it brings out extraordinary leadership qualities.
- People choose to become leaders and learn leadership skills.

People with the desire and willpower to become effective leaders can develop leadership skills through a process of self-study, education, training, and experience, but first they must have an honest understanding of who they are, what they know, and what they can do.

Followers determine if a leader is successful. If followers lack confidence in their leader, they will be uninspired. Followers also require different styles of leadership. For example, new hires require more supervision than experienced employees. People who lack motivation require a different approach from people with self-motivation.

Bosses differ from leaders. For example, managers and supervisors have the authority to accomplish certain tasks and objectives. However, this *power* does not make them leaders. Leaders make followers *want* to achieve high goals; they don't simply boss people around. Leading by example is probably the most effective way to lead. In other words, leaders shouldn't ask people to do what they are not willing to do themselves.

Overview of Activity

The participants form a loose circle. The facilitator calls out, "Freeze!" One participant moves in the space making a sound. When he stops in front of another participant, he "gives" the sound to that participant, and that participant continues. Learning how to give and take information creates leaders who can handle projects easier, faster, and more creatively.

Time

Instructions—3 minutes
Each round—5 minutes (depends on size of the group)
Debriefing—10 minutes
Total time—30 minutes

STEPS TO FOLLOW

Note: This exercise is called Give-and-Take. You need space and room to move in this perpetual-motion activity.

Round 1
1. Have the participants walk around the space in no particular pattern or rhythm. Yell, "Freeze!"
2. Now instruct them that only one person (A) can move at a time. (A) continues to move around the space in between all of the other frozen participants. (A) must also make a sound as she moves. It could be "beep, beep, beep" or any other sound or word she chooses. After a moment, (A) stops directly in front of someone else, person (B), and makes eye contact with him. (A) is essentially giving the energy to (B). (B) who was formerly frozen now unfreezes and begins to walk around the space with a different noise. "Bing, bong, bing, bong." (B) continues this action until he stops directly in front of someone else, person (C), and gives the energy to her. (C) unfreezes, and the pattern continues until everyone in the room has gone.

Round 2
After all the participants have given the energy, freeze them again. Now they can only take the energy. That means they can no longer stand in front of someone. For example, if participant (G) is moving and making a sound, he must continue to do so until someone else *takes* the energy and starts walking and moving around the space and making a sound. Only then can participant (G) freeze.

Round 3
Participants combine rounds 1 and 2. They can either give or take sounds as they want. Add the instructions that everyone must make a movement along with the sound.

Round 4

If they succeed in all previous rounds, they will now move beyond sounds and movement, and give and take sentences. If they are good at this, they can actually try to form a story as one author.

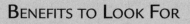

BENEFITS TO LOOK FOR

The ideas below echo the Leadership approach:

- **Leaders are made.** While it is true that some people are born with the natural personality traits of a leader, anyone who has the desire to become a leader can learn the necessary skills and qualities to become a leader.
- **A boss is not a leader.** Someone may have the authority to give instructions and tell people what to do, but this is not the same as being a leader. A leader inspires people to greatness and creates followers who want to achieve high goals.
- **Leaders set the example.** The most effective way to be a great leader is to always be willing to do what is asked of other people. People look up to people who "walk the talk."

Discussion Points

- **Q: What did it feel like in the give-and-take activity?** (*It felt weird to begin with, but once we were all involved, it was fun.*)
- **Q: What ties leaders and followers together?** (*Followers have faith in their leaders, and leaders have faith in their followers. Followers have faith that they are not being asked to do anything that the leader would not do.*)
- **Q: How does being a boss differ from being a leader?** (*A boss is given the authority to order people to do tasks, whereas a leader inspires people to achieve their goals. If a boss can become a leader, then the entire organization wins.*)

Participant Action Plan

Ask participants to find a partner and discuss what actions they will take as a result of the Leadership activity. Provide all the participants with a copy of the following action plan. Ask them to complete it, and set up a time to review their results one week later. At that time, ask them what has worked and what has not worked. What do they need to do to improve?

Leadership Actions

The actions I will take as a result of the Leadership activity are:

_____

_____

_____

_____

ONE WEEK LATER: What results have I gained from the Leadership activity?

_____

_____

_____

_____

Activity 40

Motivation

I used to think that running an organization was equivalent to conducting a symphony orchestra. But I don't think that's quite it; it's more like jazz. There is more improvisation.

—Warren Bennis, American scholar, organizational consultant, and author

Level of Risk

Low

Background and Purpose

If you don't love improvising, then get off stage because there are hundreds of people right behind you who would love to do what you are doing. If you don't love it, you will also pull the team down with your negative energy, and to top it off, you will not be fulfilled. Life is too short to moan and complain the whole way through it.

I have "phoned in" shows, and I've been indifferent and unmotivated to do a great job, and believe me, the consequences were not good. I'm actually amazed that I didn't get fired. I remember this one time playing with King Ten at iO West in Hollywood—an amazing and talented group of wonderful people. I had been improvising for over 10 years, and it was beginning to feel like "work." Keep in mind that mostly no one gets paid to improvise. People do not become improvisers for the money. They do it because they love it. Anyway, I must have done over 10,000 shows, and I was feeling bored and very much like a victim. I had wanted to be a movie star by now, and it had not happened. Actually, I just wanted to make a living doing this, but I couldn't even do that, so I was not in a good mental space.

So there I was Friday night, packed house, teammates ready to rock, and I just wanted to be home on the couch. I put in zero effort and got zero back. I could feel the resentment of my teammates growing. That's when I had to take a good look in the mirror and say, "Am I in or out?" Because being indifferent was killing me and King Ten.

I parlayed my experience in improvisation into business competencies, and I have been happy ever since. The point is, sometimes the effects of actions or the lack of actions won't unfold right away, but eventually they will unfold. Might as well enjoy what I'm doing and have lots of enthusiasm.

OBJECTIVES

By the end of this activity, people will:

- Be energized.
- Remember what it felt like to love coming to work.
- Not take things for granted and be thankful.
- See the glass as half full.

Mini Lecture

Motivating yourself and others is a crucial skill if you want to make things happen and get results. To motivate yourself, it's easier if you have a coach—someone to coerce, push, persuade, and inspire you to do something. So why not be your own coach?! It's impossible to motivate others if you cannot motivate yourself. Now is the time to get your act together, and get what you want! Here are 12 powerful tactics to help you turn on your motivation switch:

1. **Know the consequences.** Be aware of the negative consequences of not getting results.
2. **Reward yourself.** Rewards to yourself are a great way of saying, "Job well done!"
3. **Follow the instructions.** You can work better when you know exactly what to do.
4. **Be kind.** Be your own biggest fan, and be kind to yourself.
5. **Set deadlines.** Create realistic deadlines and stick to them.
6. **Develop the team spirit around you.** Create an environment of camaraderie.
7. **Focus on the outcomes.** Make it clear what you want and keep focused on your goal.
8. **Create challenges.** Give yourself the opportunity to face new and difficult problems.
9. **Demand improvement.** Keep raising the bar a little higher so you don't get bored.
10. **Have fun.** Have fun, and the positive environment will lead to better results.
11. **Communicate.** Be aware of any potential problems you can fix.
12. **Keep it stimulating.** Mix it up, and create enthusiasm for "big picture" thinking.

Overview of Activity

The participants have an opportunity to form groups and create a positive presentation based upon their answers to three work-related questions.

Time

Instructions—2 minutes
Each round—2 to 3 minutes (Depending on the number of participants, allow each participant a couple of minutes to present his or her answers)
Debriefing—8 minutes
Total time— 20 minutes

STEPS TO FOLLOW

Round 1

Ask the participants to take a few minutes to create responses to these three questions:

- What is one positive thing you believe your company does?
- How did you feel the very minute you found out you were hired, and how were you on that first day?
- Why do you truly love what you do?

Note: Tell participants that they can make up answers if they have to.

Round 2

Tell the participants that they each have a couple of minutes to present their answers to the group in a very conversational, motivational and authentic manner, as if they were talking to their friends.

▼

BENEFITS TO LOOK FOR

The ideas below echo the Motivation approach:

- **Remember that motivation begins with you.** While it's great to go to a motivational seminar or hear a motivational speaker, when we get home, we are the ones who have to motivate ourselves to do something. When we take responsibility to motivate ourselves, we can achieve what we want to achieve.
- **Don't rely on others for motivation.** When we rely on other people to motivate us, we are putting the power into their hands. And when they are not available, we feel at a loss. We don't know what to do—it's as if the electricity has gone off and there's nowhere to "plug" ourselves in.

> • **Renew your motivation every day.** Wake up every morning and motivate yourself to complete your top-priority tasks. When you do the things you need to do, rather than doing the busy work, you will feel good at the end of the day—less overwhelmed and more able to feel that you have the power to do anything you want.

Discussion Points

- **Q: What did you remember about your first day?** (*I remembered how excited I was to have this new job. I got to work early, and I was eager to learn.*)
- **Q: How do you feel about your job and company now?** (*I still love my job, and I realize that I take some things for granted.*)
- **Q: What were the benefits of talking about your job and truly loving it?** (*I realized that there are some things that I truly love about my job. I had forgotten about them because I get stressed with the things I don't like as much. I guess I just have to remind myself about what I truly love.*)

Participant Action Plan

As a group, shout out actions that will help provide motivation. Provide all the participants with a copy of the following action plan. Ask them to complete it, and set up a time to review their results one week later. At that time, ask them what has worked and what has not worked. What do they need to do to improve?

Motivation Actions

The actions I will take as a result of the Motivation activity are:

_____

_____

_____

_____

ONE WEEK LATER: What results have I gained from the Motivation activity?

_____

_____

_____

_____

Activity 41

Delegation

Level of Risk

Low

Background and Purpose

I love teaching improvisation to adults and especially to kids. The kids get it and relish the environment improv creates. I had an opportunity to start an improv class at the Raue Theatre in Crystal Lake for young teens. It was fabulous. However, I had to miss some classes. I couldn't get any of my fellow Second City instructors or iO instructors to substitute for the class because they lived in the city and Crystal Lake is far away in the burbs. I had to find someone else … but who? I asked my mother.

Now Val Gee has been a facilitator for years, and she has actually taken improv classes. However, taking improv classes and teaching improv classes are vastly different things. But I had no other choice. I had to delegate.

I first wrote down the activities in specific detail for her so that she could take notes. I read the activity to her first, and then I taught it to her as if she were my student. Then I asked her to be the teacher. It was great preparation and very helpful for Val because everything was laid out for her and she got to rehearse teaching in a hands-on way while I watched. Plus, she got to ask questions along the way.

How did she do in the class? Fantastic. I'm sure she did not deliver the activities the same way I would with the same takeaways and mannerisms, but I had to let that go. The kids got the information and loved the class, and Val had a great time doing it.

OBJECTIVES

By the end of this activity, people will:

- Build trusting relationships so that delegation can take place.
- Have a proven delegating process that works.
- See the values of delegation—less stress and workload.

Mini Lecture

Here's a rhyme on how to delegate: "Once fast, twice slow, three times together, and off we go!" Sounds simple and easy, but many people find it really hard to delegate. Maybe it's because it seems easier to do the job ourselves than take time to teach someone else how to do it. Or perhaps it's job protection—if I teach others how to do my job, I may become redundant. While most of us can't simply put our colleagues' names on a piece of paper and send it off, in many ways, Malcolm S. Forbes was right because in order for any business to grow, people must be willing to delegate.

Delegation is about giving something away. If we don't delegate, then we are not allowing ourselves or other people to grow. Imagine if we never delegated household chores—we'd end up doing all the cleaning. At work and home, delegation is about handing over a task and empowering others to do it. It's not about losing power. It's about gaining power. Delegation is about learning management and leadership skills, and here are some simple steps on how to do it:

1. **Define the task.** What task is suitable to be delegated?
2. **Select the person to do it.** What person or team is best suited and has the ability to complete the task?
3. **Tell the person what he or she will gain from it.** What will the person get out of it? What will you gain? What will the company gain?
4. **Tell the person why the task is important.** Why is the task being delegated? Why is it important, and what is its relevance?
5. **Tell the person what results you expect.** What results are required, and how will the outcome be measured?
6. **Identify resources.** Identify the task-related people, location, premises, equipment, money, materials, and other related activities and services.
7. **Set deadlines.** When must the job be completed? When are the review dates? When are reports due?
8. **Identify sources of support.** Inform others who are also involved. Warn the person about any awkward matters of politics or protocol.
9. **Provide feedback.** Let the person know how he or she is doing. Review why things worked or did not go according to plan, and deal with the problems.

When you delegate, be sure to oversee the project, but do not get so involved that you block creativity; there may be faster, easier ways of doing the task.

Overview of Activity

Participants create a group tableau based on the art of delegation.

Time

Instructions—3 minutes
Each round—2 to 3 minutes
Debriefing—9 minutes
Total time—18 minutes

STEPS TO FOLLOW

Round 1
1. Have the participants get into groups of three or four. Tell them they have five minutes to strategize and create a silent human tableau showing delegation at its worst, which they will present to the other groups.
2. After five minutes, have each group show their tableaus.
3. Everyone must participate in the tableau.

Round 2
1. Now have the participants make a different, silent human tableau that shows delegation at its best.
2. Again have each of the groups display their tableau.

   Note: The lesson here is not only about the resulting tableau, but more importantly it is also about the process of collaboration and the tools that prevent or encourage delegation. This is a cerebral activity.

BENEFITS TO LOOK FOR

The ideas below echo the Delegation approach:

Delegate the results that need to be obtained. In order to delegate in a fair and appropriate way, the people to whom you are delegating must know exactly what is expected of them. For example, if you ask people to clean a room, you must let them know what the completed task looks like. Is the floor clean and free of all garbage? Are the windows washed? Are the closets and drawers tidy? Without an accurate picture of expectations, there is no fair measure of achievement.

Be willing to give it up. Many people don't delegate because they don't want to spend time teaching other people how to do the job. In many ways this is a disservice because no one is advancing and learning new tasks. If people do not delegate, they are closing the door to new opportunities for everyone.

Give feedback. When the job has been completed, it is important to provide feedback. What worked, and what needs improvement? Always give people the opportunity to do a better job next time.

Discussion Points

- **Q: How does "Once fast, twice slow, three times together, and off we go"
 work?** (*First, I do a quick overview of the project I'm delegating, and I say why I'm delegating. Second, I go into the specific details and, if possible, I actually do the task in front of their eyes so they can watch and take notes. The third time I watch as they do it, making sure they actually understood me, and I answer any questions they have. Then I hand it off. The time I lose at the beginning I will gain by fewer mistakes occurring in the future.*)
- **Q: What are the reasons why you don't delegate? What are the consequences?**
 (*I don't trust others. Unfortunately, I am overloaded and stressed, and I don't empower anyone.*)
- **Q: What are some major points about delegation?** (*Explain the whole picture. Share resources. Demonstrate how to do the task. Provide deadlines. Give feedback.*)
- **Q: What is the worst of delegation?** (*Not getting clear instructions. No support. No deadlines or review points.*)
- **Q: What action will you take about delegation?** (*I will practice with my family and give them more chores to do. I will delegate more of my work.*)

Participant Action Plan

Provide all the participants with a copy of the following action plan. Ask them to complete it, and set up a time to review their results one week later. At that time, ask them what has worked and what has not worked. What do they need to do to improve?

Delegation Actions

The actions I will take as a result of the Delegation activity are:

_____

_____

_____

_____

ONE WEEK LATER: What results have I gained from the Delegation activity?

_____

_____

_____

_____

Activity 42

Create Your Environment

The man is a f*@#ing genius. When you walk on set and you see the environment, the costumes, and you've got the make-up, it really makes it easy.

—Orlando Bloom, English actor who had his breakthrough role in *The Lord of the Rings*, on Ridley Scott, film director and producer

Level of Risk

Low

Background and Purpose

As fun as it is to create a character that an audience can relate to and laugh about, it's also fun to create the scene onstage. In improv, we create the scenes in an opening form called *painting a picture* or *painting the room*. Basically, one by one each performer builds the room from nothing into something. We get a suggestion from the audience: coal. An improviser steps forward and begins discovering the corner of the picture. "We see a shovel that's propped up. It's filthy, and it is obviously used daily." Another improviser takes the lead as if one voice is speaking: "Beside the shovel is a furnace. It's hotter than a volcano in there, and thank goodness the door is closed." Another improviser takes over: "A man stands at the helm of the train. He's running the locomotive from Ontario to Quebec." Piece by piece, sentence by sentence, the picture is revealed. We can create any picture or environment we choose. It can be a wonderful scene at the beach with lots of laughter or a dark basement filled with rats. Everyone has a hand in it. One word or sentence can take the picture in a completely opposite direction. The joy of creating the picture is discovering it together.

OBJECTIVES

By the end of this activity, people will:

- Create a work environment that provides meaning and purpose.
- Show and tell appreciation.
- Encourage the utilization of talents to create the positive environment.

Mini Lecture

According to *Fortune* magazine, Google is *the* place to work, and it sets the standard for all other companies. Here's what they provide: 100 percent health care coverage, on-site child care facilities, 18 weeks of paid maternity leave for new moms, 7 weeks for dads, 17 cafeterias with free food prepared by top chefs for all employees ... *and* ... a rule that no staff member should ever be further away than 100 feet from a source of food.

Add to all that Google's spirit of conservation, including a department dedicated to researching "green" technologies, subsidized hybrid cars for staff, and special discounts for employees who install solar panels in their homes. Animal lovers can bring their cherished pets to work, and special meditation and prayer rooms help staff revitalize themselves in times of stress.

Nike is another socially conscious business. In their Portland office, employees volunteer as Portland Mountain Rescuers, and they respond to emergencies at a moment's notice, no matter what they are doing or how important it is. Nike's standard response to emergencies is, "What's more important? Saving lives or selling shoes?"

According to *Fortune* magazine, the top 50 businesses have one thing in common: they all realize that a company is only as good as its employees. They go out of their way to ensure that the employees are happy and content. Staff turnover is low because who wouldn't want to work for a company that rents an entire movie theater for a day so that their employees can see a blockbuster movie on its release date?

While the company you work for may not have all that companies like Google or Nike offer, you can do some things to create your environment the way you want it to be. Start with a simple thing like water; make sure you have a cup of water at your desk, and maybe a piece of fruit or some nuts. Get your company involved in local volunteer opportunities, or create a company sports team or hobby group. Encourage a "bring a pet into work day" or start a circulation of "products for sale." Whatever it is that interests you, may interest other people—and the more we can creatively bring the outside world into our work environment, the more interesting and outstanding our company will become.

Overview of Activity

The participants will get the chance to describe their environment as it is and how they want it to be. They will nonverbally and verbally communicate the best work space possible and how emotions affect the space.

Time

Instructions—1 minute
Each round—2 to 3 minutes
Debriefing—5 minutes
Total time—8 minutes

STEPS TO FOLLOW

Round 1

1. Have participants create a work office environment that they would most like to work in.
2. Ask them, if they had all the resources in the world, what kind of environment would they want to create so that they would enjoy coming to work every day?
3. One at a time, have the participants walk into the space and (mime) touching an item they think adds value to the space. For example, flowers, family pictures, sofa, mini fridge, Ping-Pong table.

Round 2

Have participants repeat the exercises, but this time they will express the work space without any physical objects. Have the participants use energy and enthusiasm. Or have them get into a character if they need to. For example, a participant walks into the space like a soccer mom, a football player who has just scored a touchdown, or a parent whose kid has just won the tournament.

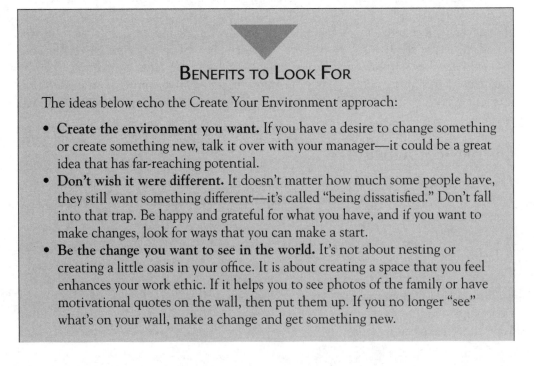

BENEFITS TO LOOK FOR

The ideas below echo the Create Your Environment approach:

- **Create the environment you want.** If you have a desire to change something or create something new, talk it over with your manager—it could be a great idea that has far-reaching potential.
- **Don't wish it were different.** It doesn't matter how much some people have, they still want something different—it's called "being dissatisfied." Don't fall into that trap. Be happy and grateful for what you have, and if you want to make changes, look for ways that you can make a start.
- **Be the change you want to see in the world.** It's not about nesting or creating a little oasis in your office. It is about creating a space that you feel enhances your work ethic. If it helps you to see photos of the family or have motivational quotes on the wall, then put them up. If you no longer "see" what's on your wall, make a change and get something new.

Discussion Points

- **Q: What kind of environment do you want as a team?** (*An atmosphere like Google. I like my family pictures.*)
- **Q: What kind of an environment do you currently have, and how can you make it better?** (*It's too cluttered, and I like clean lines. I need to throw some things out that I no longer use.*)
- **Q: What did you notice about your colleagues' environment?** (*I think we're all on the same page. We want to work in a supportive environment.*)
- **Q: What is the first thing you will do back at the office?** (*I am going to take down some of the motivational quotes that I no longer see. I am going to clean out my drawer and either recycle or throw things out. I am going to smile and make eye contact with my coworkers.*)

Participant Action Plan

Provide all the participants with a copy of the following action plan. Ask them to complete it, and set up a time to review their results one week later. At that time, ask them what has worked and what has not worked. What do they need to do to improve?

Create Your Environment Actions

The actions I will take as a result of the Create Your Environment activity are:

_____

_____

_____

_____

ONE WEEK LATER: What results have I gained from the Create Your Environment activity?

_____

_____

_____

_____

Activity 43

Out of the Box

All you're trying to do in an improvisation is get as much material as possible for the editing room.

—Martin Short, Canadian comedian, actor, writer, singer, and producer

Level of Risk

Low

Background and Purpose

After improvising for over 15 years, sometimes scenes repeat themselves, and I find myself in the same situation with the same character and the same dilemma thinking, "Okay, I've been *here* before!"

It's easy to do. For one thing we're imitating life, and sometimes life can get a little bit monotonous. We also get very comfortable with our fellow improvisers, and with that comes the problem of familiarity. So sometimes it's hard to be surprised onstage.

That's why it's really wonderful to be caught off guard by either yourself or another improviser. For example, let's say a fellow improviser usually plays a mother onstage. She is great at playing this character. She is like Betty White in the kitchen. Now, of course, she will get tons of laughs, but playing the part of a mother so often can also be limiting to the range and variety of characters she could be playing. That's why it's so nice when this improviser takes a risk and plays the opposite: a surly old man, for instance. Choosing to think outside of the box will not only take you out of your comfort zone. It will also challenge you creatively. Every now and then it's good to check in with yourself and see if there's a different way of doing it so that you can keep growing and learning.

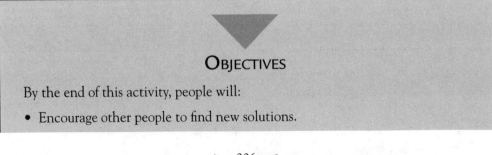

OBJECTIVES

By the end of this activity, people will:

- Encourage other people to find new solutions.

- Enable other people to view situations and people from a different perspective.
- See challenges with fresh eyes and look at the potentials in different solutions.
- Get out of their comfort zone.

Mini Lecture

Before we learn to speak and name things, our eyes act like cameras taking snapshots and storing the information in our brains. Then we attach words and label the information. Label by label we learn and understand our world and begin to experience it through common language.

A problem with labeling things is that we tend to stop seeing things as they truly are, and we end up storing only the labels in our mental box. If we continue to see things the way we've always seen them, we miss important opportunities, and our ability to act could be diminished. This sometimes gets us creatively stuck. Imagine if you were stranded on an island with a plastic gallon carton of milk. If you see it only as a milk container, you will miss its many potential uses. For example, it could be used as a rainwater collector, a flotation device for fishing, a container for storing food, a showerhead, or a drum. It's the same in the business world. With limited resources and competition knocking at the door, we have to think outside the box and see new potential.

Getting out of the box is about waking up and being willing to see things differently. I love the story about Shawn Seipler who, while sitting in his hotel room one night, pondered the question: "What happens to all those bars of barely used soap in the shower and sink?" He called a friend, Paul Till, who checked with 15 hotels in his hometown of Houston. Each said the little bars went out with the trash. Till also found on the Web that nearly 2 million children worldwide die each year from diarrheal disease. The best preventative: hand washing with soap!

Today, the men run an Orlando nonprofit called Clean the World that collects soap, plus tiny bottles of shampoo and lotion, from 125 hotels, mostly in Florida. In a mini warehouse in Orlando, crews shave off the top layer of soap and run the bars through commercial food steamers for five minutes to kill bacteria. After the bars dry, they're bundled into three-packs with plastic wrap. The group distributed more than 230 tons of soap and bath amenities to Third World nations and U.S. shelters since starting in February 2010.

It's not about just doing our job; it's about seeing it through different eyes. What can I do to be more aware and more alive? How can I collaborate with my colleagues, boss, departments, and my organization to make it the best it can be? What can I do to make a positive difference? When we step out of the box, we open up our lives to new opportunities, new challenges, and new ways to living an inspired life!

Overview of Activity

Participants will practice looking at the world with "new" eyes, by labeling familiar objects differently.

Time

Instructions—2 to 3 minutes
Each round—2 to 3 minutes
Debriefing—10 minutes
Total time—20 minutes

STEPS TO FOLLOW

Round 1
1. Have the participants pair up with a partner. One person will be (A) and the other (B). Instruct Partner (A) to lead (B) around the room by the arm and point to random objects.
2. Instruct Partner (B) to name what (A) is pointing to. The rule is that (B) must say *anything* that the object is *not*. For example, if Partner (A) points to a chair, Partner (B) will call it a "sock puppet."

Note: Remind participants to suspend judgment and go for it.

Round 2
After a while, the pairs switch.

▼

BENEFITS TO LOOK FOR

The ideas below echo the Out of the Box approach:

- **See with new eyes.** When problems or challenges come your way, it's easy to become negative or stuck. We have to be able to look at these challenges from a different perspective. Only then will we be willing to build.
- **Free your imagination.** It may be that you have not been required to use your imagination in your current job; perhaps you have submitted ideas that have been ignored. But today is a new day. Let your imagination free and have fun.
- **Respond differently.** Don't worry about saying something inappropriate—you won't. The point is to respond outside of the box and provide new solutions, creative ideas, and workable options.
- **Be fearless.** Many success stories are born out of a stream of failures. Failures are nothing more than discovering ways to not do something. The more failures you have, the more opportunities for success. So be fearless, and be willing to open your mind to creativity.

Discussion Points

- **Q: What was it like to be the one saying what the object is not?** (*It was intense. To keep coming up with random words was difficult to begin with, but after a short while it became easier. Practice made it easier.*)
- **Q: Why is it sometimes difficult to look at things differently in the business world?** (*It's easier to just see things in the same old way. Looking at something through new eyes can take effort, but it's worth it to get a new perspective. When I view something in a different way, it's hard to begin with, but then I see new opportunities.*)
- **Q: When is out-of-the-box thinking important in the business world?** (*When there needs to be a basis for fresh and creative thinking. The old ways of doing things can be improved. Improvising will remind me that sometimes I need to see things differently to find better, more effective solutions.*)
- **Q: How can you get into a creative mindset? What are some habits you can develop?** (*Take a walk. Go for a snack. Listen to music. Take a deep breath. Relax and remind myself to have fun.*)

Participant Action Plan

Ask participants to pair up and share the actions they will take to be out of the box and view things differently. Provide all the participants with a copy of the following action plan. Ask them to complete it, and set up a time to review their results one week later. At that time, ask them what has worked and what has not worked. What do they need to do to improve?

Out of the Box Actions

The actions I will take as a result of the Out of the Box activity are:

_____

_____

_____

_____

ONE WEEK LATER: What results have I gained from the Out of the Box activity?

_____

_____

_____

_____

Activity 44

Maintain Focus

It's not what's happening to you now or what has happened in your past that determines who you become. Rather, it's your decisions about what to focus on, what things mean to you and what you're going to do about them, that will determine your ultimate destiny.

—Anthony Robbins, American self-help author and success coach

Level of Risk

Medium

Background and Purpose

Some people are really good at multitasking, and they can handle all kinds of different situations. In fact, they prefer to be busy because it energizes and focuses them. If they are exercising, for example, they will think, "Why just pedal when I can talk on the cell phone at the same time." Other people don't function that way. They prefer to focus on a single task, and they get anxious if too much is "thrown" their way. One of the great things about improv training is that we have to learn to be both a person who can perform more than one task at a time and a person who is also single-minded.

For example, the Harold is a long-form improv performance piece. There are a lot of things going on in that 30-minute period: games, scenes, call-backs, openings, themes, and suggestions that have to be remembered and tied together. We are definitely multitasking in the Harold. We have to learn how to juggle all the pieces to make it an amazing Harold. With a lot practice, coaching, and determination, anybody can become good at it. Oh yes, and a little bit of focused energy helps too.

▼

OBJECTIVES

By the end of this activity, people will:

- Experience the act of maintaining focus in team activities.
- Remember to be open in the communication process.

- Practice concentrating in the midst of chaos.
- Act quickly in relation to what is going on around them.
- Learn five steps to use strength of mind to maintain focus.

Mini Lecture

This activity is a metaphor for how people interact successfully even when there are multiple things being tossed around. As more and more work piles up, how do we keep focused and ensure that we are giving and receiving successfully and not getting overwhelmed?

Maintaining focus is about creating effective processes and keeping disciplined. Here are five steps that will enable you to use your strength of mind to keep focused:

1. **Get rid of distractions.** Plan your day, clear your desk, close unrelated computer programs, eliminate background noise, and don't answer the phone.
2. **Create visual reminders.** Whether it's a big banner-style poster, a sticky note, or a statue, keeping a visual reminder of the task you are working on will keep you focused on the work.
3. **Find an interesting hook.** Be excited about the project. Have fun by creating rewards and bonuses. Plan your favorite *something* if you finish on time!
4. **Use a schedule.** Chunk the project into pieces, and make a plan and set mini deadlines.
5. **Take a break.** If you feel stuck, frustrated, or have low energy, get up and move about, take a breath, or go to a different location.

Be somewhat relaxed about your work. You can stay on task without being harsh, critical, or stressed out. Too much stress or negativity will block your productivity and creativity. Remember, it's okay to fail as long as you don't give up. Stay on top of things, and bring yourself back into alignment if you find yourself losing focus. You can maintain focus and still be excited, enthusiastic, and have fun.

Overview of Activity

With everyone standing in a circle, imaginary objects will be thrown around the circle. The objective is to stay focused while multitasking.

Time

Instructions—5 minutes
Each round—2 to 3 minutes (minimum three rounds)
Debriefing—8 minutes
Total time—22 minutes

STEPS TO FOLLOW

Round 1

1. Have the participants stand in a circle. Explain that you are holding an imaginary red ball that will be thrown around the circle. This is a game of perpetual motion. The rules are:
   - The object will never change size or shape or color.
   - Before a participant throws the ball, that person will say, "Red ball."
   - Whoever catches the imaginary ball will say, "Thank you, red ball," and she will throw it to someone else.
2. Begin to toss the red ball around!
3. After this ball has been tossed to four or five people, add more colored balls: green, yellow, orange, and purple. To put another ball into play, you can either "freeze" the group and explain that you will add more balls, or you can just catch a participant's eye and throw the new ball.
4. After the group has thrown these imaginary colored balls around, say "freeze" and ask the participants to hold up their colored balls. Find out if any of the colored balls have disappeared.
5. Have a short debriefing (discussion points for rounds 1 and 2 are shown below).

Round 2

1. Now tell the participants that they did a great job, and explain that because they are now professionals, they will do it again, but this time, additional balls of different colors and other assorted objects will be introduced.
2. The same rules apply as in round 1. Here is the order of objects being tossed around:
   - Red
   - Yellow
   - Green
   - Purple
   - Hot toaster (Be sure to mime a hot toaster in your hands.)
   - Shopping cart
   - ATM
   - Crying baby (Mime it.)
   - Electric guitar (Play it.)
3. Before you start, remind them to think about the debriefing discussion— especially to keep focused on the object. Make a goal of keeping everything being thrown around intact by the end.
4. After a couple of minutes of tossing the objects around, yell "Freeze!" Ask the participants to hold up their objects so you can count them (there should be nine).
5. Respond accordingly depending on whether objects stayed intact or they disappeared and/or morphed into other colors.

▼

BENEFITS TO LOOK FOR

The ideas below echo the Maintain Focus approach:

- **Maintaining focus is about keeping your eye on the ball.** Whether it's a tennis, golf, or soccer ball, one of the first things players learn is to keep their eye on the ball! It's the same in team projects and any communication process. As soon as we take our eye off the ball, we lose focus—and an unfocused eye often drops the ball. Keeping your eye on the ball should be done throughout the entire activity or communication: before, during and after.
- **It's good to take breaks.** Maintaining focus is not about working 24/7 or not having breaks. After intense focus, it is imperative to take breaks and regain control of the mind. After a short break, people come back refreshed and rejuvenated to continue the work.
- **Having fun can help you maintain focus.** Being serious and not enjoying a task can create unproductivity and even burnout. Today's successful companies ensure that the work environment is designed to be lively, innovative, and geared to enthusiastic productivity. People who enjoy being at work more easily maintain focus.

Discussion Points, Round 1 Questions

- **Q: What did you have to do to be successful?** (*Listen, make eye contact, be aware of who was talking to me, and physically be ready to catch the ball. Not look out the window.*)
- **Q: Was there a difference in body language between the people you threw to versus the people you didn't?** (*I threw to people who were open and looking at me versus looking away, crossing their arms, and so on.*)
- **Q: What does the red ball represent?** (*Information, whether it's verbal or nonverbal. E-mail, telephone, face-to-face, texts, and other types of information.*)
- **Q: Whose responsibility is it to make sure the ball is caught?** (*Both the sender and the receiver. And responsibility of the thrower doesn't end when the ball is released. There should be follow-up confirmation.*)

Discussion Points, Round 2 Questions

- **Q: What did you do differently the second time versus the first time?** (*I kept my arms down instead of crossed, I looked at people, I said people's names to make sure they heard me, and I actually walked across the circle so they got my object.*)

- Q: **Did some of you prefer the first round over the second?** (*I love multitasking so I preferred the second.*)
- Q: **How often do you need to keep focused at work with many things happening at once?** (*All the time.*)

Participant Action Plan

Ask players to form groups of four to five people and discuss the actions they will take that will help them maintain focus. Give all the participants a copy of the action plan. Ask them to complete it, and set up a time to review their results one week later. At that time, ask them what worked and what didn't work. What do they need to do to improve?

Maintain Focus Actions

The actions I will take as a result of the Maintain Focus activity are:

_____

_____

_____

_____

ONE WEEK LATER: What results have I gained from the Maintain Focus activity?

_____

_____

_____

_____

Activity 45

You Are Creative

We don't know where we get our ideas from. We do know that we do not get them from our laptops.

—John Cleese, English actor, comedian, writer, film producer, and member of Monty Python's Flying Circus

Level of Risk

Medium

Background and Purpose

People think they lose the ability to be creative as they get older, but that is not true. All of us are creative on a daily basis. Whether we are creatively figuring out how to solve the problem of getting the kids to work without a car or how to beat the traffic by going a different route, we are all creative thinkers.

Being a teacher at iO and the Second City, it's wonderful to see how many people from many different backgrounds, ages, and temperaments want to learn improv. I've had a 75-year-old man who thought it would be fun, a 40-something career woman who wanted to work on her presentation skills, and a single mom who wanted to widen her social network. Many times, people who "jump into" improv think they'll be terrible because they think they are not creative. Fortunately, it takes only one class for them to realize they can learn improv. Then the fun and learning begin, and they get to see just how creative they are. I've had people pretend they were pieces of corn in a stomach, a virus in a therapy session, and a snowflake on a tongue. Whatever it is, once they realize they are creative, there are no limits to where their genius will go.

OBJECTIVES

By the end of this activity, people will:

- Respond to habitual activities from a different place to create new results.
- Look for opportunities to be creative problem solvers.
- Release unproductive judgments and replace them with healthy "I can" thoughts.
- Build a life of creative thinking.

Mini Lecture

A study made by sociology professor John Mirowsky of the University of Texas, Austin, found that "creative activity helps people stay healthy. Creative activity is non-routine, enjoyable, and provides opportunity for learning and for solving problems. People who do that kind of work, whether paid or not, feel healthier and have fewer physical problems."

Mirowsky goes on to say, "One thing that surprised us was that the daily activities of employed persons are more creative than those of non-employed persons." This was true regardless of age, race, level of education, or the amount of creativity the job provided.

How do we know if we're being creative at work? According to research at the Santa Fe Institute, if you routinely call your friends from work, you're probably not being creative or happy at work. People who are solving problems at work that are challenging are being creative, and they are more likely to enjoy their work. Creativity, therefore, is a very important component of being happy, healthy, and productive. Here are three ways to make any job more creative:

1. **Believe that every job has an opportunity for creativity.** Look for ways to be creative at work. When you take responsibility for fixing your own problems in a creative way, it is empowering and satisfying. Every job has an element of creativity in it—sometimes you just need to look and be willing to do things differently.

2. **Change your response to stress.** Robert Sapolsky, a neurobiologist who studies stress at the Stanford University School of Medicine, says, "We're lousy at recognizing when our normal coping mechanisms aren't working. Our response is usually to do it five times more, instead of thinking: maybe it's time to try something new." Responding to stress by doing the same things over and over creates a rut, and as novelist Ellen Glasgow observed, "The only difference between a rut and a grave are the dimensions." Let's form new pathways by looking for creative new ways to perform routine tasks.

3. **Change the pace.** John Freeman writes in the *Wall Street Journal* that changing the pace of what we do changes what it's like to do that task. You know this intuitively from dancing or playing sports: when you change the pace, the whole game changes. It's also true of the workplace. Tasks that we often do quickly and without much thought—such as writing e-mails, answering phones, and preparing for meetings—when done at a different pace may create an enthusiastic and more productive result.

Overview of Activity

In groups of three, participants will take turns speaking in Gibberish, speaking in English, and being a translator.

Time

Instructions—5 minutes
Each round—2 to 3 minutes
Debriefing—10 minutes
Total time—24 minutes

STEPS TO FOLLOW

Round 1
1. Have participants get into groups of three and decide who is (A), (B), and (C):
   - Partner (A) speaks Gibberish.
   - Partner (B) speaks English.
   - Partner (C) speaks both languages and is the translator.
2. Partners (A) and (B) are trying to have a conversation. The problem is that (A) cannot speak English and (B) cannot speak Gibberish. Partner (A) is from a foreign country called Babble that no one has ever heard of before. The language spoken is Gibberish. Fortunately, Partner (C) can speak both English and Gibberish and will translate the entire conversation for them both.
3. The topic of discussion can be anything. They can ask as many questions as they like. The point is that both Partners (A) and (B) should try to find out as much about each other as possible: cultural differences, commonalities, histories, and so on.

Round 2

1. Have the participants switch roles:
   - Partner (C) now speaks Gibberish.
   - Partner (A) now speaks English.
   - Partner (B) now speaks both languages and is the translator.
2. Now Partners (A) and (C) are having a conversation. This time, Partner (B) will translate the entire conversation for (A) and (C).

Round 3

1. Have the participants switch roles a third time:
   - Partner (B) now speaks Gibberish.
   - Partner (C) now speaks English.
   - Partner (A) now speaks both languages and is the translator.
2. Now Partners (B) and (C) are having a conversation, which (A) translates.

Round 1 Example

Person A: "Habigabidombu!"

Person C: "He says he is very happy to be here to promote his country called Babble."

Person B: "Tell him we're very pleased to have him here—we love their unique fruits and vegetables."

Person C: "Lamburahhh!"

Person A: "Zhramada kaimiluran dimimmeeehargha cghlogmicnsudks cksiglmisin."

Person C: "They grow in green caves underground."

Person B: "We grow apples on trees."

Round 2 Example

Person A: "I'm very happy to be in your country."

Person B: "Yat."

Person C: "Yatattatatat."

Person B: "She wants to take you winderblowing."

Person A: "What's that? Do I need special clothes?"

Person B: "Yatata."

▼

BENEFITS TO LOOK FOR

The ideas below echo the You Are Creative approach:

- **What deserves your energy and focus now?** Change with intention and purpose is essential for any creative business to evolve. Be sure to look for change that enhances creativity and produces effective and rewarding results.
- **Your being creative will reduces stress.** Our body's stress response is one of our oldest possessions. Its basic architecture is similar to that of a goldfish or a red-spotted newt! While a stress response may be essential for dodging a predator, chasing down prey, or swinging through trees—in the office, not so much! The good news is that in a supportive setting, we can be innovative and create new brain synapses, which encourages creativity, which in turn reduces stress.
- **You are already capable of creative thinking.** Often the people who come up with great ideas and solutions are the most economically rewarded; try out your ideas and see what happens. Take what you know and try something else. Ask yourself, what's the worst that can happen if I'm wrong? Strip away the imaginary blocks that hinder your creativity, and let your mind go free.

Discussion Points

- **Q: How did this activity help your creativity?** (*I had to think differently as the speaker of a foreign language. I had to find creative things to say as the interpreter. It was fun to do something completely out of the box.*)
- **Q: What will you do differently as a result of this activity?** (*I will remember to be confident and more relaxed even in stressful situations. I will remember that body language and tone of voice are a big part of communication. I realized I can make a lasting impression with people based on my energy, tone, and confidence.*)
- **Q: What are the benefits of thinking you are creative?** (*I can produce different, more effective results. I'll actually use my brain more at work. I can keep learning and growing, which is important to me.*)

Participant Action Plan

Have all the participants in their groups of three discuss the actions they will take to be creative. Provide all the participants with a copy of the following action plan. Ask them to complete it, and set up a time to review their results one week later. At that time, ask them what has worked and what has not worked. What do they need to do to improve?

You Are Creative Actions

The actions I will take as a result of the You Are Creative activity are:

_____

_____

_____

_____

ONE WEEK LATER: What results have I gained from the You Are Creative activity?

_____

_____

_____

_____

Activity 46

Generate New Ideas

I said to myself, I have things in my head that are not like what anyone has taught me—shapes and ideas so near to me—so natural to my way of being and thinking that it hasn't occurred to me to put them down. I decided to start anew, to strip away what I had been taught.

—Georgia O'Keeffe, American artist and major figure in
American art (1887 to 1986)

Level of Risk

High

Background and Purpose

Some years ago, the Second City wanted to create an "all improvised" show so they pulled together some of the best improvisers in Chicago, male and female, to create this fully improvised show. It was directed by Mick Napier, author of *Improvise: Scene from the Inside Out* and founder of the acclaimed Annoyance Theatre, as well as resident director and artistic consultant for the Second City. He's a legend in improvisation circles.

Our task was to come up with brand new, short-form games, the kind that you see on the TV show *Whose Line Is It Anyway?* At the time I thought Mick was asking the impossible. I thought everything had been done before—and done well. I didn't know how we would accomplish it, but Mick had an idea.

He asked us for "the title of a game that's never been played before." I knew better than to ask for clarification so I blurted out, "Pickled People!" To my delight he said, "Great." I was so relieved. Again, this man was very impressive, and I had just said something right. Then he asked, "Now, how do you play Pickled People?"

Through major support and suspension of judgment, the ensemble created many new short-form games. We came up with titles like "Under-Blast" and "All Thumbs." After getting over the initial fear, I dove in and found the water to be very warm and enjoyable.

▼

OBJECTIVES

By the end of this activity, people will:

- Maintain and create a positive, supportive environment for themselves and their team.
- Manipulate their own energy any time of the day.
- Enjoy the personal benefits of overcoming unproductive judgments and committing 100 percent.

Mini Lecture

It's amazing how many things we take for granted, things that people once considered too bizarre or impossible to actually work. You may have heard it expressed as "an idea ahead of its time!" The problem is that if we ignore ideas, we may be losing out on "the next best thing." Here's an example of comments from people who weren't ready for new ideas:

"Heavier-than-air flying machines are impossible."—Lord Kelvin of the Royal Society in 1895

"This 'telephone' has too many shortcomings to be seriously considered as a means of communication. The device is inherently of no value to us."—An internal memo at Western Union in 1876

"Who the hell wants to hear actors talk?"—H. M. Warner of Warner Brothers films in the 1920s before he changed his mind

"We don't like their sound, and guitar music is on the way out."—The executive at Decca Recording Company about the Beatles in 1962

"The concept is interesting and well formed, but in order to earn better than a 'C,' the idea must be feasible." ——A Yale University management professor's response to a paper written by Fred Smith proposing a reliable overnight delivery service later to be called Federal Express

New out-of-the box ideas can seem weird, funny, and impractical to the logical or skeptical mind, but when people are willing to see beyond the ordinary, fantastic new products, systems, and ideas are generated. New ideas are the foundation of a thriving organization. Here are some tips on how to generate them:

1. **No critics please.** Don't be a person who says "It's impossible" or "It can't be done." Yes, at some point we need to judge an idea, but never at the idea generating stage.

2. **Assign a number to your ideas.** Quantity equals quality: the more ideas you come up with, the more likely it is that one or more of them will be a great idea. Decide to create 30 or even 100 ideas to a problem, and don't stop until you've reached the number.

3. **Turn wacky ideas to interesting to workable.** Look for as many wacky ideas as you can — the wackier the better. Now turn every wacky idea into an interesting idea. Finally, turn your interesting ideas into workable ideas. It may mean stepping back from the process a couple of times—so take a walk and then come back. The most wacky idea may turn out to be the most workable!

4. **Build on ideas.** Piggyback ideas one after another to create a new idea. Think of the example of combining an engine with a horse carriage to create the *horseless carriage*, or what we now call a car.

5. **Assign a monetary value to your ideas.** Keep doubling the value of your ideas. Give your first idea a value of 1 cent, the next idea 2 cents, the third idea 4 cents, and so on. The thirtieth idea will be worth $5,368.704. The concept is to stretch for one more idea because it may be worth thousands of dollars.

Overview of Activity

Participants form a circle, and, by overcoming judgments and being supportive, they come up with a brand new product. They give it a name, a slogan, a jingle, a celebrity, and a commercial.

Time

Instructions—6 minutes
Each round—1 to 2 minutes
Debriefing—8 minutes
Total time—24 minutes

STEPS TO FOLLOW

Instructions

Have the participants form a big circle, and explain that, in a very short amount of time, they will be creating a product from the inception of the idea to the jingle and everything in between. They will go around the circle taking turns one by one. Tell them they will create the best ad campaign ever made in the entire world:

- They will invent a product.
- They will name it.
- They will choose a celebrity spokesperson for it.
- They will create a jingle, commercials, taglines, and anything else that you want to add.

Rules

Because this ad campaign is the best ever, there are a few rules:

- There are no wrong answers. It doesn't matter if participants think an idea is the worst idea they have ever had themselves or they have ever heard, they will go for it and/or applaud it.
- Participants will embrace every idea and applaud it with great vigor.
- Participants can holler, clap, punch the air, or give a cheer for the ideas. (Have them practice.)
  1. Start by instructing the first person, a brave volunteer, to invent a product that would benefit humanity in some way. For example, fruity-smelling socks or cars that fly. Have everyone applaud the idea.
  2. Now that the group has the product, instruct the next four or five participants standing in the circle to each come up with one name for it. The names should all be different. Have everyone applaud the ideas.
  3. Instruct the next four or five participants standing in the circle to each come up with as many taglines as possible. Each participant is responsible for one tagline that everyone else will applaud.
  4. Instruct the next four or five participants to create a jingle. Again, each participant needs to come up with one that everyone else will applaud.
  5. Instruct the next four or five participants to each choose a different celebrity to make a cameo performance as the spokesperson of the product. Have everyone else applaud each of the answers.
  6. And finally, instruct the next two to three participants to each create a quick commercial. Have everyone else applaud their ideas.
  7. Repeat these steps as many times as you'd like.

Example

Step 1	"A caffeine drip."
Step 2	"IVEEEEEE!"
	"Drip Bag."
	"Liquid Bean."
	"Black Gold."
Step 3	"Awake all day."
	"No more cups."
	"Java on the Go."
	"Star ... what?"
Step 4	"Stick it in and walk around!"
	"It's no mess, no fuss."

	"One bag a day will do ya."
	"It comes in pretty, pretty colors."
Step 5	"Kathy Griffin."
	"Joan Rivers."
	"Sponge Bob Square Pants."
	"Snoop Dogg."
Step 6	"It's an office scene in the middle of the day, and everyone is sleepy. In walks Snoop Dogg with his caffeine drip awake and alive."

▼

BENEFITS TO LOOK FOR

The ideas below echo the Generate New Ideas approach:

- **Accept every idea.** When we are accepted, our creativity flows. We lose our inhibitions and act spontaneously, overcoming previous barriers. We have greater confidence, which enables us to take greater risks.
- **Recognize the value in every idea.** Imagine if the founder of FedEx had believed his Yale professor and agreed that the idea was not feasible— with that kind of thinking, we would still be delivering mail by horse. We wouldn't be driving around in cars, or flying in the air, or watching movies. Every idea has value because you never know which idea is going to turn out to be the best invention of all time.
- **Be enthusiastic.** There is nothing worse than creating an idea and having other people criticize it before it has even gotten off the ground. If someone has an idea, even if it's the wackiest idea in the world, say, "That's interesting. How do you see it working?" Let the idea's creator discover if it is workable and feasible or not. This particular idea may not be the right one, but if its creator keeps on thinking about it, he or she will eventually find one that works.

Discussion Points

- **Q: Was the activity difficult? If yes, why? If no, why not?** (*I was in my head judging myself. I was comparing too much. I just went for it and stopped listening to my judgments.*)
- **Q: How did it feel to be so enthusiastic about ideas?** (*It was great to have my ideas applauded so enthusiastically. I would love to have all my ideas get such a great response. It felt good to applaud other people's ideas—it really built team spirit.*)

- **Q: How will you relate this activity to work?** (*I will remember to generate enthusiasm when someone comes up with a new idea. I will look at the way I am doing things and create better ways of doing things. I'll keep an open mind to my own ideas and other people's ideas.*)
- **Q: Where does generating new ideas fit into work?** (*It fits in everywhere—anywhere that people are creating new ways of doing things. There's always new technology coming along to help processes run more smoothly, but maybe we can make things run better just by thinking outside the box.*)

Participant Action Plan

Have the team shout out some ideas on how to generate new ideas back at the office. Provide all the participants with a copy of the following action plan. Ask them to complete it, and set up a time to review their results one week later. At that time, ask them what has worked and what has not worked. What do they need to do to improve?

Generate New Ideas Actions

The actions I will take as a result of the Generate New Ideas activity are:

_____

_____

_____

_____

ONE WEEK LATER: What results have I gained from the Generate New Ideas activity?

_____

_____

_____

_____

Activity 47

Critical Thinking

It is easy to become deluded by the audience, because they laugh. Don't let them make you buy the lie that what you're doing is for the laughter. Is what we're doing comedy? Probably not. Is it funny? Probably yes. Where do the really best laughs come from? Terrific connections made intellectually, or terrific revelations made emotionally.

—Del Close, considered one of the premier influences on modern improvisational theater, actor, improviser, writer, teacher, and coauthor of the book *Truth in Comedy* (March 9, 1934, to March 4, 1999)

Level of Risk

Low

Background and Purpose

Del Close always said don't say the first thing that pops into your head. Say the seventh thing or the eleventh. The theory is that the seventh thing is much more interesting and thought provoking than the first. He didn't want his improvisers pandering to the audience for cheap laughs; he wanted them to play to the top their intelligence. I cherish the fact that I had Del Close as a teacher because he pushed me to be better.

It took me a long time to appreciate what Del was saying because I was always more of a spontaneous improviser. If I thought something was funny, I'd say it. Usually it was, but I wanted to go beyond laughter. Del told me to "follow my fear" into the silence of the audience and into the genius of my mind. It's easy to say something quick and easy for a laugh. It's harder to think about the state of politics, the effects of media on societies, cultural diversity in cities, and so on. In order to make any kind of statement in our shows, we had to think before we spoke, use our brains, form opinions, gather facts, read, and open our eyes and ears.

▼

OBJECTIVES

By the end of this activity, people will:

- Step back from an issue, question, or problem and figure out what to do from a reasonable standpoint.
- Reflect on the concern without having emotions skewing the outcome.
- Create purposeful, reflective judgments about what to believe or do.
- Clarify goals, examine assumptions, discern hidden values, evaluate evidence, accomplish actions, and assess conclusions.

Mini Lecture

Critical thinking is a skill that students develop as they progress in school. It requires students to set aside assumptions and beliefs to enable them to think without bias or judgment. Critical thinking involves suspending our beliefs and exploring questions and topics from a "blank-page" point of view. It also involves the ability to discern fact from opinion when exploring a topic.

When we need to work out a complex personal or business problem, critical thinking helps provide a level of confidence that is based on a credible source of knowledge. It also helps us define the right course of action to take.

Whether we are reading, writing, speaking, or listening, we can do it from a critical point of view and see patterns, make connections, and solve new problems. Critical thinking centers not on answering questions but on questioning answers. Here are a few simple steps to critical thinking:

1. **Question assumptions.** For centuries people assumed there could be no black swans and therefore "all swans were white." However, in the seventeenth century, black swans were discovered in Australia, which forced a change in people's thinking.
2. **Watch out for trends.** For example, we use more energy in the winter and take more holidays in the summer. Increased revenues may be caused by an impressive new product or service, or they may be the result of simply an increasing trend that has been going on for a few years.
3. **Look for evidence.** The Scottish philosopher David Hulme noted, "A wise man proportions his belief to the evidence." It's tempting to believe evidence that confirms our original view and dismiss evidence that challenges it, but we need to be open-minded about all the evidence.
4. **Don't jump to conclusions.** Scholar Harold Acton said, "Some people take no mental exercise apart from jumping to conclusions." Current facts may

support the original conclusion, but it's always helpful to have more evidence to support it.

5. **Deconstruct the elements of a work.** In the case of a paper or speech, look at the arguments, the evidence, the structure, and the presentation. In the case of a novel, consider the plot, the characterization, and the language. In the case of a film, think about the script, the acting, the direction, the cinematography, and the music.

6. **Keep practicing.** The British politician Barbara Castle once said: "Think, think, think. It will hurt like hell at first, but you'll get used to it." Life isn't simple, and the world is not black and white. As the Greek philosopher Socrates put it: "Confusion is the beginning of wisdom."

7. **Keep asking "why?"** Critical thinking ends in "why?" Why is this person doing this? And then question the answer … why … why … why?

Overview of Activity

In teams of five, groups will determine how the Great Pyramid of Giza was built. They will then improvise their results to the whole group.

Time

Instructions—5 minutes
Each round—3 to 4 minutes
Debriefing—8 minutes
Total time—30 minutes

STEPS TO FOLLOW

Round 1

1. Have participants form teams of five people. The task is to use critical thinking skills to determine how Egypt's Great Pyramid of Giza was built.

2. Tell them the facts:
   - The pyramid is nearly 50 stories high.
   - Researchers estimate that 2.3 million blocks were used.
   - The average weight of each block is about 2.5 metric tons.
   - The largest block weighs as much as 15 metric tons.
   - It is estimated that the Egyptians took 20 years to build it, concluding around 2560 BC.

3. Tell the teams that their job is to critically think through how the Great Pyramid was built. Each group will come up with as many theories as they want.

Round 2

1. Have each group choose their favorite theory and reenact the scene. The scene can be at any point of building the Great Pyramid, from the beginning stages of the project to the final stages. Possible examples: slaves hauling stones, aliens landing, and so on.
2. Now have each group improvise their scene in turns.

Rule

Each participant in the team should participate in some way in the scene.

Round 2 Example

Person A:	"There's a planet we can land on."
Person B:	"We must build a pyramid to show we have been here."
Person C:	"It will take only a moment to make the blocks of stone."
Person D:	"I can easily transport them with my mind control."
Person E:	"We can help. Let's all think *pyramid!*"

BENEFITS TO LOOK FOR

The ideas below echo the Critical Thinking approach:

- **Change your mind if the evidence changes.** John Maynard Keynes, a British economist, said: "When the facts change, I change my mind. What do you do, sir?" When evidence changes, many are reluctant to change their minds, but critical thinking demands that we do so.
- **Test your thinking on others.** Brainstorm your ideas with other people before starting a piece of work. Entertain challenge. Embrace change. Encourage diversity.
- **Trust your instincts.** If something doesn't feel right, even if it is in a newspaper or a television program, check it out. Strange though it may seem, the media can make mistakes, and their corrections rarely achieve the prominence of the original stories.

Discussion Points

- **Q: What did you notice about critical thinking?** (*I realized that we have beliefs that may not be true. When we questioned our assumptions, I realized that we made a lot of assumptions.*)
- **Q: Did you have enough information to use critical thinking skills?** (*I needed more information to make a good judgment. I think we made a lot of things up because we did not have enough information.*)
- **Q: What's the benefit of critical thinking?** (*It's good to use any time I am working on a major issue or problem. I can become the observer of the situation and see the bigger picture.*)
- **Q: When will you use critical thinking skills?** (*Any time I need to find a different solution or another point of view. When I need to look at something from all angles. When I am stuck in my thinking and need to examine it from outside the box.*)

Participant Action Plan

Provide all the participants with a copy of the following action plan. Ask them to complete it, and set up a time to review their results one week later. At that time, ask them what has worked and what has not worked. What do they need to do to improve?

Critical Thinking Actions

The actions I will take as a result of the Critical Thinking activity are:

_____

_____

_____

_____

ONE WEEK LATER: What results have I gained from the Critical Thinking activity?

_____

_____

_____

_____

Activity 48

Creative Inspiration

You write your first draft with your heart and you re-write with your head. The first key to writing is to write, not to think.

—Sean Connery, Scottish actor and producer, Academy Award winner,
two BAFTAs, and three Golden Globes

Level of Risk

Low

Background and Purpose

Inspiration can be found anywhere … you just have to look. Onstage, improvisers find inspiration from friends, family, and strangers. We look into our past, and we look at our current experiences. We open ourselves up to information that could come from any direction and any source, listening not only with our ears but also our eyes.

Stephanie Weir, an American actress and comedienne, best known for her membership in the recurring cast of *MADtv*, wrote a hilarious scene that was inspired by sitting on a park bench watching a father and daughter play with a ball.

Adam McKay is an American writer, director, actor, and comedian. He is most famous for directing *Anchorman: The Legend of Ron Burgundy* and *Talladega Nights: The Ballad of Ricky Bobby*. While a member of the main stage cast at Second City, he wrote and performed in that company's landmark revue *Pinata Full of Bees*. His inspiration was Noam Chomsky (American linguist, philosopher, cognitive scientist, and political activist), so he wrote several politically charged sketches, one in which he played Noam Chomsky as a substitute kindergarten teacher and another in which he played Chomsky as a hapless personnel manager informing a corporate vice president that his IQ is lower than a raccoon's.

Creative inspiration can be found anywhere; you just have to be looking for it. Opportunities are everywhere; just be open to them.

▼

OBJECTIVES

By the end of this activity, people will:

- Utilize trial and error without judgment of themselves or others.
- Be open to opposing views.
- Remember to have fun.
- Realize that creative inspiration comes from within.

Mini Lecture

Creative inspiration is the antidote to making assumptions. People with creative inspiration are willing to examine their own and others' thought processes, to reveal blind spots and predictable conclusions. Creative inspirers are also open to opposing points of view, and they are able to expand their thinking to accept new ideas. They are curious and inquisitive, and they ask thoughtful questions to seek new insight and knowledge.

Creative inspiration is about thinking beyond labels that tend to constrict the range of possible solutions. One way to increase creative inspiration is to consciously jump back from conclusions. Jumping *to* conclusions happens so fast we may not even be aware of it. Jumping *back* from conclusions forces us to inspect our thought processes more intentionally. This helps prevent assumptions that may compromise our analysis of the issue. The way to jump back from conclusions starts by asking a series of questions:

1. What conclusion have I reached so far?
2. Stepping back from that conclusion, how do I interpret the situation?
3. Stepping back again, what beliefs, experiences, or assumptions led me to that interpretation?
4. Stepping back once more, what happened to "trigger" those beliefs or assumptions?
5. Stepping back from those "triggers," what are the neutral facts?
6. Could those facts and data be interpreted in other ways?
7. Given this new perspective, how am I willing and/or able to challenge and rethink my original conclusion?

Creative inspiration is like a steady pulse that beats inside everyone. The challenge is keeping the embers alive once we have lit the fire. The first and most important rule is to never give up. Difficult tasks force our brain to invent solutions; it's what makes us human. Every problem solved sharpens our confidence and improves our brain power, so pay attention to what you're doing. Never be content to do something just because it's the way you did it yesterday. As human beings, we are here to evolve. There's no reason we can't do it on a daily basis.

Overview of Activity

Participants sit in a circle and pass around an imagined or real object. They each create a use for the object, and as the round proceeds, add to the object.

Time

Instructions—5 minutes
Each round—2 to 3 minutes
Debriefing—8 minutes
Total time—19 minutes

STEPS TO FOLLOW

Round 1

1. Ask the participants to sit in groups of 8 to 12. Give each group an "object." (It can be a real prop or an imagined object.) Simple objects are best—a comb, a fork, a rug.
2. Ask the participants to pass the object around the circle. Each person must name a new use for the object. For example, the pen becomes a mustache, a gun, beef jerky, and a baton.

Round 2

After it has gone around the circle once, then have people take it randomly to add new ideas.

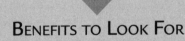

BENEFITS TO LOOK FOR

The ideas below echo the Creative Inspiration approach:

- **Practice using the other side of your brain.** If you are a logical thinker, find something that will stretch your creative side such as drawing a colorful picture of your goal or making up a jingle to highlight the main point of your project. Do the opposite of what you would normally do, and notice the results.
- **Jump back from conclusions.** We often make conclusions based on nothing but our thoughts of what's happened before, or our beliefs and judgments. However, if we step back from our conclusions and ask a new set of questions, we begin to see things differently and possibly create a more effective solution.
- **Keep stepping back.** We think that all creativity is based on moving forward, but if we are moving forward in a predictable way, we will end up with predictable results. Sometimes creative inspiration means to keep on taking a step back and be willing to see another point of view.

Discussion Points

- **Q: How did the different ideas inspire your idea?** *(When other people thought an object could be used in an unusual way, it made me think of different ways. I was inspired by other people's ideas because if they could do it, so could I.)*
- **Q: What did you do if you couldn't think of an idea?** *(I let my instinct take over. I was sometimes surprised at my ideas. I just thought of the silliest thing possible. I said the first thing that came to my mind.)*

Participant Action Plan

Provide all the participants with a copy of the following action plan. Ask them to complete it, and set up a time to review their results one week later. At that time, ask them what has worked and what has not worked. What do they need to do to improve?

Creative Inspiration Actions

The actions I will take as a result of the Creative Inspiration activity are:

_____

_____

_____

_____

ONE WEEK LATER: What results have I gained from the Creative Inspiration activity?

_____

_____

_____

_____

Activity 49

Share Your Story

You take the blue pill and the story ends. You wake in your bed and you believe whatever you want to believe. You take the red pill and you stay in Wonderland and I show you how deep the rabbit hole goes.

—Morpheus to Neo in *The Matrix* (1999)

Level of Risk

Medium

Background and Purpose

The brain communicates in stories episodically or intermittently. People don't remember facts. They remember stories. Our ancestors used stories to understand the world and to relate, connect, and move humanity forward; sharing stories is in our blood.

It's easy to make an audience laugh, but it's hard to make an audience care. Funny is great, but to have an audience think you are funny, be interested in what you have to say, and be touched in their hearts so they'll want to come back is another story. As improvisers, we must have the ability to draw the audience in. We have to connect to them beyond the funny. We do it by taking moments deeper and by giving our performance meaning. Whether it's showing vulnerability or having characters reflect and achieve insights, we gain a huge advantage when we share our story.

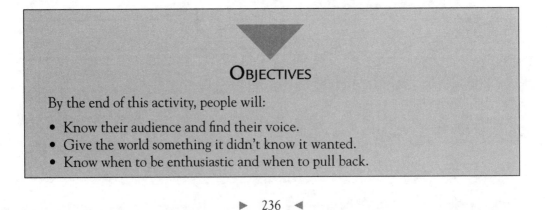

OBJECTIVES

By the end of this activity, people will:

- Know their audience and find their voice.
- Give the world something it didn't know it wanted.
- Know when to be enthusiastic and when to pull back.

Mini Lecture

If you were to write a commercial, one of the most important things to know is the value of a second. A commercial lasts 30 seconds tops, and a viewer has three to four seconds to make up his or her mind whether to watch it or not. I've seen this happen with my own family. We've recorded a program on DVR, and we'll be flipping past the commercials, when suddenly the person with the *remote* stops: "This is a great commercial!" For a few seconds we're all hooked. Stories are the same. They're very powerful, but if we don't catch people in the first few seconds, we've lost our audience.

Many corporations worldwide understand the power of real-life stories, and they use them as a way to motivate their own employees and to provide low-cost, effective training for them. Here's a story, for example, that an international telecommunications corporation shared with their own employees about one of their companies in Spain that launched a dedicated one-stop helpline to give employees, friends, and family access to information about the company's products and services.

The helpline used the company's intranet site and consulted daily with almost every department across the company to track down information. One day an employee called as a last resort; she had sent a phone in for repair two years earlier, but the phone had been misplaced and was never found. She had tried customer services and the repair center with no luck. Finally she called the helpline. Within one week they had tracked it down, but because the phone was two years out of date, they sent her a replacement. This was exceptional internal customer service—and a great story to tell other employees!

Other corporations use storytelling to overcome serious crises that involve having to reinvent business processes and how to interface with customers after a breach of confidence. Business coaches may work with teams to overcome departmental rivalries or entrenched resistance that is creating a political minefield within the corporation. The coach has employees share stories of their experiences at work. The coach then looks at the underlying dynamics by asking questions like, "What do you think they might have been thinking at that time?" "What kind of agendas, intentions, or assumptions are behind the story?" Employees begin to have insights into what was going on behind the story, and they feel they can become the change agents for creating a positive transformation for the company.

Here are some effective tips for the art of storytelling:

1. **Be brief.** Open with a strong statement. Write out the story, mark the points of strong interest, and tighten it up by taking out minor words.
2. **Give details.** Choose only the best details about each person and item in the story. Be specific in your details and comparisons.
3. **Use story twists.** A story should have surprises to keep the listeners engaged.
4. **Work the crowd.** Ask the listeners questions during the story; it keeps them involved and able to relate.
5. **Practice.** Work a favorite story into conversations with as many people as possible, but don't wedge it in unnaturally or tell the story to the same person several times. Wait for another group on another day, and work it in again.

6. **End on the biggest point.** Listeners often remember the last part of an act or story so leave the audience wanting more.

Overview of Activity

Participants decide what superhero powers they would want and why they would deserve to have them. They then share their stories with the group.

Time

Instructions—2 minutes
Each round—4 to 5 minutes
Debriefing—8 minutes
Total time—15 minutes

STEPS TO FOLLOW

1. Congratulate the participants, and tell them that they have each been chosen to become superheroes. Explain that they will now choose their own power.
2. Instruct them to think about and write down:
   - What power they would choose
   - Why they would choose this particular power
3. Instruct them to create a story about how they used their power in a certain situation.
4. Give them three to five minutes to complete the task. This is a silent process.
5. Tell them they each have a minute to stand in front of the group and share their story.

Tips
- Tell them to think about telling a story, not telling the facts.
- Tell them that the story should be emotionally engaging, invoke empathy, and be playful.

Example

Person A: "Little Fluffy had been a stray cat for most of her young kitty life. It wasn't until she was rescued by the Whyman family that she found a home and was given a name. The problem was, she had never gotten used to the vacuum cleaner. It scared her. Which is when I heard her call. She was six stories up stuck in an oak tree, and no one could hear her except me … because I have superhearing. My hearing is magnified so high that I can even hear people's thoughts. So hearing little Fluffy's cry was easy. I got into my car and drove the 500 miles to get to her. I told the Whyman family where she was. They called the local rescue squad, who climbed up and got her. Whether it's stuck kittens or lost children, my superhearing will help humanity.

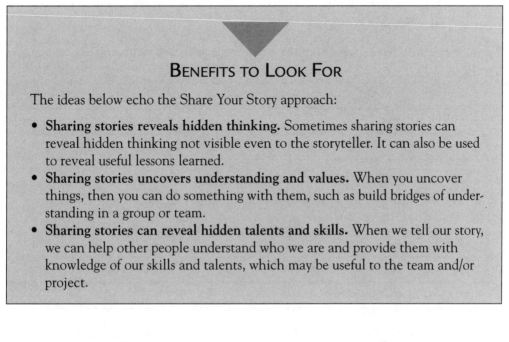

BENEFITS TO LOOK FOR

The ideas below echo the Share Your Story approach:

- **Sharing stories reveals hidden thinking.** Sometimes sharing stories can reveal hidden thinking not visible even to the storyteller. It can also be used to reveal useful lessons learned.
- **Sharing stories uncovers understanding and values.** When you uncover things, then you can do something with them, such as build bridges of understanding in a group or team.
- **Sharing stories can reveal hidden talents and skills.** When we tell our story, we can help other people understand who we are and provide them with knowledge of our skills and talents, which may be useful to the team and/or project.

Discussion Points

- **Q: What were some of your favorite stories shared and why?** *(The funniest one. The one that made me empathize. I loved the one that I could relate to.)*
- **Q: What is story?** *(It is context enriched by emotion.)*
- **Q: How can storytelling impact businesses?** *(It's a way for companies to distinguish themselves from their competition. You have to go beyond goods and services through the use of stories. Organizations can make a high-touch connection with customers. Stories capture customers' interest in ways that other marketing methods cannot.)*
- **Q: What are some examples of great business storytelling?** (One example would be Ben & Jerry's. In 1978, childhood friends Ben Cohen and Jerry Greenfield took a $5 course on ice-cream making and opened the first Ben & Jerry's in a converted gas station in Vermont. Within 5 years they had opened their first franchise. By 1987, less than 10 years after their humble beginnings, sales were at $32 million.)

Participant Action Plan

In the group have all the participants share one action they will take as a result of this activity. Provide them with a copy of the following action plan. Ask them to complete it, and set up a time to review their results one week later. At that time, ask them what has worked and what has not worked. What do they need to do to improve?

Share Your Story Actions

The actions I will take as a result of the Share Your Story activity are:

_____

_____

_____

_____

ONE WEEK LATER: What results have I gained from the Share Your Story activity?

_____

_____

_____

_____

Activity 50

Present without Scripting

What I've discovered is that in art, as in music, there's a lot of truth, and then there's a lie. The artist is essentially creating his work to make this lie a truth, but he slides it in amongst all the others. The tiny little lie is the moment I live for, my moment. It's the moment that the audience falls in love.

—Lady Gaga, American pop singer, placed number seven on the *Forbes* annual list of the World's 100 Most Powerful Women

Level of Risk

Medium

Background and Purpose

There's no money in improvising. The only way you make money is if you land a commercial, TV show, or movie. Improv is truly an art form, and the way people get into it is the same as it is for any of the arts: auditions. Having had my fair share of auditions, I can say that there is a knack to them. Most of the time you are given a script, and if you are lucky, you will have a full day, if not two, to memorize it. But sometimes, you will have only 10 minutes in the waiting room to read, memorize, and deliver an amazing audition. Either way, you have to go in and present it as if there were no script, as if the words fell naturally out of your mouth with charisma and confidence.

What I learned on my journey as an improviser about presenting without a script was to practice and practice, and then practice some more. I practiced in the car, with my husband, with anyone who would give me the time. I'd ask for feedback and listen to any helpful suggestions. The more I understood and was familiar with what I was saying, my audience, and my style, the more my chances rose. Having fun is a big part of presenting without a script. I had the honor of auditioning for a pilot with Dan Castellaneta, the voice of Homer on *The Simpsons*, and I had so much fun I landed the part! So don't discount your ability to be playful.

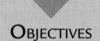

OBJECTIVES

By the end of this activity, people will:

- Think on their feet.
- Learn the power of presenting without a script.
- Practice authentic communication.

Mini Lecture

Unless they are skilled at reading from a teleprompter, effective speakers do not stand in front of an audience reading their script word for word and expecting the audience to enjoy it. But when people use webinars and web meetings, some presenters think, "They can't see me, so what does it matter?" When the material is unfamiliar, it can be nerve-racking to present without a script especially when the brain is screaming, "click here, run a poll now, read the chat," but that doesn't mean reading from a script is the best way to engage the audience.

Being read to from a script—especially when the speaker cannot be seen—is really boring. Reading from a script gives the voice a flat cadence, which quickly turns the audience off. I've seen it happen—when the presenter is reading from a script, people put the webcast on mute, then "chat" with coworkers or answer the phone, basically ignoring or even making fun of what is being said.

Professional actors who create sound recordings read through the script and mark the places where they need to pause, or make an inflection. Then they rehearse it so that it's entertaining. Presenters who are not professional actors can make their presentations interesting by using some of the following tips:

- **Use a "notes" page in PowerPoint.** Outline your presentation using bullets and bold fonts to highlight the points you need to make and questions to ask.
- **Print your outline.** Have an outline (not script) of your presentation handy. Pause to peek at it and make sure you're covering your main points.
- **Look up from your notes.** Imagine real faces in front of you and look down only to check your notes.
- **Practice, practice, practice.** If possible get online (preferably with an audience) and rehearse your presentation in real time.
- **Let your natural style move you on.** When you've covered all the points on your notes, naturally move on to the next visual.
- **Your audience doesn't know what's next.** The audience has no idea of what you're supposed to say or if you've got the wording exactly right. They don't expect perfection. They just want quality information delivered in an interesting way that doesn't waste their time.

When you sound relaxed and confident, your audience will be much more receptive to the content of your message. Know your script. Make notes and use them as reminders, and allow your natural presentation style to make it interesting, fun, and worthwhile.

Overview of Activity

Groups of players line up at the front of the room. The audience assigns the group a suggestion that the group then has to weave into a story line. All this is done on the spot.

Time

Instructions—5 minutes
Each round—2 to 3 minutes
Debriefing—7 minutes
Total time—24 minutes

STEPS TO FOLLOW

Round 1
1. Ask four volunteers to line up at the front of the room.
2. Ask the audience to tell the group their occupation. For example, an audience member would say, "They are all farmers."
3. Explain to the group of four that they alone saved the planet from aliens and that they will now together tell their story. They must work as a team utilizing the "yes, and" theory to acknowledge, validate, and build on other people's contributions to the story.

Round 2
1. Ask four new volunteers to line up and repeat round 1, using a different story line.
2. Ask the audience to give them relationships where they all know each other. For example, a teacher, student, principle, and coach.
3. Tell the four new volunteers that their characters unfortunately have just died. By incorporating the audience's suggestions, together they must offer information about how they happened to die.

Round 3
1. Ask four new volunteers to line up and repeat round 1, using a different story line.
2. Ask the audience to tell them who they are and what their skills would be.
3. Inform the group that they have done something that has landed them in jail. Together they must incorporate their audience's suggestions and explain how they ended up in jail.

Round 4

1. Ask four new volunteers to line up and repeat the previous rounds, using a different story line.
2. Ask the audience to assign each person a comic book villain and whatever powers they are capable of.
3. Inform the group that they have just executed their mastermind plan and they have taken over the world. Incorporating the audience's suggestions, the group must explain how they used their powers to dominate the world.

Round 1 Example

Person A: "I was outside feeding the chickens when it all happened."

Person B: "I was baling the hay."

Person C: "Yeah, there was a hole in the barn's roof, so I was fixing the hole on the roof."

Person D: "Someone's gotta feed this bunch so I was in the kitchen cooking up some grits."

BENEFITS TO LOOK FOR

The ideas below echo the Present without Scripting approach:

- **Practice.** There's a reason professional actors rehearse—no audience wants to see someone just stand up and read the script. The audience expects the actors to know the script and give it energy. It's the same with a presenter. Even when you have a script and highlighted notes, practice the script so that you are confident and energized.
- **Be comfortable with your natural style.** When we present without a script, we can allow our natural style to come through. Our natural voice inflections, enthusiasm, and passion will enliven the presentation and keep the audience's interest alive.
- **Use notes, not scripts, for webinars.** Professional actors who make sound recordings for films read through their script and mark it with lots of inflections and pauses so that when the time comes to read it live, it sounds interesting and fresh. To make a webinar or web meeting interesting, know the script, make notes, and then rehearse it. When the time comes to present it live, you can present without scripting and just refer to your notes from time to time.

Discussion Points

- **Q: What did you notice about making things up for this activity?** (*I'm not a writer so I don't have a big imagination. It was hard, but I enjoyed it by the end. I thought it was easier because my team was a big inspiration. Some of the things they came up with were easy to follow.*)
- **Q: How can you use what you learned back on the job?** (*I really feel that I pushed out of my comfort zone today, and I was okay with that. I can do that more at work. I learned that as a team, we can do anything.*)
- **Q: How important is it to present without scripting?** (*Audiences are more interested when the presenter is speaking naturally than when he or she is reading from a script. It makes for authentic communication. Energy and enthusiasm are created from presenting without a script.*)

Participant Action Plan

Have the teams discuss what they can do to present without scripting. Provide all the participants with a copy of the following action plan. Ask them to complete it, and set up a time to review their results one week later. At that time, ask them what has worked and what has not worked. What do they need to do to improve?

Present without Scripting Actions

The actions I will take as a result of the Present without Scripting activity are:

_____

_____

_____

_____

ONE WEEK LATER: What results have I gained from the Present without Scripting activity?

_____

_____

_____

_____

Activity 51

The Power of Questions

You can tell whether a person is clever by their answers. You can tell whether a person is wise by their questions.

—Naguib Mahfouz, Egyptian writer who
won the 1988 Nobel Prize for Literature

Level of Risk

Medium

Background and Purpose

Beginner improvisers ask questions as a way of escaping the scene because they don't know what to say. They ask questions out of fear. But as improvisers learn and practice more, they learn that they can ask questions to move the scene forward. Improvisers realize the power of asking questions to gain a deeper insight into the characters or the theme. When I do two-person scenes where we have time to invest in the characters, I use questions to find out more about my partner's character. Questions always reveal something that is interesting and useful onstage. They allow the scene to go on twists and turns that previously were not thought of. With experience, questions can take a scene from being funny to being funny and interesting.

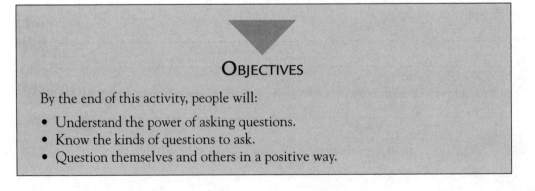

OBJECTIVES

By the end of this activity, people will:

- Understand the power of asking questions.
- Know the kinds of questions to ask.
- Question themselves and others in a positive way.

Mini Lecture

When most people think about asking questions, they think of questions they ask other people, but understanding the real power of questions starts with the questions we ask ourselves. For example, one vacation, we were on a beach in Mexico, and we saw a magnificent home with a wrap-around deck, swimming pool, and rooms with beautiful large windows overlooking the sea. Every day as we walked along the beach, I thought how wonderful it would be to have a home like that, and I asked myself, "Can I afford it?"

The answer that came back was, "No, you cannot." The Powerful Question would have been, "*What has to happen* so that I can afford my dream home?"

Powerful Questions drive you and others to take action that will achieve the results you want. For example, suppose you are thinking, "I don't earn enough." Now change it to a Powerful Question: "*What has to happen* to double or triple my income?" Whenever you are stuck wondering about what Powerful Questions to ask yourself or another person, just add "What has to happen?" If you are still stuck wondering what Powerful Questions to ask, take a look at the list below:

- What are my best achievements?
- What are the best compliments I have received?
- When did I laugh so much, tears rolled down my cheeks?

Our brains love questions because they have the power to shift our mindset. A Powerful Question will drive knowledge, provide growth, and fuel creativity and critical thinking. The best way to start using Powerful Questions today is to ask the what, where, who, when, and why questions:

1. "What are emperors?"
2. "Where do they hang out?"
3. "Who gets invited to court?"
4. "When do ordinary people get to see them?"

Develop the habit of questioning. Question everything. Become comfortable with unanswered questions. Don't see them as problems. Welcome them. Play with them. Your brain will thank you.

Overview of Activity

Participants form two lines facing each other, and through the process of elimination, they practice asking questions.

Time

Instructions—2 minutes
Each round—depends on the number of people
Debriefing—8 minutes
Total time—20 minutes

STEPS TO FOLLOW

Create two groups and have them stand in two lines facing each other but far apart from each other. Inform the participants that this is an elimination activity. The last person standing wins. The two people standing at the front of the lines will start. One will begin the scene by asking a question. The other player will answer with a question. Then explain the rules.

Rules
- You can only ask questions.
- You cannot ask the same question twice.
- You cannot hesitate for more than two seconds.
  If any of these rules are broken, that person is out!

Tips
- Inform the participants that they will judge each other, and they will holler and clap when they feel someone has broken the rules.
- Every time someone is out and is replaced by a new person, give the new person a word and a location to begin their scene. This will ensure that no one is thinking of questions beforehand and that each scene will be different. They will truly be improvising.

BENEFITS TO LOOK FOR

The ideas below echo the Power of Questions approach:

- **Powerful questions are usually open-ended.** Asking open-ended questions allows us to gain information and knowledge. If we are talking, then we are giving away information. If we are listening, then we are gaining knowledge and power.
- **Ask open-ended questions.** Any question that begins with what, where, who, why, or when is an invitation for the other person to talk. A closed-ended question elicits a yes or no response, and we don't learn very much.
- **Ask, "What has to happen?"** Asking our customers questions is obviously important, but what about asking ourselves questions? The Powerful Question can make the difference between creating positive results and negative ones. "What has to happen for me to get a promotion?" creates a dialogue that inspires action, and action creates results.

Discussion Points

- **Q: What kinds of questions did you ask?** *(Because we had to ask the questions within two seconds, I just asked the first thing that came into my head. I wanted to just ask open-ended questions, but they were mostly closed-ended questions.)*
- **Q: How did it feel to be onstage for a long time?** *(In some ways it was comfortable, and in other ways it got more and more intense. I got to ask only a couple of questions. My mind just went blank.)*
- **Q: What is the most important thing about asking Powerful Questions?** *(The most Powerful Questions are the open-ended ones that make the other person talk more. Closed-ended questions are great for stopping people rambling, but we don't get much information from them.)*
- **Q: Why are questions so important?** *(I gather information. I listen more to what my customers really want. I make them do most of the talking, which means I can gather the facts to determine what the customers really need.)*

Participant Action Plan

Have the participants work with someone they don't know well and share what they intend to do as a result of this activity. Provide all the participants with a copy of the following action plan. Ask them to complete it, and set up a time to review their results one week later. At that time, ask them what has worked and what has not worked. What do they need to do to improve?

The Power of Questions Actions

The actions I will take as a result of The Power of Questions activity are:

_____

_____

_____

_____

ONE WEEK LATER: What results have I gained from The Power of Questions activity?

_____

_____

_____

_____

Activity 52

Negotiation Skills

If women ran the world, we wouldn't have wars, just intense negotiations every 28 days.

—Robin Williams, American actor and comedian who
won the Academy Award for Best Supporting Actor
for his performance in the 1997 film *Good Will Hunting*

Level of Risk

Medium

Background and Purpose

Writing shows is a process. Some people find it to be really easy, and others find it to be a little bit more difficult. Director Doug Sarine, the ninja on *Ask A Ninja*, a series of comedy video podcasts about a ninja, once said, "You can't produce a diamond without a little bit of pressure."

Part of the writing process is negotiating with the director and fellow ensemble players for your scenes to get stage time. If done well, the end result is a win-win situation for everyone. All the players involved in the show feel like rock stars, and they feel good about their part in the show. The scenes are the products of agreements reached through discussions (debates) in which the director and ensemble players consider all the different perspectives.

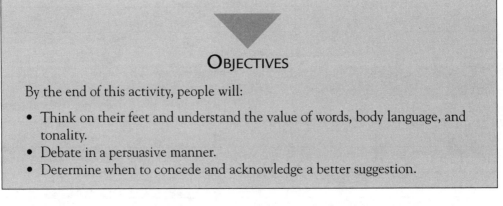

OBJECTIVES

By the end of this activity, people will:

- Think on their feet and understand the value of words, body language, and tonality.
- Debate in a persuasive manner.
- Determine when to concede and acknowledge a better suggestion.

Mini Lecture

The goal of negotiation is to create a win-win outcome for both parties. Each side should feel positive once the negotiation is over. Negotiation skills are useful in all kinds of situations from struggles with authority, to one group of people taking advantage of another group, to sales large or small. Depending on the circumstances and the different styles of negotiation, it is always useful to *plan*. Without planning, you are flying without a compass. Here are a few tips that will help you plan your negotiations:

- **Goals.** What do you want? What does the other person want?
- **Trades.** What do you have to trade, and what are you comfortable giving away?
- **Relationships.** Is there a history, and will it impact the negotiations?
- **Hidden issues.** What hidden issues might influence the negotiations?
- **Expected outcomes.** Are there any past outcomes and precedents?
- **Consequences.** What are the consequences of winning or losing for each party?
- **Power.** Who has what power in the relationship? Who controls resources?
- **Possible solutions.** What possible compromises might there be?
- **No deal below or beyond (NDB).** What is the least or most you are willing to negotiate?
- **Best alternative to a negotiated agreement (BATNA).** What course of action will the parties take if the negotiation fails?

Whatever the negotiation, stay detached and discuss emotions as if they belong to someone else. Remember, people are rarely as opposed as they first might seem—the other person may have very different goals from the ones you expect! Three important tips for negotiation are:

1. **Realize that knowledge is power.** The more they talk, the more information and power you have.
2. **Let the other party go first.** Don't be the first to make an offer, and never give your best offer first.
3. **Trade small first.** Start off with what you can offer that is free to you and valuable to them.

Leave time at the end of a negotiation to build the relationship, or the negotiation process will seem cold. If this relationship is important, then you must continue to build rapport.

Overview of Activity

Players form two lines facing each other. Everyone takes turns debating; players are eliminated according to certain rules.

Time

Instructions—2 minutes
Each round—Depends on the size of the group
Debriefing—10 minutes
Total time—35 minutes

STEPS TO FOLLOW

1. Participants form two lines facing each other. This is an elimination game. The two people at the front of the line step forward. The topic will be daylight savings. The left side is *for*; the right side is *against*.
2. Instruct the participants to debate. The challenge is to get the other person to concede first. Both participants tell their position, for or against, as quickly and as persuasively as possible.

Rules
*   If one of the participants is too slow and takes more than three seconds to speak, she is eliminated and must go to the end of the line. (*The other player stays while the next person in line joins them and continues the debate.*)
*   If one of the participants concedes, he is eliminated and must go to the end of the line. (*The other one stays while the next person in line joins her and continues the debate.*)
*   If a participant talks too much and gives too much information away, she is eliminated and must go to the end of the line. (*The other participant stays while the next person in line joins him and continues the debate.*)
*   If a participant repeats himself, he is eliminated and must go to the end of the line. (*The other one stays while the next person in line joins her and continues the debate.*)

Note: When the participants run out of steam with this particular debate topic, here are some other issues to keep them going:

*   Cats versus dogs
*   White onions versus red onions
*   Snickers versus Milky Ways
*   Vanilla versus chocolate
*   Thin crust versus thick crust pizza
*   Something related to their company

BENEFITS TO LOOK FOR

The ideas below echo the Negotiation Skills approach:

*   **Plan your negotiations.** Having clear goals is a key to creating win-win situations. What do you want? What does the other person want? What are you comfortable giving away?

- **Improve your debating skills.** Knowing both sides of a negotiation in terms of what can be lost or won helps with debating skills. Whatever the expected outcomes, both parties will make concessions in order to achieve a win-win situation.
- **Talk less, listen more.** The more the other party talks, the more information you receive, and the more information you have, the more power you have. Knowing what they want helps you determine what you are willing to comfortably give.

Discussion Points

- **Q: Did you consider the relationship when deciding what you could give away?** (*I always think about ongoing relationships, so yes. I've seen people have difficult times with people because of a bad negotiation so I always work on building rapport at the beginning and closing of the negotiation to keep it "human."*)
- **Q: Did you discuss the limits and boundaries of the participants' role when negotiating?** (*Sometimes we went over the boundaries. The three-second rule made it difficult to think. It was important to know the boundaries—without that knowledge, we could easily have created a lose-lose situation.*)
- **Q: How did you establish the climate?** (*The climate was established early on because we both wanted a win-win outcome. I could tell by our smiles and tone of voice that we were good.*)
- **Q: Where did you leave time for rapport and catch-ups?** (*At the end of the negotiations. Rapport building is something I sometimes forget to do, so I am making that a priority in future.*)

Participant Action Plan

Provide all the participants with a copy of the following action plan. Ask them to complete it, and set up a time to review their results one week later. At that time, ask them what has worked and what has not worked. What do they need to do to improve?

Negotiation Skills Actions

The actions I will take as a result of the Negotiation Skills activity are:

_____

_____

_____

_____

ONE WEEK LATER: What results have I gained from the Negotiation Skills activity?

_____

_____

_____

_____

Activity 53

Persuade

Even within the band, if I cannot manage to persuade the members of what I see to be the next course of action, how do you expect the group to deal with the expectations of thousands of people? It is not possible.

—Robert Fripp, English guitarist, composer, and record producer, best known as guitarist in King Crimson

Level of Risk

Medium

Background and Purpose

Headshots are the improviser's calling card. It puts a face on the product. When we are creating our headshots, we are trying to persuade the casting directors, *especially if we have no relationship with them,* that we are the ones best suited for the jobs or the parts. Of course, a lot of cast selection is random and luck. If they need an Asian male, obviously I can't do that; but if they are looking for a white female in her thirties to forties, I need to make sure I have a chance.

So my headshot has to catch them. When I am in the photography studio, I have to make sure the message I want to send is coming through my facial expression and my body language. I have to be thinking certain thoughts when the photographer is snapping the picture. For example, I have to look into the camera and picture my best friend, or my nephew and niece, and be thinking of something they did that made me laugh, so that the smile that is captured is authentic, real, and sincere—which are some of the basic keys in the art of persuasion.

▼

Objectives

By the end of this activity, people will:

- Demonstrate ways to incorporate ethos and pathos into conversation.
- Select words that are clear, concise, accurate, and impacting.
- Practice persuasive delivery techniques, including nonverbal skills.
- Have more confidence in their public speaking abilities.
- Have better critical listening skills.

Mini Lecture

Being persuasive is one of the most important skills we can learn because it is useful in countless situations. At work, at home, and in our social life, our ability to be persuasive and influence others is instrumental for achieving goals and being happy. There are some key elements to being persuasive. When we persuade someone to our way of thinking, we have to be sincere. Our presentation, talk, or document needs to look real, smell real, and *actually be real*. The following basic principles will help us to persuade more people to do what we want:

- **Be sincere.** When Susan Boyle first sang "I Dreamed a Dream" on reality TV, her sincerity shone through, and millions were persuaded to give her their vote and ultimately send her CDs to number one, worldwide.
- **What is your most wanted response (MWR)?** Know in advance what you want your audience to do and you will be better able to persuade them to your way of thinking.
- **What do they want?** How is your request going to benefit them? It has to be something that they *want* to do.
- **Match the benefits you are offering to their wants.** When you've figured out what they want, tie in what they want with what you want.
- **Let them know the benefits.** When you want to persuade others, identifying the benefits to them is the *most important* thing you can do.

The more you get inside other people's heads, the more you will be able to persuade them. What is it they want? What is it that, if you offered it to them, they couldn't refuse? Give them benefit after benefit that they will receive if they do what you want. Get to their emotions. And before you know it, they'll be begging to do what you want. Other techniques to persuade people include:

- **"Yes" questions.** Begin the conversation with questions that generate a "yes" response. "Nice day today, isn't it?" When you get someone saying "yes," it's easy to get them to continue, up to and including "Yes, I'll buy it."
- **Scarcity.** Advertisers commonly make opportunities seem more appealing because of their limited availability.

- **Reciprocity.** When someone does something for us, we feel compelled to return the favor. If you want someone to do something nice for you, why not do something nice for them first? In a business setting, maybe you pass the other person a lead.
- **Timing.** People are more likely to be agreeable at the end of the workday or on their way out the door. Whatever you ask them, their likely response will be, "I'll take care of it tomorrow."
- **Congruence.** In most people's minds, a handshake equates to a closed deal. By offering a handshake before a deal actually closed, a salesperson is more likely to actually close it. For example, if you were out and about with a friend and you wanted to go see a movie but the friend was undecided, you could start walking in the direction of the theater while your friend was considering it. Your friend is more likely to agree to go once he or she is walking in the direction you set.
- **Fluid speech.** "Ummm" or "I mean" have the unintended effect of making us seem less confident and sure of ourselves, and thus less persuasive. If you're confident in your speech, others will be more easily persuaded by what you have to say.

Remember, we are more likely to be persuaded by someone we like or by someone we see as an authority. An effective way to use this tendency is to make yourself be seen as a leader. Even if you don't have the official title, be charming and confident, and people will place greater weight on your opinion. If you're dealing with a superior in the workplace, casually praise a leader who that person admires. By triggering positive thoughts in that person's mind about a person she looks up to, she will be more likely to associate those qualities with you.

Overview of Activity

Participants must persuade each other to let go of a $1 million voucher.

Time

Instructions—2 minutes
Each round—5 to 10 minutes
Debriefing—5 minutes
Total time—30 minutes

STEPS TO FOLLOW

Round 1

Have the participants find a partner. The partners with the longest hair will be the (A) partners. (If they are two bald men, ask for the longest arm hair.) Tell the (B) partners that they are millionaires and they have a voucher for $1 million. Tell the (A) partners that they have 5 to 10 minutes to persuade the millionaire (B)s to give them this $1 million voucher. The improvisation ends when either the (B)s keep or the (A)s win the voucher.

Round 2

Now switch! This time the (A)s will have the power. Tell the (A)s that they are the parents, and tell the (B)s that they are the teenagers. Inform them they are arguing over something the teenagers want to do. It can be anything: staying out late, getting a car, start dating, getting a tattoo. The teenager (B)s have to try to persuade the parent (A)s to give in to their demand. The improvisation ends when parents or teenagers win.

Round 1 Example

Person A: "It would be great if I could get that $1 million voucher."

Person B: "I bet. Why should I give it to you?"

Person A: "Good question. I'm going to do something amazing with it."

Person B: "Like what?"

Person A: "Buy myself a house, a car, and a boat, and if there's any money left over, I'll go out to dinner at a really nice restaurant."

Round 2 Example

Teenager: "I want to stay out until midnight on Friday."

Parent: "Well, you can't."

Teenager: "I know 11 p.m. is my curfew, but this Friday is a special night."

Parent: "How special?"

Teenager: "Well, it's Janet's birthday! And she's my best friend. And everyone's going be there. And you'll be a terrible parent if you don't let me go."

BENEFITS TO LOOK FOR

The ideas below echo the Persuade approach:

- **Persuasive argument.** Select words that conjure images in the minds of your audience. Notice the difference between "Having a cell phone will keep you out of trouble" and "Having a cell phone will keep you safe." Which word is more effective for your message: "trouble" or "safe"?
- **Mirroring.** Mimicking the movements and body language of the person you are trying to persuade creates a sense of empathy, which is a powerful persuasive technique. Mirror hand gestures, lean forward or away, or echo various head and arm movements, but be subtle, and delay two to four seconds in your mirroring of the other person's movements.

> • **Man's best friend.** Sounds strange, but a picture of you with a dog (it doesn't even have to be your dog) gives the impression that you're loyal, and it inspires others to be loyal to you. It can make you seem like a team player. But don't go overboard; putting up too many pictures looks unprofessional.

Discussion Points

- Q: **Were you clear, convincing, compelling, and credible in your approach to persuading the other participants?** (*Yes, I used persuasive words, and it worked very well.*)
- Q: **What techniques helped or hindered you from getting your desired outcome?** (*I was sincere, and it really helped. When I got too confident, I sounded harsh, and it did not work. I should have used more body language.*)
- Q: **What techniques could you have used to make you a more successful persuader?** (*I could have used mirroring of their movements more. I could have found out more about what they wanted and then matched their needs.*)

Participant Action Plan

Have participants work with someone they don't know too well and share what they intend to do as a result of this activity. Provide all the participants with a copy of the following action plan. Ask them to complete it, and set up a time to review their results one week later. At that time, ask them what has worked and what has not worked. What do they need to do to improve?

Persuade Actions

The actions I will take as a result of the Persuade activity are:

_____

_____

_____

_____

ONE WEEK LATER: What results have I gained from the Persuade activity?

_____

_____

_____

_____

Activity 54

Customer Service

Customer Satisfaction could be the only sustainable advantage in the New Economy.
—John Chambers, CEO, Cisco "Collaboration Market"

Level of Risk

Medium

Background and Purpose

In improvisation, the product is the show, and the customer is the paying audience. If I want to be service oriented, the show has to be amazing. I want to walk off the stage with standing ovations, patting my fellow improvisers on the back and feeling as though I couldn't have done it any better. In that sense, I am serving the customer because I have the passion to create an amazing show for them. I want to make them laugh so hard they bust a gut.

How do I know I've succeeded? I know the answer to that the minute I walk off the stage. I know if I've "phoned it in" or if I've given it my all. Of course, there's nothing better than hearing from an audience member. Jesse Thorn, American public radio show host and creator, saw my Batman Riddler sketch and five years later ran into a friend of mine and quoted me. I ended up being interviewed on his talk show … that's what customer service is about. I want to be my best onstage—for me, for my team, and for my coach. I want to connect with my audience and my ensemble members, be present, and have fun. I want to be interesting, technically proficient with my improv skills, and emotionally involved in the show. Those are the best ways I can serve the audience.

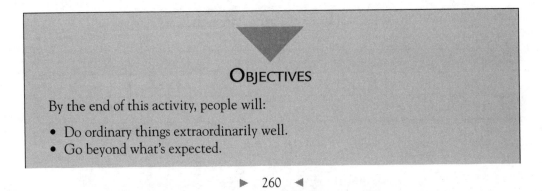

OBJECTIVES

By the end of this activity, people will:

- Do ordinary things extraordinarily well.
- Go beyond what's expected.

- Add value and integrity to every interaction.
- Be at their best with every customer.
- Surprise themselves with how much they can do.

Mini Lecture

One of the hardest things to accomplish after we've delivered training to a company is to demonstrate measureable results. The company needs to have a baseline to begin the measurement process, but not all companies have that. Fortunately, Snap-On Tools in Crystal Lake did, and that is how we were able to accurately measure the results of our customer service training!

We went to Snap-On Tools in Crystal Lake and delivered a two-day customer service workshop that we had designed and developed from our book *Super Service: Seven Keys to Delivering Great Customer Service, Even When You Don't Feel Like It, Even When They Don't Deserve It!*

Right off the bat, as soon as the program was finished, the managers noticed a difference: customer service had improved. Not only that, the people who had not been doing so well turned their attitude around so much that the lowest-performing representative was now the highest-performing representative in terms of customer satisfaction and sales. We asked Snap-On Tools to give us a chart of their findings. It was true. After the customer service training—even up to five months later—sales from customer service had doubled.

Providing customer service training works on many levels. Employees are better motivated, managers receive more outside support and inspiration, customers receive better service, and revenues increase. Here's an excerpt from our book *Super Service*, second edition, page 43, by Val and Jeff Gee:

How to Show a Desire to Serve

1. **Be in control of your attitude.** If you wake up with a bad attitude or something triggers it during the day, become an actor for a while. Think of a person who has a positive attitude. See him or her in your mind. Imagine how the person sits, stands, walks, and talks. Feel yourself become like that person.
2. **Let your anger go.** Anger is poisonous and feeds on itself. If anger comes up, simply take a deep breath, hold it for the count of 3, and then let it go. Feel the anger release with your breath. We breathe not just to bring in oxygen but also to release carbon dioxide. Let your anger go when you exhale.
3. **Maintain a positive attitude.** If you want to feel satisfied in your job and experience energy and fulfillment at the end of your day, have a positive attitude. Think good thoughts. Do the right thing. Make better choices.
4. **Affirm your day.** When you wake up in the morning, brush your teeth, look at yourself in the mirror, and say out loud, "Today is going to be a great day. No matter what I am doing, I am going to do it with the desire to serve. I will be positive, upbeat, and ready to be the best for my customer."

Overview of Activity

In groups, participants will broaden their perspective of the customer point of view by brainstorming solutions to make the customer's experience better.

Time

Instructions—5 minutes
Each round—5 to 10 minutes
Debriefing—10 minutes
Total time—60 minutes

STEPS TO FOLLOW

Round 1

1. Have the participants think of the challenges they are currently facing in two categories: (1) the challenges they are having in providing excellent customer service and (2) the challenges the customers are having in receiving excellent customer service. (**Note:** A customer can be either internal or external.)
2. Have the participants count off in 4s; then all the 1s form a group, all the 2s, and so on. Have all the participants share with their group their two challenges. Have a notetaker from each group write down the challenges on two separate papers (or flip charts).
3. Have each group pick one challenge for both categories that will be the most beneficial to solve. Write them down on a piece of paper (or flip chart).

Round 2

1. Have each group pass their top two challenges to the group on their right— counterclockwise. Each group has five minutes to brainstorm and write down as many possible solutions for the other group's challenges as possible. (*Remind all the participants not to edit or judge themselves or each other. This round is about quantity of solutions, not quality of solutions. There is no right or wrong solution.*)
2. After the brainstorming session, give the solutions back to the original group.

Round 3

After reading all the solutions, each group must then vote on the solutions for the two categories they think are the most viable to build on. They will have to present this to the rest of the class. Each group must incorporate these elements into their presentations:
- Steps (for example: Step 1. Remain calm. Step 2. Remember to smile. And so on).

- Competencies (that is, empathy, enthusiasm, balance, and so on).
- A motto (for example: Discover new ways to delight those I serve).
- A quote (for example: I'll take care of my customer as I would take care of my grandmother).

Round 4

Present your creative solutions to the class.

▼

BENEFITS TO LOOK FOR

The ideas below echo the Customer Service approach:

- **Show a desire to serve.** There's nothing worse than going into a store and feeling like you are bothering them. It's a way to *not* guarantee customer loyalty. Be helpful, smile, and look as though you care. If that's impossible for you to do, then maybe it's time to find a different job.
- **Build rapport.** People buy from people they like. They also recommend people they like, do things for people they like, and go one step further for people they like. That's why building rapport is so important. It establishes relationships in which your customers know that they are important to you and that you value them as individuals, not just dollar signs.
- **Check information.** Paraphrase and ask questions to make sure nothing falls through the cracks. You don't want to waste your time and energy or anyone else's on miscommunication. And if you need to repeat policies and procedures for the benefit of the customers, do so. There's nothing worse than being in the dark or having expectations shattered.

Discussion Points

- **Q: How did the brainstorming go?** (*It was fun. I kept on wanting to judge, but I held my tongue. I felt very free to say anything because I knew there was no wrong answer.*)
- **Q: How can you utilize and implement all the creative work you've done?** (*Print out the steps and post them on my wall. Have weekly follow-up calls with my group to make sure we are doing it.*)

Participant Action Plan

Provide all the participants with a copy of the following action plan. Ask them to complete it, and set up a time to review their results one week later. At that time, ask them what has worked and what has not worked. What do they need to do to improve?

Customer Service Actions

The actions I will take as a result of the Customer Service activity are:

_____

_____

_____

_____

ONE WEEK LATER: What results have I gained from the Customer Service activity?

_____

_____

_____

_____

Activity 55

Think on Your Feet

You going from being on your toes on every play at second base and then suddenly you are just out there. You have to see the way the ball comes off the bat—the different reads you have to take, the different jumps you have to get. It's still a work in progress. I can't say that I do everything right. It's just a matter of working on it.

—Brandon Eric Watson, American outfielder and Pacific League
All-Star who bats left-handed and throws right-handed

Level of Risk

Medium

Background and Purpose

A big component of thinking on your feet is being flexible and adaptable. If I'm too stuck with what I am saying and doing, or if I am too serious with what's going on, I won't be able to adapt and change, and I definitely won't be able to think on my feet and improvise.

For example, the Harold, a 30-minute long-form improvisation, can go along at such a quick pace that it's imperative that the players think on their feet. I can be on the sidelines watching a two-person scene when they look at me and say, "You're our crazy Uncle." I have to quickly become that crazy uncle and come up with something funny: "I've got 21 hamsters. They're all called Hamster. Come here, Hamster." I've got to listen, get out of my head and stop the judgments, and be open and ready to move and support what's going on.

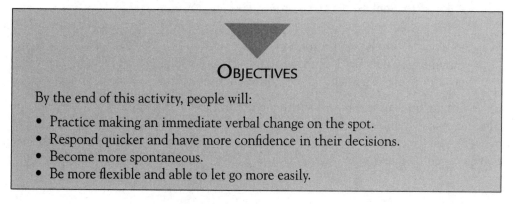

Objectives

By the end of this activity, people will:

- Practice making an immediate verbal change on the spot.
- Respond quicker and have more confidence in their decisions.
- Become more spontaneous.
- Be more flexible and able to let go more easily.

Mini Lecture

The tools improvisers use onstage can help make any conversation more engaging. You can rehearse in front of a mirror, but the moment another person is involved, the script goes out the window. If you want to make an impression, you have to be able to think on your feet—to fling yourself into the moment and improvise.

One of the secrets to thinking on your feet is to be prepared for various contingencies. Here are some tips and tactics that will help you be prepared for situations that might put you under pressure:

- **Relax.** To help your voice stay calm and your brain to "think," take deep breaths, take a second to give yourself a positive message, and clench invisible muscles (thighs, biceps, feet) for a few seconds and release.
- **Listen.** Understand the question before you reply. To listen more effectively, look directly at the questioner. Observe his or her body language, and remember that the questioner is interested.
- **Please repeat the question.** The questioner then has an opportunity to rephrase, and you have time to think.
- **Please rephrase the question.** Give yourself time to think and clarify what is being asked.
- **Please clarify.** Force the questioner to be more specific.
- **Use silence.** Silence can be used to your advantage. It helps you control your thoughts and tells your brain to slow everything down.
- **Stick to one point.** If your answers are too short, the conversation can slip into interrogation mode. If your answers are too long, you may lose people's interest, come across as boring, or give away too much.
- **Ask "What if?"** Take time to brainstorm the most difficult questions that people might ask. Prepare and rehearse good answers.
- **Practice clear delivery.** How you speak is almost as important as what you say. If you mumble, "umm" or "ah" between every second word, your listeners' confidence in you plummets:
  - Speak in a strong voice.
  - Pause to emphasize a point or slow yourself down.
  - Vary your tone.
  - Use eye contact appropriately.
- **Summarize and stop.** Use expressions such as *in conclusion* and *finally*, and wrap up with a quick summary. Don't fill the silence with more information.

Thinking on your feet means staying in control of the situation. Ask questions, buy time for yourself, and stick to one point. When you can zoom in on the key areas of concern, you'll answer like an expert and impress your audience, and yourself, with your poise and self-confidence.

Overview of Activity

In trios, two participants will have a conversation. Sporadically, the third participant will "buzz," and the two participants will have to "take back" what they just said and replace it with something new.

Time

Instructions—2 minutes
Each round—2 to 3 minutes
Debriefing—5 minutes
Total time—16 minutes

STEPS TO FOLLOW

Round 1

Have the participants form trios (groups of three). Ask for one of them to raise her hand. Inform this volunteer that she will be the Buzzer. The other two people in the group, Partners (A) and (B), will have a conversation. Randomly in the conversation, the Buzzer will clap her hands, and whoever spoke last must *take back* the last line of the dialogue he just said and replace it with something new. Give them this example:

- If I said "I have a dog" and the Buzzer said "Buzzzzzz!" I would immediately say something new like "I have a cat." And if the Buzzer buzzed me again, "Buzzzzzz!" I'd say something new yet again: "I have a cat that looks and acts like a dog."

Rules

- The Buzzer can buzz one person as many times as he likes (within reason).
- The Buzzer must give equal buzzing opportunities.

Round 2

Have the participants switch roles! The Buzzer switches roles with one of the participants in the conversation. They start a new topic of dialogue.

Round 3

Have the participants switch roles again so that everyone gets a chance to be the Buzzer.

Round 1 Example

Person A: "I cooked a really great meal last night from my grandma's recipe. It was delicious."

Person B: "What was it?"

Person A: "Lasagna."

Buzzer: "Buzzzzz!"

Person A: "Meat loaf."

Buzzer: "Buzzzzz!"

Person A: "Potato chips. Yeah, she made real mean potato chips."

▼

BENEFITS TO LOOK FOR

The ideas below echo the Think on Your Feet approach:

- **Follow the "yes, and" philosophy.** Using "yes, and" responses shows interest and helps keep the conversation moving in a positive way.
- **Relax.** Help your voice stay calm and your mind clear by taking a breath and maintaining positive self talk.
- **Ask what-if questions.** Think about the most difficult questions that people might ask, and take time to prepare and rehearse good answers.
- **Practice your delivery.** How you say it is almost as important as what you say; be aware of your tone and body language.

Discussion Points

- **Q: Was it easy or difficult to substitute something new?** (*It was easy to begin with, but later as the buzzer went faster, it got harder. I enjoyed the game. It made me really think.*)
- **Q: What made it easy or difficult?** (*It was fun. It helped me overcome my fear of thinking on my feet.*)
- **Q: How did it feel to "wing it"?** (*It was great. I don't normally wing it, so it was good to get out of my comfort zone.*)
- **Q: How was it to be the Buzzer?** (*Great. I wish I could do that in every conversation!*)
- **Q: How did the new piece of information affect the conversation?** (*Every new piece of information took the conversation in a completely different direction.*)

Participant Action Plan

Provide all the participants with a copy of the following action plan. Ask them to complete it, and set up a time to review their results one week later. At that time, ask them what has worked and what has not worked. What do they need to do to improve?

Think on Your Feet Actions

The actions I will take as a result of the Think on Your Feet activity are:

_____

_____

_____

_____

ONE WEEK LATER: What results have I gained from the Think on Your Feet activity?

_____

_____

_____

_____

Activity 56

Drop Inhibitions

The ultimate is finding a place where you have no inhibitions, nothing to hide, where you can learn from one another.

—Jennifer Aniston, American actress, film director and producer, and winner of an Emmy Award, Golden Globe Award, and Screen Actors Guild Award

Level of Risk

High

Background and Purpose

There's a great story about Chris Farley, *Saturday Night Live* (SNL). Bob Odenkirk, an American actor, comedian, writer, director, and producer, wrote the part of a fictional motivational speaker called Matt Foley for Chris Farley. The problem was, everyone at the time was doing comedy bits about motivational speakers, so people thought it wouldn't work. If the writers had listened to the naysayers, we would have missed out on Chris Farley's destroying pieces of furniture with his girth.

It's about dropping inhibitions and not listening to the inner judge and going for it. Yes, it's good to listen to advice, but sometimes it's better to listen to your own instincts. Sometimes it's easier to ask for forgiveness than it is to get permission.

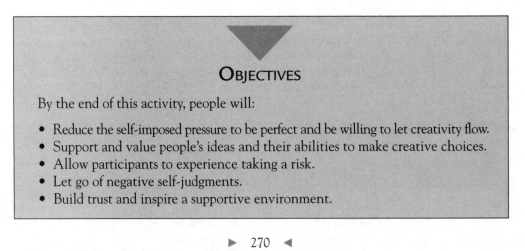

OBJECTIVES

By the end of this activity, people will:

- Reduce the self-imposed pressure to be perfect and be willing to let creativity flow.
- Support and value people's ideas and their abilities to make creative choices.
- Allow participants to experience taking a risk.
- Let go of negative self-judgments.
- Build trust and inspire a supportive environment.

Mini Lecture

When you drop inhibitions, you let go of things that hold you back from saying and doing what you would normally do if you weren't thinking about the consequences or repercussions. For example, people who drink alcohol release their inhibitions because the alcohol stops them from being inhibited by conscious thoughts telling them what to say and do. Fortunately, there are other ways to release our inhibitions, and these include:

- **Find the best solution.** Sometimes we inhibit creativity because of our fear of failure. Instead of being afraid, put your newfound knowledge toward finding the *best solution*. Build more prototypes, test them out on people, gather feedback, and make changes.
- **Escape.** Sometimes our best ideas come to us in the shower or while we're alone. Escaping to a different environment can give us access to our creative energy and trigger new solutions. Einstein used to take long walks to think and solve problems. Experiment and find what works for you.
- **Jot down your thoughts.** Keep a journal or a notepad handy to jot down your thoughts and ideas. Many innovators and creative people have some method to capture their thoughts, to think on paper, to drop their inhibitions, and start the creative process. Leonardo da Vinci's famous notebook was purchased by Bill Gates for $30.8 million!

Whether it is a presentation or a stand-up routine, audiences respond to one of two triggers: the unexpected and the common experience. So, for example, admitting that you get road rage on the way to work will get a laugh. Some will laugh because they didn't expect it, and others will laugh because they do the same thing but keep it quiet. Every day, people play to social norms and expectations, and you stand out when you let go of those inhibitions and explore your creative freedom. Of course, in the business world you have to know your limitations and your audience.

When we have inhibitions, it tends to make us feel limited and stuck. When we feel inhibited, it limits our thinking, and we become closed to new ideas and solutions. Freeing ourselves from these self-created constraints begins by removing assumptions and restrictions, and it has more to do with psychology than intellect. It is what we refer to when we talk about "thinking outside the box."

Overview of Activity

In groups of 8 to 10, participants go around a circle retelling a classic joke and improvising the punch line.

Time

Instructions—2 to 3 minutes
Each round—5 to 8 minutes
Debriefing—5 minutes
Total time—15 minutes

STEPS TO FOLLOW

1. Have the participants form groups of 8 to 10. Explain that they will put on their creative minds and go around their circle retelling a classic joke and improvising the punch line. Give them the joke format:
   "1,001 *blanks* walk into a bar, and the bartender says, 'We can't serve 1,001 *blanks*.' The *blanks* say, 'Why not?' And the bartender says, '*Punch line.*'"

2. Say to the participants, "I will give you an object for your joke, and it's a simple game of fill in the blank. Basically, incorporate the object into the joke, and add an ending and/or a punch line. Don't worry about what the ending is. It does not have to be funny. Just say anything, and avoid 'umms' and 'ahhs.' Let the joke flow as if you've told it 1,001 and times! ALSO, after each person finishes the joke, the rest of the group must go wild with laughter and applause in support of their colleague. I'll give you the first example. Can I get an object?"

3. After you have successfully told the joke and the participants have applauded you, say, "Now here's your first object: a light bulb. Anyone can start. Go!"

Objects for Suggestions
Comb, mushroom, treasure chest, pen, glasses, and so on.

Example

Person A: "1,001 forks walk into a bar. The bartender says, 'We don't serve forks here.' The forks say, 'Why not?' The bartender says, 'Fork off before I call the police.'"

Person B: "1,001 doors walk into a bar. The bartender says, 'We don't serve doors here.' The doors say, 'Why not?' The bartender says, 'Morrison is dead.'"

BENEFITS TO LOOK FOR

The ideas below echo the Drop Inhibitions approach:

- **Label yourself differently.** Often we tell ourselves that we are shy or not self-confident, and then we that way, which keeps reinforcing the label. If you want to impress people or stand out from the crowd, use your imagination to transform your own beliefs about your identity. Begin by imagining how you would like to be perceived by other people. Approach other people with an open mind.

- **Don't let failure stop you.** "I have not failed. I've just found 10,000 ways that won't work."—Thomas A. Edison. If Edison had allowed failure to stop him from moving forward, he might have stopped progress on some of the greatest inventions the world has ever known including the phonograph, the motion picture camera, and the long-lasting, practical electric light bulb!
- **Keep a notebook.** It can be as simple as using Post-it notes or a paper napkin, but when you have a great idea, jot it down. When J. K. Rowling moved to Edinburgh, Scotland, to be near her younger sister, she brought with her a suitcase half-filled with her notes on her ideas for the first Harry Potter book.

Discussion Points

- **Q: Do you put pressure on yourself to be creative and why?** (*A lot of times I don't think my ideas will work. I've failed at things in the past, and I don't like failure. I'm a bit of a perfectionist.*)
- **Q: What is it like to be creative when you know your idea will be valued?** (*It feels good to have ideas affirmed. Even if an idea doesn't work exactly how I think it will, it's good to be appreciated.*)
- **Q: How can you quiet the inner judge more?** (*I think of myself as a creative person. I write things down. I go for a walk. I exercise. I create a new dish for dinner.*)

Participant Action Plan

In groups of four, discuss ideas that will enable you to be more creative. Provide all the participants with a copy of the following action plan. Ask them to complete it, and set up a time to review their results one week later. At that time, ask them what has worked and what has not worked. What do they need to do to improve?

Drop Inhibitions Actions

The actions I will take as a result of the Drop Inhibitions activity are:

_____

_____

_____

_____

ONE WEEK LATER: What results have I gained from the Drop Inhibitions activity?

_____

_____

_____

_____

Activity 57

Self-Awareness: Identify Emotions

Emotional intelligence is the capacity for recognizing our own feelings and those of others, for motivating ourselves, for managing emotions well in ourselves and in our relationships.

—Daniel Goleman, author of more than 10 books on psychology,
education, science, and leadership; and science journalist (*New York Times*
for 12 years) specializing in psychology and brain sciences

Level of Risk

High

Background and Purpose

Do I hog the stage, get angry if I have a bad show, and make other people angry at a show or rehearsals? Do I still have some habits onstage that I promised myself I would stop years ago? How far could I go as an improviser if I eliminated one or two counterproductive behaviors? How much time and energy do I spend feeling jealous, inadequate, worried, or anxious?

Many improvisers ask these kinds of questions in order to become successful. It's about having self-awareness. And the great thing is that you can start to ask these questions at any point in your life. Experts agree that no matter where you are in life, you can improve your level of *emotional intelligence* (EI). You can go from being an emotional wreck to an emotional genius. And even small improvements will help your career. No matter what your emotional starting point is, if you improve your level of EI, you will do a better job of managing your work life.

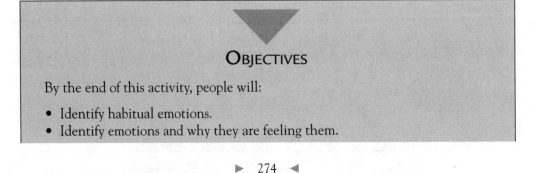

OBJECTIVES

By the end of this activity, people will:

- Identify habitual emotions.
- Identify emotions and why they are feeling them.

- Recognize the links between thought, feelings, and behaviors.
- Understand how feelings affect performance.

Mini Lecture

Having self-awareness and identifying emotions are crucial to personal development. It is possible to build self-awareness simply by finding out more about ourselves: How do we relate to the world around us? Why do we feel the way we do? What beliefs do we have? What beliefs are holding us back, and what beliefs work for us? For example, a person raised by an angry parent tends to view any type of anger or frustration as something to fear. Or someone who is smart but has never been encouraged to feel smart might believe he is stupid. It takes a lot of work to look at yourself and identify the beliefs that are affecting your life in a negative manner. However, knowing your beliefs will give you a good basis for emotional freedom because the only person who can change what you feel is you.

A simple activity to build self-awareness is to question your actions, thoughts, feelings, and responses and to look at yourself through the eyes of the world. As we question ourselves about why we do things the way we do, we can uncover a lot of things we did not know about ourselves. That is called *awareness*, and awareness is always the first step in any behavior modification. If we don't know what we are doing, how can we even begin to change it?

For example, if you ask yourself "Why am I afraid of speaking in public?" which is a fear many people have, you may find that it is simply a belief that you hold about yourself. As you question it more, you are likely to realize that this belief can be changed, modified, or adapted—and when you change the belief, you will realize that you can actually speak in public without fear!

Emotions play a big part in self-awareness. Emotions control thoughts, behavior, and actions, and they operate on many levels. They have a physical aspect as well as a psychological aspect. Emotions are good indicators of how our life is working out. They help keep us on track by making sure that we don't use only our intellectual faculties of thought, perception, reason, and memory to make decisions.

Emotional self-awareness is the ability to recognize our emotions and feelings and their effects on ourselves and other people. It is the ability to effectively read how we react to cues in the environment and be aware of how our emotions affect our performance. Having awareness of our emotions includes understanding our feelings and what triggers our emotions. We might not always be able to control or even change our feelings, but when we are aware of them, we can at least begin to make subtle changes in our lifestyle and change how we react to things.

Overview of Activity

This is a process whereby the participants move about in the space and personify a wide variety of different emotions.

Time

Instructions—5 minutes
Each round—5 minutes
Debriefing—10 minutes
Total time—35 minutes

STEPS TO FOLLOW

Round 1

1. Have participants discuss all of the different types of emotions a person can have in a day and a lifetime and the magnitude of the emotions.
2. Instruct the participants to walk around the space. Tell them you will call out an emotion that they should immediately express and personify as they walk around the space. For this first round, have them explore these emotions in silence. Emotions to call out to the participants:
   - Love, joy, surprise, anger, sadness, fear
3. Be sure to encourage eye contact. They can inspire each other's emotional state.

Tip

If some participants are not fully exploring an emotion for whatever reason, ask them to rate themselves on a scale 1 to 10—1 being not feeling the emotion and 10 fully feeling it. Ask them to go to a 10.

Round 2

Freeze the moving participants, and explain that they can now verbalize their thoughts as they walk around the room and explore these emotions. Call out these emotions:
   - Irritation, indifference, grouchiness, nervousness, disappointment, disgust, horror, excitement, curiosity, pride, contentment, and so on

Round 3

1. For the last phase, divide the group in half. Explain that half of the group will watch while the other half of the group continues to walk around the space.
2. After half of the group has sat down, instruct the group walking around the space to individually feel and display an emotion not yet explored. Encourage emotions that they see in their everyday personal and professional lives.
3. After a short while call out, "Freeze!" Instruct the group watching to guess and identify what emotions each participant is personifying. "What emotion is Jamie expressing?"

Round 4

Have the participants switch. Have the group sitting down walk around while the other group determines what their emotions are.

▼

BENEFITS TO LOOK FOR

The ideas below echo the Self-Awareness: Identify Emotions approach:

- **Emotional triggers.** Marketing messages are created to appeal to consumers' emotions. Think about how you feel the next time you hear a marketing message and how those feelings affect your own buying decision. What emotional triggers move you to action: fear, guilt, trust, value, belonging, competition, instant gratification, leadership, trendsetting, or time?
- **Learn your triggers.** There are many emotional triggers that evoke feelings and move people to action. People see a lot of marketing messages every day, and those messages are targeted to making you feel something. Feelings are powerful, and copywriters tap into that power and leverage it to control your reactions. Next time you watch or read a commercial, identify your own personal trigger—it will help you realize and understand what makes you tick.

Discussion Points

- **Q: What effect do emotions have on you?** (*I definitely felt some emotions that did not make me feel great. I much prefer to feel the positive emotions rather than the negative ones. Emotions are difficult to control.*)
- **Q: What behaviors do certain emotions produce?** (*Anger makes people do things they often regret. Frustration makes people talk loudly and aggressively or even cry. Happiness makes people smile. Joy makes people laugh, have fun, and tell jokes.*)
- **Q: In the final round, what did you notice about the perception of what you thought people's emotions were versus what they actually were?** (*Most of the time we recognized the emotion. Body language had a lot to do with recognizing the emotion. People who were happy were open, and people who were sad were crunched over.*)
- **Q: Why is it important to think about your own emotions and how they are being expressed—consciously or unconsciously?** (*I'm not sure I can always control my emotions, but if I am aware of the triggers, I don't have to react in a negative way. The more I know about my emotions, the more I can modify them. I don't have to express my anger by shouting. I can go work out!*)

Participant Action Plan

Provide all the participants with a copy of the following action plan. Ask them to complete it, and set up a time to review their results one week later. At that time, ask them what has worked and what has not worked. What do they need to do to improve?

Self-Awareness: Identify Emotions Actions

The actions I will take as a result of the Self-Awareness: Identify Emotions activity are:

_____

_____

_____

_____

ONE WEEK LATER: What results have I gained from the Self-Awareness: Identify Emotions activity?

_____

_____

_____

_____

Activity 58

Identify Triggers

Anyone can become angry—that is easy. But to be angry with the right person, to the right degree, at the right time, for the right purpose, and the right way—this is not easy.

—Aristotle, Greek philosopher, student of Plato and teacher
of Alexander the Great, and an important figure of
Western philosophy (384 BC to 322 BC)

Level of Risk

Low

Background and Purpose

Everybody has triggers, or boiling points. Even comedians have them. It doesn't matter what career you're in, people and situations can make other people upset. In the improv community, triggers include: improvisers who aren't on time to rehearsals and improvisers who hog the stage, who don't listen, who constantly go into conflict, or who always have potty mouths. All these things can tend to make an improviser hot around the collar.

There are healthy and unhealthy ways of dealing with these triggers. Unhealthy ways are talking about people behind their back or passive aggressively making fun of them with sarcasm—unless, of course, the people are aware they will hear the sarcasm and get it. Without a doubt, however, the best way to deal with triggers is to identify them and be responsible enough to not react negatively.

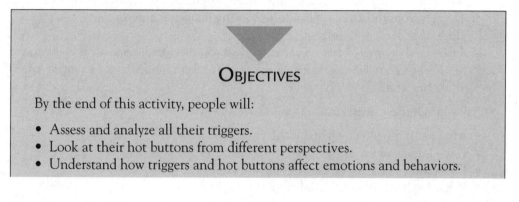

Objectives

By the end of this activity, people will:

- Assess and analyze all their triggers.
- Look at their hot buttons from different perspectives.
- Understand how triggers and hot buttons affect emotions and behaviors.

> - Stop projecting onto others what they feel inside.
> - Recognize when something is emotionally draining or energizing, identify the reason why, and make an informed decision about their continued involvement with a person, activity, or organization.

Mini Lecture

Imagine a busy airport with flights landing and taking off 24/7. It's the same with our thoughts—they land and take off in our mind all day long. The problem is that sometimes we allow negative thoughts to stick, and we end up interviewing all the passengers on board as well. Here's an example: Bertha is alone in her kitchen one evening preparing dinner. She's slicing and dicing when suddenly a thought of her ex pops into her mind. "That Bob! He's probably out right now, wining and dining and having a great time, and his sister, she's as bad as he is!" Bertha feeds those negative thoughts and suddenly cuts her finger. "Now look what they made me do!"

It may sound simple, but if you think about your own life, there are certain triggers that set off a particular train of thought that can end up wrecking your entire day. You feel awful, and meanwhile the proverbial Bob is "out having a great time!"

Once we identify triggers, we have the possibility to stop our thoughts running on and on in our minds, like a computer virus. Identifying triggers is comparable to downloading antivirus software. Consider the above scenario with Bertha once she has identified her trigger—Bob! "That Bob! He's probably out right now …" Bertha realizes Bob is a trigger; she takes a deep breath and refocuses her thoughts. "I am so glad I am preparing this dinner. It's really good for my health, and I enjoy being healthy."

Once you identify your triggers, you have an opportunity to change your thoughts and thereby your actions. It's not always easy to do, but the more you do it, the easier it becomes. Once you have identified your triggers, here's some ways to stabilize them:

1. **Get back to now.** Triggers are products of a past event. Stay focused on the present. Take a few deep breaths to generate a sense of relaxation.
2. **Take ownership.** Do not give your power away to someone or something else. The only way to move on and fully let go is to empower yourself to do so.
3. **Detach from the drama.** Substitute healthy images, words, or memories for those that cause you distress.
4. **Learn and grow.** You have a *choice* in how you react to situations. If you know your buttons are being pushed, check your reaction immediately, examine your thoughts, and choose peace.

Ask yourself these questions:

- Am I thinking too much about the past?
- Have I done all I could to make things right?
- Do I want to give my power to someone else?
- What happy thing can I think about?

- Which path do I want to go down?
- Do I choose to be happy, productive, and healthy or angry, nonproductive, and unhealthy?

Overview of Activity

After discussing all the different types of emotional triggers or hot buttons people can have—they could be ideas, people, places, situations, or institutions—the participants will rant about them. (*Rant:* a monologue in which the person is emotionally invested in the topic and is speaking passionately and with great gusto.)

Time

Instructions—5 minutes
Each round—1 to 2 minutes
Debriefing—8 minutes
Total time—15 minutes

STEPS TO FOLLOW

Round 1

1. Before the activity starts, ask the participants to shout out all their hot buttons and triggers. For example, tardiness, loud talkers, or their husband. Write their answers on a flip chart so they can refer to them later. Comment that this list could go on and on and on, and ask, "Why do you think that is?"(*Possible answers include: "There are more negative triggers than positive ones." "People know their triggers." "Being around people all day creates lots of triggers.")*

2. After the discussion of triggers, instruct the participants to partner up, preferably with someone they don't know very well. Have them decide who is Partner (A) and who is Partner (B). Explain that the (A) partners will choose one of their personal triggers or hot buttons to rant about for one to two minutes.

3. Tell the (B)s that their job is to silently observe.

Tip

The (A)s can pick as many triggers as they need to fill up one to two minutes. If they think they have no hot buttons, have them pretend: Pretend that the trigger is the most diabolical, miserable situation in the world and in their life!

Round 2

After a minute or so, have the participants switch.

Round 1 Example

Person A: "I just hate people who are late! I mean, it's so rude. I've waited 15 minutes or more for late people. I have work that I could be doing! Is my time not as important as theirs? But we can't start the meeting because of them. And don't even get me started on apologies. If I hear one more 'I'm sorry,' I'll close my ears for good. I mean, don't get me wrong. 'Sorry' is good if you say it once in a while, but when it becomes a habit … it's less than useless."

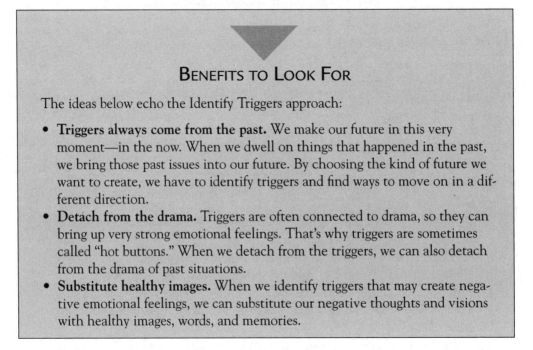

Benefits to Look For

The ideas below echo the Identify Triggers approach:

- **Triggers always come from the past.** We make our future in this very moment—in the now. When we dwell on things that happened in the past, we bring those past issues into our future. By choosing the kind of future we want to create, we have to identify triggers and find ways to move on in a different direction.
- **Detach from the drama.** Triggers are often connected to drama, so they can bring up very strong emotional feelings. That's why triggers are sometimes called "hot buttons." When we detach from the triggers, we can also detach from the drama of past situations.
- **Substitute healthy images.** When we identify triggers that may create negative emotional feelings, we can substitute our negative thoughts and visions with healthy images, words, and memories.

Discussion Points

- **Q: Why is it important to know other people's personal triggers and your own?** (*So I can start to take a look at whether they are useful to me or not. Now I know how to handle people better and how not to unintentionally push their buttons.*)
- **Q: How do you feel about some of your triggers now? Do you feel more or less attached to them?** (*I think my triggers are ridiculous. I really want to try and not get so plugged into things. It's just not good for my overall health.*)

Participant Action Plan

Provide all the participants with a copy of the following action plan. Ask them to complete it, and set up a time to review their results one week later. At that time, ask them what has worked and what has not worked. What do they need to do to improve?

Identify Triggers Actions

The actions I will take as a result of the Identify Triggers activity are:

_____

_____

_____

_____

ONE WEEK LATER: What results have I gained from the Identify Triggers activity?

_____

_____

_____

_____

Identify Reactions

Emotional intelligence emerges as a much stronger predictor of who will be most successful, because it is how we handle ourselves in our relationships that determines how well we do once we are in a given job.

—Daniel Goleman, author of more than 10 books on psychology, education, science, and leadership; and science journalist (*New York Times* for 12 years) specializing in psychology and brain sciences

Level of Risk

Medium

Background and Purpose

Emotional reactions, when used correctly, are great tools for improvisers. They can take a very boring scene and turn it into an "can't take my eyes off you" scene, or focus a scene when it's gone off track. However, emotional reactions if not used at the proper time or in the proper way can take a perfectly good scene and ruin it. Let's say there's a great scene happening with a husband and wife talking about starting a family. Suddenly, the man starts screaming and yelling and acting like a lunatic. It's not funny because it came out of nowhere, the actor is trying too hard, and the audience cannot relate! They just sabotaged the show.

Using reactions to your advantage is a skill that most improvisers must be taught, and it must be practiced. We teach students that at any point in time they can choose to react strongly to what their scene partner said or did and dramatically change the direction of the scene. We take them through a variety of emotions in a variety of different activities to show the power of emotional reactions. The key is knowing when and when not to use them and the degree of the reaction to play. In the beginning, they often get that part wrong, but with experience and lots of practice, they can make reactions work for them instead of against them.

▼

OBJECTIVES

By the end of this activity, people will:

- Assess situations and see all possible reactions.
- Choose the most appropriate reaction that will yield the best outcome.
- Identify reactions and think about the results they will get—good and bad.
- Eliminate the emotions that are not working for them.

Mini Lecture

The way we react to an event is our choice, and I get to see this clearly during an exercise called Magic Marker. There are three ways any person can react: positive, neutral, or negative (and the varying degrees between them). If someone handed me a pen, I could react really happily: "How did you know this is my favorite type of marker!!! It smells great, and it's got one of those slanted tips that make it so sharp and defined. You are wonderful. Thank you very much." If this same person handed me the exact same pen again, I could react with no emotion: "Thank you very much." If that same person handed me the same pen a third time, I could act really angrily: "What is this? It smells terrible, and it's a black marker. I want a red one. I'm so upset. I want one with a rounded tip. I like those better. You've ruined my day!"

Who was responsible for turning the events into positive, neutral, and negative experiences? In life we are the ones who choose to react to events. The question is, how do we want to react?

Maybe you've noticed it: life is just a series of events. We wake up in the morning—event number 1. We go through the day event by event until the end of the day when we climb into bed and fall asleep—event number 51, depending on how busy our life is. The events in themselves do not have triggers. We put the triggers on the events. When we get a promotion, we feel good! And when we get a speeding ticket, we feel bad—sometimes for a long, long time. But what if we are in charge of our reaction to each event? We're not expecting to celebrate a speeding ticket, but could we be thankful that it's not something worse?

If life is just a series of events and we have the power to choose how we react to the events, we can wake up in the morning and choose to feel alive, enthusiastic, and full of energy, or we can wake up in the morning and choose to feel tired, unhappy, and grumpy.

If driving to work is an event, we can choose to react in a way where we enjoy the drive, and we have a good time even if the traffic is bad! Or we can choose to react by being frustrated and getting into road rage when somebody pulls out front of us. Having a job is an event, and we can choose to react by having a great time, or we can choose to react by not liking it and getting upset.

By being aware of the fact that we can choose how we react to events, we gain control and in turn unleash our personal greatness. We no longer have to be at the mercy of whatever comes our way. We can take an active role in our life and move toward greater achievements.

Overview of Activity

In pairs participants discuss triggers they experience or observe in others. They then come up with five different possible reactions they can use that are positive, negative, or neutral. Each pair decides on a reaction that creates a positive outcome for all.

Time

Instructions—2 minutes
Each round—3 to 5 minutes
Debriefing—10 minutes
Total time—22 minutes

STEPS TO FOLLOW

Round 1
1. Have the participants pair up. Then have them take two to three minutes to discuss triggers and/or hot buttons they have experienced or noticed in other people, for example: "Angry drivers." "People talking on cell phones in restaurants." "Loud music." "People with 20 items standing in the 10-item line."
2. Give each pair a couple of minutes to *come up with* five different possible emotional reactions to the triggers they identified. These reactions can be thoughts, actions, or behaviors. They must have at least one negative, one positive, and one neutral reaction.

    Note: Using what-if statements is helpful: "What if I said, 'Stop talking on the cell phone?'" "What if you told them they were in the wrong line?"

Round 2
After a minute or two yell, "Freeze!" Explain to the participants that now that they've come up with five possible reactions, they need to choose the one that is the most likely to yield the best possible outcome for all parties.

Round 1 Example

Person A: "A negative reaction would be … I could scream at the person and slam the door on my way out."

Person B:	"What if I don't do anything and just ignore the problem? That can be a neutral reaction."
Person A:	"What if we choose to react in a positive way and apologize and ask the person if we can help her?"
Person B:	"What if I escalate the problem and go to her boss?"
Person A:	"What if I say, 'I can't talk right now. Can we schedule this conversation later?'"

Round 2 Example

Person A:	"One of the best reactions is to take responsibility for a positive outcome: 'I know you love playing loud music. Maybe you can use these headphones so you can play it as loud as you want.'"
Person B:	"I like that reaction."

▼ BENEFITS TO LOOK FOR

The ideas below echo the Identify Reactions approach:

- **Life is a series of events.** From the moment we wake up in the morning, life is a series of events. We choose to react to each event as good or bad. Some people view waking up and getting out of bed and going to work as a bad event; others see it as a great opportunity and are very thankful. We are the ones who choose our reaction.
- **We can choose our reaction.** When we realize that we choose our reaction to every event in our life, we empower ourselves to live a happier, more fulfilled life. Instead of being grumpy in the morning, we can wake up feeling great and ready to have a wonderful day. It's all a choice, and the choice is ours.
- **Choosing how to react is empowering.** It's disempowering to have other people in charge of our reactions, and yet that is what many people choose to do: "If my spouse would only …" "If my children would just …" "If I just got more …" When we come from a place of feeling disempowered, we keep taking it into our future. We may get the promotion, and our children may get good grades … but after a while we feel unhappy again! Choosing to have a positive reaction to events is empowering, and it starts now.

Discussion Points

- **Q: What was the difference between the possible reactions you got?** *(Some reactions will create problems, and some will actually be useful. The best reactions are the ones that create a positive outcome for everyone involved.)*
- **Q: What effects will positive, negative, or neutral reactions have on you and your relationships?** *(Negative reactions will create ongoing problems and issues. Neutral reactions can also seem negative at times—especially if someone wants a positive outcome.)*
- **Q: What helped you or hindered you in this exercise?** *(It was helpful to come up with positive reactions that I can use. I did get caught up a bit in the triggers—some triggers are difficult to overcome. Reacting to a trigger in a positive way is hard.)*

Participant Action Plan

Provide all the participants with a copy of the following action plan. Ask them to complete it, and set up a time to review their results one week later. At that time, ask them what has worked and what has not worked. What do they need to do to improve?

Identify Reactions Actions

The actions I will take as a result of the Identify Reactions activity are:

_____

_____

_____

_____

ONE WEEK LATER: What results have I gained from the Identify Reactions activity?

_____

_____

_____

_____

Activity 60

Emotional Self-Control

What lies in our power to do, it lies in our power not to do.

> —Aristotle, Greek philosopher, student of Plato and
> teacher of Alexander the Great, and an important
> figure of Western philosophy (384 BC to 322 BC)

Level of Risk

High

Background and Purpose

When you don't land the audition, don't get your sketch in the show, have a bad show, or get passed over for a promotion, it's easy to let emotions get the better of you. I've seen people quit the show, bad-mouth other players, reach for the bottle, and in one case punch a hole in the wall of the stage. Of course, none of these behaviors help in the long run.

In every career there will be events that happen that we don't expect, like, or have any control over. When we practice self-control, we continue to learn, grow, and form great, productive relationships.

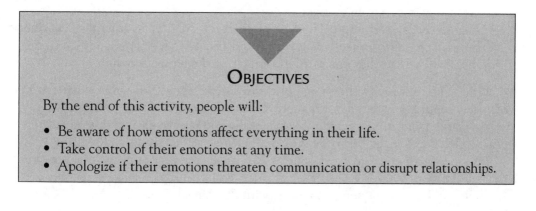

OBJECTIVES

By the end of this activity, people will:

- Be aware of how emotions affect everything in their life.
- Take control of their emotions at any time.
- Apologize if their emotions threaten communication or disrupt relationships.

Mini Lecture

When we lose control, we activate a series of events that starts with a trigger, a strong emotion, an instant reaction, and later, a feeling of regret that we've done something that impacted our value and effectiveness.

When we learn emotional self-control, we are able to keep our impulsive feelings and emotions under control. When we are provoked, we can restrain our negative actions; and when faced with opposition, hostility, or pressure, we can maintain our sense of calm and composure.

Of course, it's easy to talk about being calm when things are going well, but for many of us, each day is like an emotional rollercoaster. When things go well, we feel happy. When they don't, we feel angry, sad, and disappointed. In fact, we can get so accustomed to experiencing negative emotions that we think our lives will always be that way. Fortunately there are ways to improve our emotional self-control such as:

- **Deep breathing.** Take a deep breath and hold it for six seconds. Repeat this as many times as needed. Deep breathing helps release the endorphins into the body. Endorphins are the body's natural painkillers, and they are extremely useful in relieving overall physical pains and aches. Deep breathing is also the trigger in the parasympathetic nervous system that evokes the relaxation response. Recent neuropsychological studies have shown that deep breathing is likely to affect the stress response system in individuals while calming the mind and body.
- **Five-step freeze-frame technique.** Recognize stressful feelings and freeze-frame them. Take time out! Make a concerted effort to shift your focus away from the racing mind or disturbing emotions. Be calm and recall a positive, fun feeling that you have had and re-experience it. Ask your heart, What's a more effective response to this stressful situation? Listen and do what your heart says.
- **Global processing.** Focus on the forest instead of the trees: see the big picture and your specific actions as just one part of a major plan or purpose. For example, someone trying to be healthy should focus on the ultimate goal and how each individual decision about what to eat and when to exercise contributes (or detracts) from that goal.
- **High-level categorization.** Think about high-level concepts rather than specific things. Long-term projects can easily get bogged down by focusing too much on the details of everyday processes and forgetting the ultimate goal.

With a little creativity the same principles can be applied to many situations in which self-control is required. Ultimately these four techniques are different ways of saying much the same thing: avoid thinking locally and specifically and instead practice thinking globally, objectively, and abstractly. Increased self-control should follow.

When we learn emotional self-control, it changes the beat of every situation and every relationship. It takes two people to dance, but when you change your step, it is impossible for the other person to continue with the same dance.

Overview of Activity

This activity is performed in groups of three. Person A talks about a topic that is slightly annoying to him, but he can be swayed into either accepting the situation or getting more annoyed. Person B is the emotional *hijacker* who spurs on (A) to be more annoyed. Person C is the emotional *self-control* person, who coaches (A) to think before he speaks and choose appropriate emotions to handle the situation.

Time

Instructions—4 minutes
Each round—2 to 3 minutes
Debriefing—8 minutes
Total time—21 minutes

STEPS TO FOLLOW

Round 1

1. Have participants form groups of three.
2. Have each group sit in three chairs and form a triangle so they are fairly close to each other. Assign the person nearest the door to be Partner (A), assign the person to her right to be Partner (B), and the last person is Partner (C).
3. Have (A), the speaker, choose a topic that is frustrating to her. She can choose an issue from her own experience or from the list below:
   - People who are chronically late
   - Photograph-enforced traffic lights
   - People texting while driving
   - People taking pens and not bringing them back
   - Being put on an e-mail list that you don't need to be on
   - People who don't look up from their computer to answer you
   - People who don't say please or thank you
4. Partner (A) is the *speaker*, and she will talk about the issue. After a minute or so, Partner (B) and (C) interrupt: Partner (B) is the emotional *hijacker*, and he will spur (A) on to be more angry and upset. Partner (C) is the *self-control*, and she will coach (A) to remain cool and be wise.

Round 2

1. In the second round they will repeat round 1, but they will all change roles. Partner (B) will be the *speaker*, (C) the emotional *hijacker*, and (A) the emotional *self-control*.
2. Partner (B) will choose a different topic.

Round 3

In this round, Partner (C) will be the *speaker*, (A) the emotional *hijacker*, and (B) the emotional *self-control*. (C) will choose a different topic.

Round 1 Example

Person A (the speaker): "I hate it when people are late. It seems to happen mostly at meetings. I waste like 20 minutes waiting for people to arrive."

Person B (the hijacker): "You should call these people out and humiliate them any way possible. Call them selfish and say, 'Thanks for wasting my time,' and storm out."

Person C (the person with self-control): "Well, I don't know if that's going to get you the results you want. You have to ask yourself what you want from the situation and think about how you can solve the problem. Maybe introduce incentives so people will arrive on time. Maybe bring your work to the meeting."

Person A: "I guess I never thought about bringing my work to the meeting. I'd be able to get my work done, and it would send a message that my time is important."

Person B: "No, no, no! Here's what you do ... You start being late! In fact, don't show up to meetings at all."

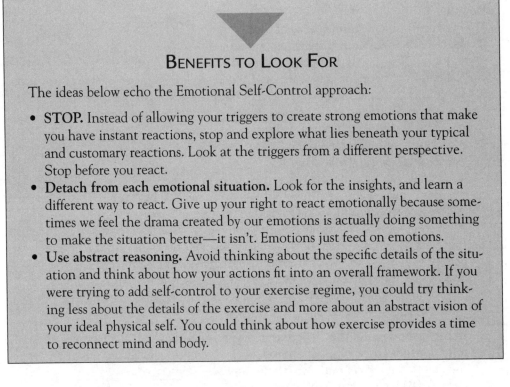

BENEFITS TO LOOK FOR

The ideas below echo the Emotional Self-Control approach:

- **STOP.** Instead of allowing your triggers to create strong emotions that make you have instant reactions, stop and explore what lies beneath your typical and customary reactions. Look at the triggers from a different perspective. Stop before you react.
- **Detach from each emotional situation.** Look for the insights, and learn a different way to react. Give up your right to react emotionally because sometimes we feel the drama created by our emotions is actually doing something to make the situation better—it isn't. Emotions just feed on emotions.
- **Use abstract reasoning.** Avoid thinking about the specific details of the situation and think about how your actions fit into an overall framework. If you were trying to add self-control to your exercise regime, you could try thinking less about the details of the exercise and more about an abstract vision of your ideal physical self. You could think about how exercise provides a time to reconnect mind and body.

Discussion Points

- **Q: Was it easy to gain control after you had been emotionally hijacked?**
  (*It wasn't too hard because I had my coach giving me lots of help.*)
- **Q: What other techniques besides taking a deep breath will help you gain emotional self-control?** (*I can think globally instead of focusing on the details.*)

- **Q: What conversation did you have with yourself to gain emotional control?** (*I was thinking about how I didn't want to get angry or annoyed. I kept my eye on the goal of being calm.*)
- **Q: What are the consequences of losing control?** (*There is a feeling of guilt that I've done something that has impacted effectiveness.*)
- **Q: What are the benefits to gaining control?** (*I feel empowered. It feels great to overcome my triggers and emotions.*)

Participant Action Plan

Have the groups discuss what actions they will take as a result of this activity. Provide all the participants with a copy of the following action plan. Ask them to complete it, and set up a time to review their results one week later. At that time, ask them what has worked and what has not worked. What do they need to do to improve?

Emotional Self-Control Actions

The actions I will take as a result of the Emotional Self-Control activity are:

_____

_____

_____

_____

ONE WEEK LATER: What results have I gained from the Emotional Self-Control activity?

_____

_____

_____

_____

Activity 61

Adaptability

Reasonable people adapt themselves to the world. Unreasonable people attempt to adapt the world to themselves. All progress, therefore, depends on unreasonable people.

— George Bernard Shaw, an Irish playwright and the only person to
have been awarded both a Nobel Prize for Literature (1925) and
an Oscar (1938) (July 26, 1856, to November 2, 1950)

Level of Risk

Medium

Background and Purpose

If an improviser holds on to her one sketch idea or character and refuses to work in the present, she will be doomed. As in life, change is constant, and we have to adapt to those changes. I remember I had a scene idea that I really wanted to put into a show. The problem was that it was about five years out of date. It was a parody of the *Sopranos*. I won't even begin to tell you about it because I won't do it any justice. But the point is that the *Sopranos* had come and gone, but I was determined to throw it in a show. Sure it was funny, and I know it would've gotten tons of laughs, but the problem was that it was way past the due date. It was time for something new, fresh, competitive, edgier, and possibly even better. And if I continued to live in the past and not look at the present cultural, social, and political times, I'd be a dodo.

OBJECTIVES

By the end of this activity, people will:

- Push the limits of their ability to adapt to change beyond what they think is possible.
- Identify their natural response to adapting to change.
- Learn new skills to become more adaptable.

Mini Lecture

Adaptability is the skill to be flexible and work effectively within a variety of situations with individuals or groups. Being adaptable means understanding and appreciating different perspectives on an issue and adapting our approach as the situation changes. It is the ability to accept changes in the organization or job requirements.

People who have this competency willingly change their own ideas or perceptions on the basis of new information or evidence. They change standard procedures where necessary, and they juggle multiple demands. Sometimes it also involves the ability to change the overall strategies, goals, or projects in response to changing situations.

One of the keys to being adaptable is to encourage the small details that enable change. Here's a checklist for becoming more adaptable:

1. **Enable good ideas.** Who spots trends? How are they translated into products and services? What was your last innovation? Build some flexibility into product development so that new trends can be addressed quickly.
2. **Challenge people to generate the new from within.** If you've been doing business the same way for years with few or no changes, you can see the results. You don't have to bungee jump off the top of a mountain, but you can take a leap in a new direction.
3. **Check your personal comfort level with change.** If you dislike change, you're probably communicating that to others. Look within and challenge yourself to model the behavior you desire in your team. Put yourself in one new situation a day so that you are consciously meeting change on an ongoing basis.
4. **View change as an opportunity.** If competition keeps ahead of you, take a look at your team. Ask for their input and listen. Find opportunities to get closer to current customers and get the word out to people who will benefit from what you offer.

Change is constant and difficult to predict. Managers need to be able to adapt their plans as the environment changes. Successful managers anticipate and adjust to circumstances, and they must be proactive instead of reactive. For example, the social trends toward the healthy lifestyle took a lot of managers by surprise. The trend created opportunities for businesses such as gymnasiums and fruit drink bars, but at the same time it created threats for many takeaway food businesses. McDonald's managers were flexible and quickly adapted the business to the changed environment, stocking fruits and salads ... and that's adaptability!

Overview of Activity

Participant will pair up, and they will be asked to make changes in their appearance and then have their partner guess the changes.

Time

Instructions—1 minute
Each round—3 to 5 minutes

Debriefing—10 minutes
Total time—16 minutes

STEPS TO FOLLOW

1. Have the participants stand in two lines facing each other. Make sure each person is opposite a partner. Ask them to look at each other and notice as much as they can about each other.
2. After 30 seconds, say to them, "Please turn around so that your backs are facing each other." After they have turned around, tell them to change three things in their appearance.
3. When everyone has changed three things (three to five minutes), ask them to turn back around so they are facing each other.
4. Tell them to each guess the changes their partners made.

Tip
Take mental notes of the comments you hear so you can replay them back.

▼

BENEFITS TO LOOK FOR

The ideas below echo the Adaptability approach:

- **It's often harder to think about doing something than it is to actually do it.** Things are never as hard as we think they are. And when we actually do the task, whatever it is, we ask ourselves why we worried so much. Change can be easy or hard depending on how much time we spend in denial, anger, or resentment. Get beyond the negative emotions, and be curious and commit.
- **Don't be insane.** The definition of insanity as defined by Einstein is doing the same thing over and over again but expecting different results. When change happens and we have the same thoughts about it or we keep reacting the same way to it, we are impractical. We have to get out of mental traps and be more adaptable.
- **Go with the flow.** Change is going to happen whether you like it or not. Sometimes it is more mentally, emotionally, and physically healthy to just go with it.

Discussion Points

- **Q: How did it feel when you had to look at each other?** (*That was really hard because I don't really like being looked at. I felt embarrassed looking at someone.*)

- **Q: How did it feel when you had to change three things?** (*I thought it was difficult until I saw what the people beside me were doing. Then I got on board. I was stumped at first, and then I got over myself and went for it.*)
- **Q: How can you adapt better to changes in your life?** (*I can make small daily changes to get used to change. I can invite ideas.*)

Participant Action Plan

Provide all the participants with a copy of the following action plan. Ask them to complete it, and set up a time to review their results one week later. At that time, ask them what has worked and what has not worked. What do they need to do to improve?

Adaptability Actions

The actions I will take as a result of the Adaptability activity are:

_____

_____

_____

_____

ONE WEEK LATER: What results have I gained from the Adaptability activity?

_____

_____

_____

_____

Activity 62

Achievement

Be a yardstick of quality. Some people aren't used to an environment where excellence is expected.

—Steve Jobs, inventor, American business magnate, cofounder and CEO of Apple, previous CEO of Pixar Animation Studios

Level of Risk

High

Background and Purpose

The Chicago improv community is saturated with teams and groups performing every night of the week. There's also a variety of improvisation to choose from: musicals, Shakespeare, long forms, short forms, sketches, two-person shows, three-person shows, and a series of others. There is no shortage of improvisation shows in Chicago. That means competition, and that makes it a little bit harder to gain a loyal following of fans (customers). If you want to become one of the best teams or players, you have to rise above the rest. That means your shows have to be funnier, more intelligent, and somehow edgier. You cannot get there without talent and of course hard work and goals.

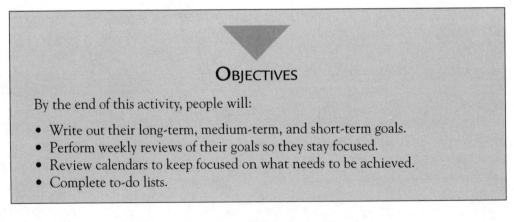

OBJECTIVES

By the end of this activity, people will:

- Write out their long-term, medium-term, and short-term goals.
- Perform weekly reviews of their goals so they stay focused.
- Review calendars to keep focused on what needs to be achieved.
- Complete to-do lists.

Mini Lecture

The standard for achievement may be measured by our own past performance (striving for improvement); an objective measure (the results); our outperforming others (competitiveness); challenging our goals; or our surpassing what anyone has ever done (innovation). However, achievement is not just about accomplishing things; it is accomplishing things through our own effort, against a clear and challenging standard of excellence. This competency is most effectively engaged in situations that provide immediate, concrete feedback from a credible source. One of the best ways to boost our achievement is to do a powerful Weekly Review. Here are four simple steps:

1. **Review long-term and medium-term goals.** Write your goals down. What is your life goal? What do you want to accomplish this year, and in the next few months? Refocusing on your goals will keep you on track and keep your attention and energy where it should be.
2. **Review your calendar.** Look back at last week's calendar items to see what needs to be moved forward. Look over your upcoming week's calendar to see if there are any tasks that need to be done.
3. **Review your lists.** Look over your to-do list to make sure it's up-to-date. Cross off completed items. Review your follow-up list, your someday/maybe list, and your project list.
4. **Set your short-term goal.** List the minitasks you want to accomplish this week, and schedule them on your calendar. Schedule them for early in the morning. These tasks should have the highest priority each day. Only put one or two on each day's schedule.

Spend no more than five minutes on each step. Clear away all distractions, turn off e-mail and the Internet (unless your lists and calendar are online), and turn off your phone. By doing these essential tasks at your Weekly Review, you will keep your system together, and you will stay focused on your goals. *Focus on one goal at a time, and you are more likely to achieve it*. Print it out, and post it up if necessary. Send yourself e-mail reminders. Tell everyone about it. Put it on your blog. However you do it, maintain that laser focus, and you will achieve everything you want to achieve.

Overview of Activity

The first activity is building a story from random sentences; the second is creating a sentence from random words (which you have written down on index cards).

Time

Instructions—5 minutes
Each round—5 to 10 minutes
Debriefing—10 minutes
Total time—45 minutes

STEPS TO FOLLOW

Round 1

1. The participants will improvise a short story. They will begin by standing in a line and stepping forward one by one to create a new front line and provide a sentence that helps build a story.
2. Have one volunteer step forward and form the beginning of the front line. She will provide a story starter, for example: "Once upon a time in a land far away …"
3. Have another volunteer come forward and stand at the end of the front line (so there is enough space between the beginning and end of the line for every participant to join in). The volunteer says the last sentence of the story. For example: "And everyone lived happily ever after."
4. Another participant will now step forward and stand at any random point in the front line and contribute another sentence to add to the story. (*There will now be three participants in the line, one at each end and one randomly near the middle.*)
5. The next participant will step into the line at a random place and contribute another sentence to the story.

Rule

Every time someone steps forward, each participant standing in line must repeat his sentence in order from beginning to the end. This helps the rest of the participants not yet involved to remember what has been said and to see the gaps in the story.

6. When everyone is standing in line, repeat the story one last time from beginning to end. (It is usually very funny to hear the outcome.)

Round 2

Materials Needed

Index cards with a word written on each one.

1. Explain that in this round the participants will have index cards with different words on them and together they must form a coherent sentence. (Create the same number of index cards as participants.) There are 20 words here:

- Harry
- after
- graduating
- in
- medicine
- from
- came
- back
- to
- his
- home
- city

- a
- Chicago
- suburban
- university
- in
- Atlanta
- to
- practice

Harry, after graduating in medicine from a Chicago suburban university, came back to his home city in Atlanta to practice.

2. Add the pressure of time restraint and begin.

Note: If you want to send a message, you can make the sentence more applicable.

Round 3

Have the participants repeat round 2 with this new sentence except add the pressure of no talking:

- Mary Shelley wrote *Frankenstein*. The monster of Frankenstein formed inspiration for Dean Koontz's *Frankenstein* series.

Note: Again you can substitute the words to send a message to your participants

BENEFITS TO LOOK FOR

The ideas below echo the Achievement approach:

- **Do more than the minimum.** It's so easy to "phone in" your job, life, relationships. And have you noticed what you put out is what you get back? Set goals that are attainable but that challenge you to "up your game." Write the goals down with due dates in your calendar. According to studies, people who write down their goals and put them in the calendar are 100 percent more likely to achieve their goals!
- **Review your goals.** Write your goals down. What do you want to achieve in your life? What do you want to accomplish this year, and in the next few months? Refocusing on your goals will keep you on track and help you achieve what you want to achieve.

Discussion Points

- **Q: What emotional response did you have to this activity?** (*It seemed complicated to begin with. I was nervous about making up a story. The longer I stayed in the back line, the more difficult it got to contribute to the story.*)

- **Q: What did you do as a team to achieve this task?** (*We all had fun and kept it together as far as the story line went. We motivated each other to contribute.*)
- **Q: What did you do individually to achieve this task?** (*I just did my best to make the story flow. I remembered what I had said, which made it easier.*)
- **Q: Do you consider yourself an overachiever, perfectionist, or too competitive with goals?** (*I'm an overachiever. I always push myself to do more. I like to keep my goals in line with what I can achieve. If my coworkers are achieving more than I am, I can get really competitive.*)

Participant Action Plan

Have participants pair up and discuss what action they will take as a result of this activity. Provide all the participants with a copy of the following action plan. Ask them to complete it, and set up a time to review their results one week later. At that time, ask them what has worked and what has not worked. What do they need to do to improve?

Achievement Actions

The actions I will take as a result of the Achievement activity are:

_____

_____

_____

_____

ONE WEEK LATER: What results have I gained from the Achievement activity?

_____

_____

_____

_____

Activity 63

Positive Outlook

Believe you can and you are half way there.
—Theodore Roosevelt, the twenty-sixth president of the United States

Level of Risk

Medium

Background and Purpose

Many people don't understand how a person could become an improviser. I agree. Most often, there's no money in it, you've got to be consistently funny, and you have to handle rejection on a daily basis. It's hard to stay positive when you see it from that point of view. But what if you looked at it from this perspective? Improv makes people's lives, if only for a minute, less stressful and more enjoyable. Improv creates magic in front of people's eyes. The rules of improv generate an environment that's supportive, nonjudgmental, and creative. What a difference perspective can make.

OBJECTIVES

By the end of this activity, people will:

- Stay positive through all types of adversity.
- Be persistent in pursuing goals despite obstacles and setbacks.
- Demonstrate resilience.
- Operate from a hope of success rather than a fear of failure.
- Learn from setbacks.

Mini Lecture

A *positive outlook* is persistence in pursuing goals despite obstacles and setbacks. People who strive to reach a goal that they truly desire are most likely to focus on the positive outcomes of that goal. Practice keeping your thoughts focused on the positive outcome you wish to achieve. Positive thinking is contagious. People sense our feelings and are more disposed to help us if we are positive. Here are some tips on enabling a positive outlook:

- Visualize favorable and beneficial outcomes.
- Use positive words in your inner dialogue or when talking with others.
- Smile a little more because this will help you think positively.
- Disregard any feelings of laziness or a desire to quit. If you persevere, you will transform the way your mind thinks.
- Expect only favorable outcomes, and circumstances will change accordingly. It may take some time for the changes to take place, but eventually they do.

We recently developed a workshop based on positive outlooks because some of the major benefits to people who focus on positive outcomes is that they enjoy better health, they live longer, they are liked by more people, they have better relationships, and they achieve more at work and on the general playing field of life. Here's a chart to show the differences between people who have positive outlooks and those who do not:

Positive Outlooks	Negative Outlooks
Focus on the good things around them.	Focus on the negative or bad things around them.
See the good things as permanent and pervasive.	See any good as temporary and specific to the current situation.
Work to see the good in every situation.	Do not work to see the good in every situation.
See bad things as temporary and specific to the situation.	

When good things happen to people with a positive outlook, they say things like, "I always believed in our team. We played this game really well. I think my own skill really contributed to our success."

When bad things happen to people with a positive outlook, they are more likely to say, "I made an error in the way I presented the information. With practice, I won't do that again. The next time, I will be right on top of this."

Overview of Activity

The participants stand in a large circle. They are given **no** instructions and are introduced to obstacles. Will the participants maintain a positive outlook throughout or get frustrated and give up?

Time

Instructions—0 minutes
Each round—as long as needed
Debriefing—10 minutes
Total time—20 minutes

STEPS TO FOLLOW

There are *no* instructions to this game.

Round 1

1. Gather all the participants into a large circle so that they can all see each other. Without any instructions they must figure out the game.
2. Clap and say the name of someone who is standing in the circle. Make eye contact with her when you do this.
3. That person must clap and say someone else's name. If this doesn't happen, silently start over—again with no instructions or advice or feedback on what went wrong.
4. After the group catches on and you play this for a while, you can start round 2. Wait for someone to call your name to start. If it takes too long for your name to be called, you can find another way to start round 2.

Round 2

1. Without warning, clap and say a person's name, but this time point to a different person. The actual person who is supposed to speak is the person you point to. Make eye contact with the person you are pointing to.
2. The person you just pointed to will then clap, say another person's name and point to yet a different person. If this doesn't happen, silently start over—again with no instructions or advice or feedback on what went wrong.
3. After the group catches on and you've played it for a while, round 3 will begin. Again, you will start it. Wait for someone to point to you. If that takes too long, you can find another way to start round 3.

Round 3

Without warning, clap and say a person's name, but this time say something about the appearance of the actual person who is supposed to speak next, for example: yellow shirt, head band, mustache.

Tip

This can go on and on with as many different obstacles as you like. For example, say someone's name, point to another person, but make eye contact with a third person who is supposed to speak next.

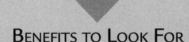

BENEFITS TO LOOK FOR

The ideas below echo the Positive Outlook approach:

- **Bounce back.** Demonstrate resilience. Persist in seeking goals despite obstacles and setbacks.
- **Be optimistic.** Operate from a hope of success rather than a fear of failure. Attribute setbacks to manageable circumstances rather than innate personal flaws or unalterable environmental factors.
- **Learn and grow.** Everyone makes mistakes. Learn from them. Don't let them become your chains. They are just little setbacks.

Discussion Points

- **Q: How difficult or easy was this activity having been given no instructions?** (*It was easy. It was hard.*)
- **Q: Did you manage to stay positive throughout?** (*At first I was curious and open, but as the activity progressed, I found myself getting a little bit frustrated. By the second round I got it—and it was easy to be positive.*)
- **Q: How do you stay resilient and overcome the obstacles in your life?** (*I'm always thankful and I try not to take anything for granted. I look for the good in things, and when bad things happen, I see them as temporary.*)

Participant Action Plan

Provide all the participants with a copy of following action plan. Ask them to complete it, and set up a time to review their results one week later. At that time, ask them what has worked and what has not worked. What do they need to do to improve?

Positive Outlook Actions

The actions I will take as a result of the Positive Outlook activity are:

_____

_____

_____

_____

ONE WEEK LATER: What results have I gained from the Positive Outlook activity?

_____

_____

_____

_____

Activity 64

Empathy and Organizational Awareness

I won't belong to any organization that would have me as a member.
—Groucho Marx, American comedian, actor,
and singer (1890 to 1977)

Level of Risk

Medium

Background and Purpose

When I was directing the Second City graduate class or directing first-time sketch writers, I could always tell who was emotionally ready and who was not. The ones who were positive and inspired and who were enjoying the process would always come in with a smile. They'd sit near others and be attentive to the group's needs. If volunteers were needed, they'd be the first ones to raise their hand. Everyone loved being around them, and the writers would write scenes for them or put them in their scenes. They helped create a great atmosphere to work in and thus a great show.

The people who were not feeling good about themselves, the group, or the process would come to rehearsal in dark glasses and wearing their sweatshirt hood up, and they'd sit in the back row. They alienated themselves and others. No one wrote for them or put them in their sketch. They learned little and left with nothing.

Both types of people created a reputation for themselves—one being easy to work with the other not. And it always showed in their performances. The ones who were aware of the group and their role in supporting the group always seemed to come out on top. They checked their ego at the door and put their heart and soul into the work, which took their careers further than those who didn't.

Objectives

By the end of this activity, people will:

- Sense others' feelings and perspectives.
- Take an active and ongoing interest in others, not being interested only when there is a problem.
- Increase their focus on communicating.
- Deeply listen and read situations.

Mini Lecture

Empathy is having the ability to understand other people. It is the ability to accurately hear and understand the unspoken or partly expressed thoughts, feelings, and concerns of others. To have empathy means taking an active interest in other people's concerns. It measures the increasing complexity and depth of understanding of others, and it may include cross-cultural sensitivity.

People with empathy are constantly picking up emotional cues, knowing what is being felt and thought even when it is not being said explicitly. They adjust their behavior according to these cues. They can appreciate not only what people are saying but why they are saying it. At the highest levels they also understand where people's feelings are coming from.

Organizational awareness is the ability to understand and learn the power relationships in their own or other organizations (the organizations of their customers, suppliers, and so on). People with organizational awareness can identify who the real decision makers are and who influences them, and they can predict how new events or situations will affect individuals and groups within these organizations.

People who have this competency naturally think about power relationships, and they enjoy analyzing formal and informal structures and dynamics. If they choose to act on this understanding, people high in this competency can be very effective at influencing organizational events. At minimum, they tend not to violate or offend organizational norms.

Overview of Activity

During a mingle process, participants improvise low and high status.

Time

Instructions—10 minutes
Each round—5 to 10 minutes
Debriefing—15 minutes
Total time—30 minutes

STEPS TO FOLLOW

Round 1
1. Have participants form two lines facing each other about 18 feet apart.
2. Tell the participants in the left line that they are high status and ask them these questions:
   - What types of jobs or occupations do high-status people usually have? (There are no wrong answers.)
   - What attitudes and inner thoughts do high-status people usually have? (Again, there are no wrong answers.)
3. Ask the participants in the left line to demonstrate with body language what high status looks like.

Tip
If they need more encouragement, have them rate themselves on a scale of 1 to 10: 1 = low status, 10 = high status. Have them push it to a 10.

4. Inform the right line that they are low-status people, and ask them these questions:
   - What types of jobs or occupations do low-status people usually have? (There are no wrong answers.)
   - What attitudes and inner thoughts do low-status people usually have? (Again, there are no wrong answers.)
5. Ask the participants in the right line to demonstrate with body language what low status looks like.

Materials Needed for Rounds 2 and 3
Deck of cards

Round 2
1. Now tell the participants that they will go to a cocktail party where they will role-play being either low-status people or high-status people as they all mingle with one another. Their fate will be determined by what card they pick from the deck of cards. *They will not show their card to anyone.* If they pull out a 2, they will role-play a person who is the lowest of low status. If they pull out an ace, they become a person of the highest status in the world. If they pull out a 7 or 8, they will be right in the middle and thus have average status. After they pull a card and see what status they will role-play, they will have a couple of seconds to get into character. They can make up their name, occupation, nationality, family history, social life, wealth, and health and everything in between in accordance with the card. For example, if someone picks a jack, she might be a director of sales in a small company in Dallas looking for more opportunities. If someone picks a 2, he might be a homeless person begging for change.

Rules

- Tell participants to not show their card to anyone. Tell them to keep it a secret.
- Have the participants mingle, meet, and converse with as many people as possible. (Every minute instruct them to meet someone new.)
- Have the participants converse with no more than three people at a time. No group discussions.

2. After they have interacted with as many people as possible, ask the participants to form a semicircle or line up from low status to high status *without* saying or asking the card number. It should be based on observation of what others said and did.

3. Conduct a debriefing.

Round 3

1. Have the participants repeat round 2 except this time they cannot look at the card they pull. Tell them to pick a card and put it up to their forehead or hold it up for the other participants to see.

Rules

Tell participants to help each other guess what card they are holding by subtly informing others of their status. Participants need to give each other ideas. They shouldn't just say, "Your card is a 10."

1. Have them line up again.

2. Conduct a debriefing.

Round 1 Example

High-status answers	Occupations	"Presidents." "Celebrities." "CEOs." "CFOs."
	Attitudes	"Very confident." "Cocky." "Reserved." "Outgoing." "Positive."
	Body language	"Makes eye contact." "Offers firm handshake." "Strong voice."
Low-status answers	Occupations	"Bums." "Students." "Staff." "Shy." "Passive." "Indifferent."
	Attitudes	"Careless." "Frustrated."
	Body language	"No eye contact." "Slouched shoulders." "Small voice."

Round 2 Example

Queen: "It's so good to see you again. I'm sorry I was late. I just came back from
                our vacation home in Cabo San Lucas."

Ace: "No worries. I'm going out of town tomorrow. I'm flying on my private jet
                to one of the islands I own in Fiji."

Card 4:   "Excuse me for the interruption, but can I get anyone a beverage? Wash
                your car? Pick up your dry cleaning?"

▼

BENEFITS TO LOOK FOR

The ideas below echo the Empathy and Organizational Awareness approach:

- **Deeply listen.** Read the situation. Read the body language. See what elements are out of place or missing. It's about listening with not only your ears but your eyes. This awareness will allow you to adjust or modify communication to benefit all players.
- **Don't jump to conclusions.** Everyone has problems. There are just varying degrees of them. Other people's problems might seem trivial to you, but to them they are hard to manage. Don't assume you understand others people's problems completely and can solve them with a snap of a finger. Listen to what is really going on. You might see a different perspective.
- **Be of service.** Most of us are so focused on ourselves and our problems and our forward momentum that we forget about other people. Remember to get out of your head and be of service.

Discussion Points

- **Q: How did people inform you that you were low status, and how did it feel?** *(It felt horrible. Someone literally looked me up and down and turned away in disgust. Jill asked me to leave. Someone said my breath smelled.)*
- **Q: How did people inform you that you were high status, and how did it feel?** *(They smiled and came right up to me. People's body language said it all. I felt respected. People wanted to do anything for me. It felt great.)*
- **Q: How many of you secretly wished you were an ace, and why?** *(All of us! Because people treat the aces well. People want to be around the aces. People smile at the aces. The aces feel special and important.)*
- **Q: What are some qualities we can emulate from a high-status person?** *(I notice that effective high-status people include everyone. They make sure to know every person's name. They are positive. They don't form clicks. They are aware of even the smallest details.)*

- **Q: How does empathy play a part in awareness and status?** *(It's the golden rule—treat others the way you would like to be treated. When I have empathy, I can put myself in other people's shoes and be aware of what is going on.)*

Participant Action Plan

Provide all the participants with a copy of the following action plan. Ask them to complete it, and set up a time to review their results one week later. At that time, ask them what has worked and what has not worked. What do they need to do to improve?

Empathy and Organizational Awareness Actions

The actions I will take as a result of the Empathy and Organizational Awareness activity are:

_____

_____

_____

_____

ONE WEEK LATER: What results have I gained from the Empathy and Organizational Awareness activity?

_____

_____

_____

_____

Activity 65

Influence

You don't have to be a "person of influence" to be influential. In fact, the most influential people in my life are probably not even aware of the things they've taught me.

—Scott Adams, American cartoonist, creator of the *Dilbert* comic strip, and author of satire, commentary, business, and general speculation

Level of Risk

High

Background and Purpose

In most comedic theaters there's probably a bar. And if you improvise there, you probably will get some sort of a discount on the cheap beers. Everyone around you drinks, so it's hard not to be influenced by it. I could say the same about being onstage. If I would be performing with improvisers who had no depth and always used potty humor, it would be hard to play at the top of my intelligence. So how did I stop myself from becoming an alcoholic woman with a mouth like a sailor?

I had to make strong choices and never undervalue myself. I had to have a goal: become a great improviser in Chicago. By surrounding myself with the kind of improvisers I admired, the chances are that I'd start performing like them. I also had to align myself with the decision maker, who at iO was Charna Halpern, founder of iO Chicago and iO West. She had the power to pull the plug on any improviser or team at any time. I had to work on all these skills if I was going to succeed.

OBJECTIVES

By the end of this activity, people will:
- Experience the difference between manipulation and influence.
- Learn tools to help influence others.

- Show support in order to keep communication positive and flowing.
- Understand that all communication has the potential to be useful and important.

Mini Lecture

Having influence is having the ability to positively persuade, convince, or impact other people to go along with or support your agenda. One way to understand influence is to look at the people we hang around with. The people we spend our time with determine what conversations dominate our attention and what observations, attitudes, and opinions we are repeatedly introduced to.

Associations with other people don't necessarily push us in one direction, but they do nudge us over time: "Associations are both subtle and powerful" (Jim Rohn, American entrepreneur and author).

One way to evaluate and shift our associations is to take a closer look. There are three types of associations that influence your life. Take a look at the list below and choose where your power of influence is most affected:

- **Disassociations:** Break away from certain negative influences that affect you. Decide the quality of life you want to have, and surround yourself with the people who represent and support that vision.
- **Limited associations.** You can spend three hours with some people, but not three days. Others you can spend three minutes with, but not three hours. Decide how much you can "afford" to be influenced based on how you feel around these people.
- **Expanded associations.** Whatever stage of life you are in, you want to see improvement. Find people who represent the success you want, the work ethic you want, the parenting skills you want, the relationship you want, and the lifestyle you want, and spend more time with them. Join organizations, clubs, businesses, and health clubs where these people are, and make friends.

Overview of Activity

In pairs, the participants must get their partners to say or do something without instructing them directly.

Time

Instructions—2 minutes
Each round—2 to 3 minutes
Debriefing—5 minutes
Total time—10 minutes

STEPS TO FOLLOW

Round 1

1. Have the participants find a partner and decide who is Partner (A) and Partner (B).
2. Instruct the pairs that one partner will have a couple of minutes to influence the other partner to say or do something—for example, cluck like a chicken. Tell the partner trying to exert influence that she can use any method except telling the other partner flat out what she is trying to get him to do. She can only hint.
3. (A) goes first and has to come up with an objective for Partner (B) to say or do.
4. Once every (A) has an objective, begin the activity.

Round 2

Have the participants switch. Now the (B) partners will get a chance to influence the (A) partners to do or say something.

Round 1 Example

Person A: "What is that Chinese dish that ends with 'choy'?"

Person B: "Bok choy?"

Person A: "Yes! That's it. I love how you say 'bok.'"

Person B: "Bok?"

Person A: "Can you say 'bok,' like 10 times in a row really fast? I bet you can."

Person B: "Sure. Bok, bok, bok, bok, bok, bok, bok, bok, bok, bok."

Person A: "That's it. I wanted you to cluck like a chicken! And you did!"

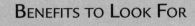

BENEFITS TO LOOK FOR

The ideas below echo the Influence approach:

- **Listen and learn.** Every communication has the potential to be useful, important, and a learning experience if given a chance. So find a way to indicate your support in order to keep communication positive and flowing.

- **Be a storyteller.** Grab people's attention, and impart something to them in a way they want to hear. Take people who know nothing about a subject, get them interested, and send them away feeling they have learned something important or useful. People with this competency know how to make others stand up and listen.
- **Expand your associations.** Hang out with people who represent the kind of influence you want in your life. Whether it's in your personal or business life, you are influenced by the people you spend the most time with. Make the top five people in your life be the influence you want to see in your life.

Discussion Points

- **Q: Which did you find more difficult: influencing or being influenced? Why?**
  (They were equally difficult. It was difficult to think of an objective—I finally came up with taking off like a duck on water.)
- **Q: What is the difference between manipulation and influence?**
  (Don't know. Influencing someone is more nonthreatening whereas manipulation is more controlling.)
- **Q: What are some of the things in your work life that you have control over and want to influence more, and how can you do that?** *(I would like to stop the gossip more, so I'm going to say, "I don't want to talk badly about people anymore." I want to influence myself to get more work done, so I'm limiting my drop-in visitors. I want to influence the attitudes around me, so I'm going to smile more.)*

Participant Action Plan

Provide all the participants with a copy of the following action plan. Ask them to complete it, and set up a time to review their results one week later. At that time, ask them what has worked and what has not worked. What do they need to do to improve?

Influence Actions

The actions I will take as a result of the Influence activity are:

_____

_____

_____

_____

ONE WEEK LATER: What results have I gained from the Influence activity?

_____

_____

_____

_____

Activity 66

Coaching and Conflict Management

Make sure that team members know they are working with you, not for you.
—John Wooden, American basketball coach, National Coach
of the Year, winner of the NCAA national championships

Level of Risk

High

Background and Purpose

Coaches are invaluable to improvisers. They give individual and team feedback and inspire groups to success. They listen to improvisers' problems real or imaginary and give them advice. They see gaps in performance and make adjustments with the players accordingly.

Without coaches or directors, groups and teams would not last long because they don't have the experience and long-standing relationships to fall back on. Conflicts would soon arise: Individuals would start giving unwarranted notes. There'd be power struggles. There would be disagreements over the direction of where the shows should go, and personalities would clash. And unless there were a set of skills and techniques in place to manage these problems, the teams would fall apart. That's why it's important to have both a coach and a system in place to cope with any potential conflicts.

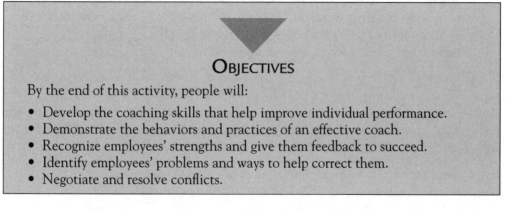

OBJECTIVES

By the end of this activity, people will:

- Develop the coaching skills that help improve individual performance.
- Demonstrate the behaviors and practices of an effective coach.
- Recognize employees' strengths and give them feedback to succeed.
- Identify employees' problems and ways to help correct them.
- Negotiate and resolve conflicts.

Mini Lecture

One of the first rules in coaching and conflict management is to take an active interest in others' development needs and bolster their abilities. Conflict situations occur when the interests, needs, goals, or values of involved parties interfere with one another. Conflicts are common in the workplace because different stakeholders often have different priorities.

Conflicts may emerge between team members, departments, projects, organizations and their clients, bosses and their subordinates, and organizations and the personal needs of their employees. Conflict is not necessarily bad; it often presents an opportunity for improvement. Therefore, it is important to understand (and apply) various conflict resolution techniques as shown below:

- **Compromising.** A compromise is a practical and mutually acceptable solution that partially satisfies both parties. Compromise is effective when the parties have moderately important goals, when the parties can live with temporary settlements on complex issues, or when people do not know each other well or haven't yet developed a high level of mutual trust.
- **Forcing.** This type of resolution is used when an individual firmly pursues her own concerns despite resistance. This may involve pushing one viewpoint at the expense of another or maintaining firm resistance to another person's actions. Parties can use force when they need to stand up for their own rights or when they need to resist aggression and pressure. However, force is usually used as a last resort to resolve a long-lasting conflict.
- **Win-wins.** Also known as *collaborations*, win-wins involve attempts to work with the other party to find win-win solutions that best satisfy the concerns of both parties. The win-win approach sees conflict resolution as an opportunity to come to a mutually beneficial result. It includes recognizing the underlying concerns of both parties and finding an alternative that meets all concerns.
- **Withdrawing.** Also known as *avoidance*, withdrawing is used when one of the parties does not pursue his own concerns or those of his opponent. Withdrawing is a tactic used to avoid the conflict and/or sidestep or postpone the issue. It is sometimes useful when the issue is so trivial it is not worth the effort.
- **Smoothing.** This technique requires one party's putting the other party first, ahead of her own concerns. Smoothing can provide a temporary relief from the conflict or buy time until the smoothing party is in a better position to respond or push back. It useful when the issue is not as important to one party as it is to the other.

If you view conflict as something that shouldn't happen, something that harms relationships, it becomes negative. Then you avoid it and hope it will go away. But if you see conflict as a fact of life and as an opportunity to strengthen relationships, you have a way of resolving conflict by turning it into something creative. Try these effective ways to resolve conflict:

1. Agree on a mutually acceptable time and place to discuss the conflict.

2. State the problem as you see it and list your concerns:
   - Make "I" statements.
3. Withhold judgments, accusations, and absolute statements ("always" or "never").
4. Let the other person have his say:
   - Do not interrupt or contradict.
   - Do not get defensive—this is her point of view.
   - Do not allow name-calling, put-downs, threats, obscenities, yelling, or intimidating behaviors.
5. Listen and ask questions:
   - Ask fact-based questions ("Who?" "What?" "Where?" "When?" "How?") to ensure that you understand the information.
   - Ask fact-finding questions ("What if?" "Is there a different solution to our problem?" "What if we did such-and-such?" "Are there other alternatives to this situation?").
   - Avoid harsh why questions ("Why are you like that?").
6. Use your own words to restate what you think the other person means and wants.
7. Acknowledge the other person's feelings and perceptions.
8. Stick to one conflict at a time:
   - Do not change the subject or allow it to be changed.
   - "I understand that concern, but I'd like to finish what we're talking about before we discuss it."
9. Seek common ground:
   - "Let's summarize what we agree on."
   - "Let's list our shared concerns."
   - Brainstorm solutions that allow a win-win solution.
10. If you want them to "stop doing" something, suggest an alternative action:
    - "Perhaps we could …"
    - "What if …"
    - "Maybe this would work …"
11. Agree to the best way to resolve the conflict and a timetable for implementing it:
    - Who will do what by when?
12. If the discussion breaks down, reschedule another time to meet and consider bringing in a third party (a coach).

Overview of Activity

Participants have the chance to watch and role-play a conflict situation and also figure out the *relationship*, the *problem situation*, and the *location* of where the miscommunication happened. They must come up with as many possible ideas to diffuse the situation.

Time

Instructions—10 minutes
Each round—10 to 20 minutes
Debriefing—10 minutes
Total time—30 minutes

STEPS TO FOLLOW

Round 1

1. Inform the participants that this is a guessing game. You will need three brave volunteers: one to guess and play the Coach and two to play the participants in a problematic relationship (Players A and B). As soon as you have the three volunteers, ask the Coach to leave the room. You will call him back in later.

2. Once the Coach is gone, get suggestions about a single conversation that has two different stories about what really happened. Identify the:
   - **Relationship.** For example, a boss and an employee.
   - **Problem situation.** For example, an employee didn't get a promotion she thought she was going to get. Her boss didn't think she was qualified.
   - **Location.** For example, a company lunch room where the miscommunication occurred.

3. After the suggestions have been taken, ask Players A and B which role they would like to play—for example, Player (A) will play the boss, and Player (B) the employee.

4. After that has been decided, bring the Coach back into the room and explain the full game to all participants: The Coach will have 30-second intervals marked by your watch or clock to interview each player and figure out the *relationship*, the *problem situation*, and the *location* of where the misconstrued conversation happened. They have unlimited 30-second intervals, but if the Coach is not catching on, you can intervene and give clues.

Round 2

Once the Coach has established all three facts, inform all participants including the audience that they must come up with as many different possible ideas to diffuse the situation. Here are some questions to ask the audience:
- What are some different ways to approach the problem situation as a coach?
- What could potentially happen if the problem is ignored?
- What are some of the advantages and disadvantages to these ideas?
- Which idea would lead to the best result?
- Is there anything that could have prevented this conflict?

Round 1 Example

Coach: "So, Player A, I'll start with you. How long have you known Player B?"

Player A: "Since I hired him two years ago."

Coach: "Okay. So he's one of your staff members?"

Player A: "Correct."

Coach: "Great. But obviously, there's some sort of a problem between you. Can you tell me a little bit about what has happened?"

Player A: "Well, there was a promotion that Player B wanted. Unfortunately, he didn't get it."

Coach: "I understand, and from your perspective, how was the process handled? Did you communicate with Player B about his not getting the promotion? Was there a review?"

Player A: "No. I didn't have time."

YOU: "Time! Coach, you now have 30 seconds to interview Player B."

▼

BENEFITS TO LOOK FOR

The ideas below echo the Coaching and Conflict Management approach:

- **Support learning and growth.** Coaches want to improve their employees' performance over the long term, and they spend time helping them find their own way to excellence by providing detailed feedback on current performance, knowledgeable support, and meaningful assignments.
- **Focus on behavior, not personality.** People who manage conflict bring disagreements into the open, effectively communicating the positions of those involved without emotionality. They focus on the issues rather than the people, which essentially deescalates the conflict.
- **Seek win-win solutions.** They also find solutions that all parties in a conflict situation can endorse.

Discussion Points

- **Q: What methods did the Coach use to find the *relationship, problem situation,* and *location?* (*She just asked open-ended questions, which allowed the players to express and communicate. She was nonjudgmental. Her body language and tone were calm and collected, which allowed both parties to relax and give information.*)

- **Q: When diffusing a situation, what are some important lessons to use?**
  (*I have to listen. I can't interrupt. I can't take anything said personally. I have to see the others' perspective through empathy. I need to listen and learn from the feedback. I can't get defensive. I can't get angry. I need to aim for a win-win solution.*)
- **Q: What qualities make a good coach?** (*Understands people's motivations and grasps the big picture by becoming a great listener and questioner. Is willing to make people accountable by having a structure that supports their doing what they said they were going to do. Practices self-awareness and continues to learn.*)

Participant Action Plan

Provide all the participants with a copy of the following action plan. Ask them to complete it, and set up a time to review their results one week later. At that time, ask them what has worked and what has not worked. What do they need to do to improve?

Coaching and Conflict Management Actions

The actions I will take as a result of the Coaching and Conflict Management activity are:

_____

_____

_____

_____

ONE WEEK LATER: What results have I gained from the Coaching and Conflict Management activity?

_____

_____

_____

_____

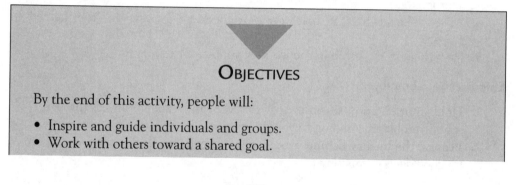

Activity 67

Inspirational Leadership and Teamwork

It ain't what they call you; it's what you answer to.
      —W.C. Fields, an American comedian, actor, juggler, and writer

Level of Risk

Low

Background and Purpose

I always remember the improv gods like Rich Talarico, TJ Jagodowski, and Craig Cackowski (comedians, actors, writers, and Second City alums) walking through the theater on their way to the green room before their show. Students and fans would literally casually line up at the bar hoping to just brush arms against them. They were idols. And these amazingly gracious guys would stop, thank the students and fans for coming, and ask them how they were doing … using their name! You could literally see the fans and students melt. Like deer in the headlights, they froze in shock because (a) their heroes actually stopped to talk with them and (b) they knew their name!

Great leaders in improv are aware of themselves. They know the importance of talking with not only their peers but also the fans and the students as well. They make a point to remember people and names, and they find out what's going on in the improv community and how they can help to make it better. They also challenge themselves to make the improv form better.

Objectives

By the end of this activity, people will:

- Inspire and guide individuals and groups.
- Work with others toward a shared goal.

- Create group synergy in pursuing collective goals.
- Set aside personal agendas in conversations.
- Focus on communicating with the group.

Mini Lecture

Inspirational leadership is the ability to take a role as the leader of a team or other group. It implies a desire to lead others. Inspirational leadership is generally, but certainly not always, shown from a position of formal authority. The "team" here should be understood broadly as any group in which the person takes on a leadership role, including the enterprise as a whole.

Teamwork is the ability to work cooperatively with others, to be part of a team, to work together as opposed to working separately or competitively. It means working with others toward shared goals and creating group synergy in pursuing collective goals. For this competency to be effective, the intention should be genuine. There are many tips on how to be an inspirational leader. The most important tips, however, are to look at your leadership style in terms of what employees want and need:

What Employees Want from a Leader

1. **Trust.** Be trustworthy and extend trust.
2. **Two-way communication.** Be a good listener.
3. **Challenge.** Set your vision and goals, and allow your team to use their creativity and authority to meet your goals.
4. **Accountability.** Hold your team accountable, and measure your own performance.
5. **Recognition.** Offer praise and express appreciation at every opportunity.

Lead Employees to "Own" Their Work

1. Include your team in long- and short-term planning.
2. Ask for input on projects for which they are responsible.
3. Include them in top-level discussions, conferences, and meetings when appropriate.
4. Allow them a byline for their work or to speak at a presentation they helped prepare.
5. Help them to be vested in the work by asking for their opinion.

Empower Your Employees

1. **Hold an orientation session.** Answer FAQs, and walk employees through solving problems common to your business.
2. **Provide the history behind procedures and policies.** Background is essential for good decision making.

3. **Furnish the necessary resources.** Give your employees the opportunity to succeed.
4. **Let employees know where to turn.** If they can't solve a problem, let them know who can.
5. **Delegate tasks.** Build confidence and teach employees the necessary steps to follow in your business.

Practice Hands-on Leadership

1. **Be there.** A successful business can slip when the owner isn't there part of every day.
2. **Set an example for working hard.** Arrive early and do what needs to be done.
3. **Don't micromanage.** Set objectives and offer guidance, but don't make employees do every little thing your way. Gauge what they do by the results.
4. **Understand your business to the last detail.** The founder of a restaurant chain visits the restaurants and spends time doing each job (selling, clerking, and so on) and observing customers' reactions.
5. **Stay in touch with stakeholders.** This includes customers, employees, and suppliers.

Overview of Activity

Have the participants get into teams, and have each team design, build, and test a brand new game. Then they must teach their game to another team.

Time

Instructions—2 minutes
Round 1—20 minutes
Round 2—20 minutes
Round 3—10 minutes
Debriefing—10 minutes
Total time—60 minutes

STEPS TO FOLLOW

Materials Needed

Note: Add or subtract to this list as needed.

Index cards, staplers, tape or glue, markers, deck of cards, ruler, plastic cups, dice, pipe cleaners, Popsicle sticks, cotton balls, balloons, plastic or rubber balls, paper clips, foam core boards, and additional miscellaneous items

Round 1

1. Have participants get into teams of any size, but make sure there is an even number of teams in all: two teams, four teams, six teams, and so on. Tell them they have 10 minutes to brainstorm ideas for a game that has never been invented. Each participant must pitch a game idea, and the group then determines which idea or combination of ideas they ultimately will build.

Variation

Each team game can be assigned a corporate issue, strategy, or client group.

2. Using a variety of provided supplies, the teams must design their game, create the elements of the game, and test their game. They have 10 additional minutes to design, build, and test.

Variation

Give them zero supplies, and allow the teams to gather their own supplies from work space and/or office. (Give any boundaries you feel necessary.)

Round 2

At the end of round 1, each team will pair up with another team and learn each other's games. Give them 5 minutes to teach their game to another team. 10 minutes total.

Teaching time

5 minutes

Playing time

5 minutes

Round 3

(This round is optional.) Have each team explain the other team's game to the rest of the group.

▼

BENEFITS TO LOOK FOR

The ideas below echo the Inspirational Leadership and Teamwork approach:

- **Build coalitions.** Bring people together to get the job done. Aim for a goal, not as a single person but as a team, and get others to commit to it. Use hard information and enlightened self-interest to convince others.

- **Focus the whole group.** Build a sense of belonging in the team. Lead others to feel they are part of something larger than themselves. If you see any feuds arising, stomp them out because those can be detrimental to the good of the team.

> • **Enjoy interdependency.** Working separately or competitively is out. Start to enjoy common goals and feel a shared responsibility with others. Teamwork is not simply enjoying working around other people; it is enjoying shared responsibility and rewards for accomplishments. Teamwork is not passively going along with others; it is about actively participating.

Discussion Points

- **Q: What did you do to accomplish your objective?** *(I asked questions and listened to the team. I dropped some ideas that weren't working.)*
- **Q: What caused the success or failure of your objective?** *(We worked as a team, and it all came together. Whenever something didn't work, it was because we were being competitive with each other.)*
- **Q: What tools can you take away from this exercise to use and implement in your life?** *(I realize that more heads are better than one. I learned to drop my ego and not take things personally if my idea didn't take hold with the team.)*

Participant Action Plan

Provide all the participants with a copy of the following action plan. Ask them to complete it, and set up a time to review their results one week later. At that time, ask them what has worked and what has not worked. What do they need to do to improve?

Inspirational Leadership and Teamwork Actions

The actions I will take as a result of the Inspirational Leadership and Teamwork activity are:

_____

_____

_____

_____

ONE WEEK LATER: What results have I gained from the Inspirational Leadership and Teamwork activity?

_____

_____

_____

_____

Activity 68

Effective Meetings

A meeting is an event where minutes are taken and hours wasted.

—James ("Jim") Tiberius Kirk, a fictional
character in the *Star Trek* media franchise

Level of Risk

Medium

Background and Purpose

All of us, at some point in our life, have to attend meetings. Even improvisers have to sit through them. It usually happens when we are creating an improvised or written sketch show. And let me tell you, our meetings can be as unproductive and annoying as yours. I remember being in Las Vegas with Second City, and we were creating a show. One of the actors, who is now on *Saturday Night Live*, had a vision for a scene that he pitched to us in a meeting. He literally talked and talked and talked about how great the scene was, how brilliant the idea was, and how it would kill. Fifteen minutes went by. I remember looking at our director who just stared at him with an "Are you finished yet?" look. I have to thank this actor because I learned a what-not-to-do lesson.

Director Mick Napier got so tired of us actors that he wrote a chapter for us in the *Second City Journal*: "How to Be the Perfect Actor in a Show." His number one rule was ... Shut up! He found that improvisers wasted a lot of time talking for all sorts of insecure reasons.

The best thing to do is to ask yourself, "Is it necessary to speak right now? Is it valid to the conversation at hand? Do I know what I'm talking about?" Good rules to live by.

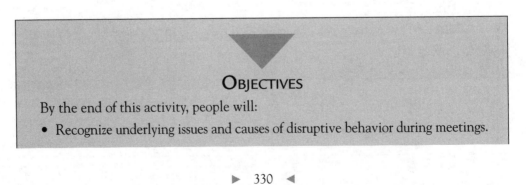

OBJECTIVES

By the end of this activity, people will:

- Recognize underlying issues and causes of disruptive behavior during meetings.

- Eliminate disruptive behaviors in meetings.
- Manage the need to reduce or control others' behavior.
- Create personal accountability.

Mini Lecture

The way to run effective meetings is to follow the basic rules. These are the simple, easy-to-follow, proven guidelines that should be followed every time your group meets. These basic rules can be followed before, during, and after your meetings:

1. Hold a meeting only when necessary.
2. For sensitive meetings, invite a neutral facilitator.
3. Have clear objectives and create an agenda that includes:
   - Topics for discussion
   - Discussion leader for each topic
   - Time allotment for every topic
4. Circulate meeting information to all participants prior to the meeting, and include:
   - Agenda
   - Location, time, and date
   - Background information
   - Assigned items for preparation
5. Start meetings on time.
6. Be well prepared.
7. Be concise and to the point, and participate in a constructive way.
8. Record meeting notes, and document decisions and action items to be done.
9. Appoint appropriate people to follow up and complete action items.
10. Review the effectiveness of the meeting at the end of each meeting with suggested improvements for the next meeting.

Meetings can easily get off track and bogged down in a variety of ways including straying off topic, participants' losing interest, and disruptive people. Here are some tips on how to deal with disruptions:

When People Lose Interest

- Summarize the discussion, and link progress to the objective.
- Bring the discussion back into line by posing a question that relates to the agenda item.
- Propose a success-guaranteed, short-term task to be completed.
- List the achievements of the group to date.
- Introduce a related theme to encourage a more active response.
- Check that individual participants are still in agreement with the group's goals.

When People Are Reluctant to Speak

- Ask questions that you know they can answer.
- Compliment them for the views they have offered.
- Ask everyone, in turn, to express an opinion.

When It Gets Overheated

- Summarize the hot issue, giving participants the chance to calm down.
- Appeal to other members, thus using group pressure to restore order.
- Suggest that the current issue be dropped for a while and another line of discussion be pursued.
- Call firmly for order, stating the need for objective reasoned discussion.
- Suggest a coffee break.

When There Are Side Talkers, Pencil Tappers, and Paper Shufflers

- Ask the disrupters a relevant question.
- Tackle them in public, and indicate that they are making it difficult for the group to get through the agenda.
- Take a break, and discuss the problem with the offenders in private.

When Argumentative People Are Taking Over

- Request that positive and helpful contributions be made.
- Give them a job to do—take minutes, record points on the whiteboard, or something else.
- Break the meeting into small groups.
- Politely interrupt the speakers and suggest that it is now time to hear from other participants.
- Say, "I think we have been over this before."
- Fire a different question at the offenders to halt the flow of words.

Knowledge is power, so whenever possible, know and understand the people who are involved in the meeting. If you don't know the members personally, be on the lookout for certain disruptive behaviors that may emerge, and have your strategy ready. That way, you will remain in charge, and the meeting can start and end on time with positive outcomes for all!

Overview of Activity

Participants think of the most disruptive behaviors that occur before, during, or after meetings, and then they get to play a scene using those specific behaviors. They then play a scene in which they use the opposites of the previous behaviors.

Time

Instructions—4 minutes
Each round—2 to 3 minutes
Debriefing—8 minutes
Total time—21 minutes

STEPS TO FOLLOW

Round 1

1. Have participants form groups of five to six players.
2. Have every individual within each group think about the most annoying or disruptive or ineffective behavior that someone can do before, during, or after a meeting.

Round 2

1. Each group will now hold a meeting about any subject they choose.
2. Every player will play one of his or her undesirable behaviors to the fullest.

Round 3

Each individual will now think about the opposite behavior to the one he or she just acted out. The behavior could also be a productive behavior that should happen in meetings.

Round 4

1. Each group will hold a meeting about any subject they choose.
2. Every player will play the opposite or productive behavior.

▼

BENEFITS TO LOOK FOR

The ideas below echo the Effective Meetings approach:

- **Refocus meetings when necessary.** Sometimes people with certain personality types will try to take over meetings. If this happens, refocus the meeting by summarizing the meeting goals. If it becomes a chronic problem, take the disruptive people aside and discuss the issues.
- **Manage the disrupters and fidgeters.** People can disrupt meetings in many different ways—shuffling papers, tapping pencils, texting, side talking, and so on. When this happens, it is best to nip it in the bud by asking a direct and relevant question to the person or people involved. Make sure that the meeting has an agenda with topic leaders and times allotted for certain topics. If it becomes a chronic problem, talk to the disrupters outside the meeting and find out what the problem is.
- **Address the action items.** Often when a meeting is over, the most critical part is overlooked: appointing the appropriate people to follow up and complete action items. Before you hold the meeting, ask the leaders of each topic to make sure they address the action items, and make sure the allocation of jobs is spread evenly across the board.
- **Review the effectiveness of the meeting.** Always review the effectiveness of the meeting at the end of each meeting with suggested improvements to the next meeting.

Discussion Points

- **Q: What was the biggest difference between meetings that were disrupted and those that were not?** (*It was like chalk and cheese—the first meeting was impossible. I couldn't hear what anyone was saying. The second meeting, everyone listened. It felt calm and peaceful. I felt we could accomplish something in the second meeting. The first meeting was a waste of time.*)
- **Q: What are the human needs behind the disruptive behaviors?** (*I noticed that people who disrupt a meeting just want attention. People who talk loudly want to be heard. People who ask lots of questions don't listen to the answers—they just want to appear smart. Sometimes they are bored or feel they do not need to be there and that the meeting is a waste of time.*)
- **Q: What specific actions can you take to stop disruptive behavior during meetings?** (*Create team ownership of the meeting by giving people jobs: help in setting the agenda, being a time keeper, keeping group notes, and so on. Collaborate with the disruptive person or people by having a premeeting to gather ideas about how to make the meeting more productive from their point of view. Set time limits. Have a post-meeting to discuss the results. Ask people if they needed to be there.*)

Participant Action Plan

Have participants pair up with someone they don't know very well and share what they intend to do as a result of this activity. Provide all the participants with a copy of the following action plan. Ask them to complete it, and set up a time to review their results one week later. At that time, ask them what has worked and what has not worked. What do they need to do to improve?

Effective Meetings Actions

The actions I will take as a result of the Effective Meetings activity are:

_____

_____

_____

_____

ONE WEEK LATER: What results have I gained from of the Effective Meetings activity?

_____

_____

_____

_____

Prioritizing

The most difficult thing is the decision to act; the rest is merely tenacity. The fears are paper tigers. You can do anything you decide to do. You can act to change and control your life; and the procedure, the process, is its own reward.

—Amelia Earhart, American aviation pioneer, author, recipient
of the Distinguished Flying Cross for being the first woman
to fly solo across the Atlantic Ocean (1897 to 1937)

Level of Risk

Medium

Background and Purpose

Every time we went on the road with the Second City Tour Company, I was thankful that our stage manager had a to-do list. That way nothing got missed. He always had a rehearsal schedule copy for us so we knew exactly where to be and when and a master list of all our props and a contact list with phone numbers in case we got lost. When we moved into the theater, he would always bring a toolbox that included various objects for emergencies like flashlights, string, scissors, and many different kinds of tape. You'd be surprised at what things can go wrong or break during a performance. Once in the theater, he'd have a to-do list for things like "spike the set of the floor with tape" so we would know where to stand for the spotlight and "set props and costumes in reachable places." Then he would actually run the show from top to bottom (T's and B's) for light and sound cues. Then there would be a to-do list for after the performance called *striking*.

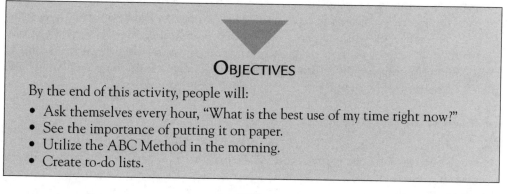

OBJECTIVES

By the end of this activity, people will:

- Ask themselves every hour, "What is the best use of my time right now?"
- See the importance of putting it on paper.
- Utilize the ABC Method in the morning.
- Create to-do lists.

Mini Lecture

There are so many workshops given and books written on how to prioritize that everyone should get an A+ on the subject. Yet time and again, we come across people who simply can't make a decision about the most important thing they need to do next. Or they know what to do, but they don't do it.

For example, I know a single guy called Bill, who, instead of washing his dishes after each meal, puts them into plastic bags to be done at a later time! I've never been to Bill's home, but I'm sure it's not a pretty site—a kitchen filled with plastic bags stuffed with dirty dishes. It seems a simple but necessary cleanliness priority for homeowners to wash their dishes after a meal—but not for Bill.

There's another person called Mary, who, rather than pay or even think about her bills, stashes all her mail in the trunk of her car—as if not opening the mail will make the problem go away! Of course, it never does. In fact, it just gets worse and worse. Wouldn't it be easier to open the mail and deal with it—even if dealing with it is to put them into neat piles?

Prioritizing seems to be associated with things we absolutely must do but absolutely do not want to do. Providing detailed ways of how to prioritize may be good for people who already do prioritize. But for people who don't want to prioritize, well, they need something simpler—a basic way to remind themselves about the thing they *must* do next.

One of the simplest ways to prioritize the important tasks is to ask at the top of every hour, "What is the most effective use of my time right now?" Or, if you spend more time doing busy work than handling the important tasks, ask, "Is what I am doing right now the most important thing I need to do?"

If you are walking around with a long to-do list in your head, why not put it down on paper? Just write down the "broad strokes" of what you would like to accomplish. Now that you have a clear picture of the things you want to do, you can prioritize them using the ABC Method and create your ABC list:

A **priorities** are must-do tasks that support your values, goals, and mission statement. These activities also have a negative consequence factor if not completed on time.

B **priorities** are should-do tasks with a lower urgency but high importance.

C **priorities** are could-do tasks with low urgency and low importance.

After organizing your tasks, you can then further prioritize using a number sequence for each prioritized group. If you have four A tasks, you can then prioritize them using A1, A2, A3, and A4. This sharpens your sense of importance for each group of tasks. I often do my C things in the evening while watching TV or when I just need a break from completing my A and B list. Prioritizing tasks turns into completed tasks, and there's no better feeling than a job well done and completed on time!

Overview of Activity

Participants stand in a circle, and someone calls out an occupation. The other participants then call out various tasks related to that occupation. The person who called out the occupation then asks, "What's the most effective use of your time right now?" People respond with their answers.

Time

Instructions—4 minutes
Each round—2 to 3 minutes
Debriefing—8 minutes
Total time—27 minutes

STEPS TO FOLLOW

1. Have the participants stand in a circle.
2. Someone in the circle will yell out an occupation, for example, "Baker!" The other participants must immediately start to do an activity related to that occupation. For example, one person might start baking bread in a big oven. Another person might roll dough. Someone else might put the buns in the window.
3. The person who just yelled out the occupation will then ask the group, "What's the most effective use of your time right now?"
4. Anyone can yell out an answer—for example, "Knead the dough!" or "Add yeast!" or "Put the bread in the oven!"
5. Repeat steps 2 to 4 as many times as needed.

   Note: Asking, "What's the most effective use of your time right now?" encourages prioritizing.

▼

BENEFITS TO LOOK FOR

The ideas below echo the Prioritizing approach:

- **Ask, "What's the most effective use of my time right now?"** Sometimes we get caught up doing busy work—work that needs to be done but is not a priority. For example, if it's 9 a.m. and you have to create an agenda for a 1 p.m. meeting, is it best to answer e-mails or create the agenda? Answer: Create the agenda, and then answer e-mails. If you get caught up in e-mails, the agenda may not get written!
- **Get your to-do list on paper.** Any time you are carrying a to-do list in your head, you are in danger of being overwhelmed and not completing any of the tasks. Write your to-do list on paper so that you have a clear picture of what needs to be done. Use the ABC Method, and create a list of A's, B's, and C's. Complete your A list before moving on to your B and C lists.

Discussion Points

- **Q: What's the best use of your time during your first hour of work?** (*Depends from day to day. For me, making sales calls because that's when I'm most likely to catch clients. Entering data. Making my to-do list first thing in the morning is good for me because then I can see my whole day ahead of me.*)
- **Q: What's the best use of your time the hour after lunch?** (*Making phone calls because that's when I know people are in. My energy is low, so it's a good time to answer e-mails.*)
- **Q: What things stop you from making the best use of your time? And what can you do about that?** (*Procrastination. Overwhelmed with too much stuff. It's not a habit for me. Drop-in visitors. Pointless e-mails. Meetings. I can put a sign on my door saying "Come back at 3 p.m." I can wait to look at my e-mails until the afternoon. I can bring my work to the meetings and at least get some of it done in the waiting time before the meetings start. I can get into a habit of creating a to-do list in the morning.*)

Participant Action Plan

Have participants pair up with someone they don't know very well and share what they intend to do as a result of this activity. Provide all the participants with a copy of the following action plan. Ask them to complete it, and set up a time to review their results one week later. At that time, ask them what has worked and what has not worked. What do they need to do to improve?

Prioritizing Actions

The actions I will take as a result of the Prioritizing activity are:

_____

_____

_____

_____

ONE WEEK LATER: What results have I gained from the Prioritizing activity?

_____

_____

_____

Activity 70

The Power of No

It [innovation] comes from saying no to 1,000 things to make sure we don't get on the wrong track or try to do too much.

—Steve Jobs, inventor, American business magnate, cofounder and CEO of Apple, previous CEO of Pixar Animation Studios

Level of Risk

High

Background and Purpose

This of course is the exact opposite of the "yes, and" philosophy. But I will try to explain why sometimes it's okay to say no. For example, you could be onstage with a wild card who thinks it's funny to hurl his body at you. That's a time when you say no. I don't need to be roughhousing onstage with someone I don't trust. No, thank you. Or what if your scene partner literally starts taking off his shirt and says, "Join me." No, thank you. Go ahead if you'd like, but I'm comfortable right where I am.

It's about taking care of yourself. The Annoyance Theatre in Chicago is a place that really embraces that philosophy. And they are right because if I don't take care of myself first, how can I take care of my scene partner and the scene and the show. I've got to make sure I'm rested, awake, alive, and ready to rock and roll. If not, then I'm not able to do anything for anyone else, and the show could suffer. I have no problem saying "No, thank you."

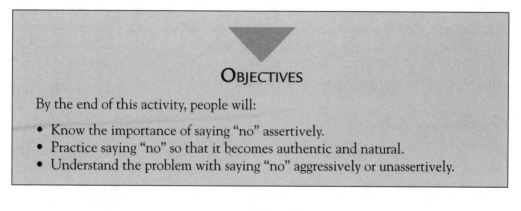

OBJECTIVES

By the end of this activity, people will:

- Know the importance of saying "no" assertively.
- Practice saying "no" so that it becomes authentic and natural.
- Understand the problem with saying "no" aggressively or unassertively.

Mini Lecture

One of the basic rules of improv is to say "yes, and." In a collaborative process, the "yes, and" technique works really well to create acceptance and agreement. In the business world, however, sometimes we have to say "no." It should be easy since "no" is one of the first words we learn to use as children, but for lots of people, it's hard to do.

Many of us grow up to be *people pleasers*; the word "no" drops out of our vocabulary, and we find ways to be friendly and keep others happy. The bottom line is that when we say "no" to authority figures, we believe it may cost us a lot in our adult life. There are many ways to say "no," and here's an overview:

> **Unassertive "no."** Often accompanied by weak excuses and reasons to convince the other person that you mean it, this type of "no" can sound ineffective when you need to justify your stand.
> **Aggressive "no."** Sometimes this type of "no" includes an attack such as, "Get your own coffee—who do you think I am?"
> **Assertive "no."** Simple and direct, this sounds like "No, I won't be able to help with that." A short and simple explanation can be added such as, "I've already made a commitment for Monday morning." The assertive "no" is effective in the workplace because it allows both parties to communicate truthfully and be authentic.

Strategies to make the assertive "no" easier to say are as follows:

1. It's okay to ask for time to think a request over: "Give me a couple of hours, and I'll get back to you."
2. Use a firm voice and look the person in the eyes as you shake your head and say, "No."
3. If you say "no" to someone you would normally say "yes" to, use empathy: "No, Jen, I can't stand in for you today. I know it must be hard to find someone, but I've got meetings and I won't be able to help you."
4. Start with the word "no." It's easier to keep your word if "no" is the first word out of your mouth.

When people say "yes" when they mean "no," they can end up feeling resentful, which costs them energy and discomfort. Practice saying "no" so that it comes naturally. For example, say "no" to the telemarketer who disturbs your dinner, to the store clerk who asks for your Zip code, and to your friend's pet when he jumps up on you, and you'll soon be assertively saying no with ease—naturally and authentically.

Overview of Activity

In round 1, participants write down random questions. In round 2, during a mingle process, participants ask and respond to questions. In round 3, participants assertively say, "No."

Time

Instructions—5 minutes
Each round—2 to 3 minutes
Debriefing—8 minutes
Total time—22 minutes

STEPS TO FOLLOW

Round 1

Before you start and as soon as the participants enter the meeting, give them five separate note papers. Instruct them to write down five different excuses, reasons, or apologies why they couldn't or didn't do something. The reasons can be excuses they have used in the past, real ones, or fictitious ones. Give an example of each: "My dog ate my homework" or "A dragon ate me yesterday and spit me out too late." Gather up all of the note papers and mix them up.

Round 2

Have the participants each grab five random note papers, and tell them not to read them just yet. (Put them in their pockets if they need to.) Tell them they will now have a mingle process whereby they must speak to five different people. In each of these five interactions, one person asks a random question and the other person replies using one of their note papers.

Round 3

Have participants continue with the mingle process. Each participant must speak with three different people. In each interaction, the participants will take turns: one participant will ask a random question, and the other person will respond with an assertive "No," adding:
- "I would prefer not to."
- "I would rather not."
- "I am not willing because …"
- "I don't want to right now because …"

Round 2 Example

Person A: "Will you get me a coffee?"
Person B: (Reading the note paper) "The nurse told me not to leave the sick office."
Person B: "Will you iron my shirt?"
Person A: (Reading the note paper) "Grandpa woke me up too late."

Round 3 Example

Person A: "Will you come for a walk?"

Person B: "No, I would rather not."

Person B: "Will you make the call?"

Person A: "No, I don't want to right now because I will be late for my appointment."

▼

BENEFITS TO LOOK FOR

The ideas below echo The Power of No approach:

- **Aggressive "no."** People who say "no" aggressively are often trying to push other people around. Whether by anger, coercion, or manipulation, they don't want to comply with the needs of others. It's okay to say "no," but there is no need to be aggressive about it.
- **Unassertive "no."** When people behave unassertively, they are failing to express their honest feelings, thoughts, and beliefs, or they are expressing their thoughts and feelings in such an apologetic, diffident, or self-effacing way that others can easily disregard them. An unassertive "no" is just a "yes" in disguise.
- **Assertive "no."** Assertiveness is part of a healthy relationship. A simple and direct "no" is okay. In fact, it's more than okay—it is a necessary skill in being authentic. People pleasers can sometimes end up feeling resentful, which costs them energy and makes them feel uncomfortable.

Discussion Points

- **Q: How was it different in round 3 when you said "no"?** (*Saying "no" felt uncomfortable. It was just an exercise, but it felt assertive to say "no." I am often a people pleaser but saying "no" felt authentic and less stressful than agreeing to something I don't want to do.*)
- **Q: What did it feel like in the mingle activity?** (*The first round was fun. I enjoyed reading the notes. In the third round it was more intense because we were saying "no."*)
- **Q: What do you think about saying "no"?** (*It's important to be able to say "no," instead of just saying "yes" to everything and then not being able to follow through. Saying "no" is empowering.*)

Participant Action Plan

Provide all the participants with a copy of the following action plan. Ask them to complete it, and set up a time to review their results one week later. At that time, ask them what has worked and what has not worked. What do they need to do to improve?

The Power of No Actions

The actions I will take as a result of The Power of No activity are:

_____

_____

_____

_____

ONE WEEK LATER: What results have I gained from The Power of No activity?

_____

_____

_____

_____

Activity 71

Diversity

I consider myself a Hindu, Christian, Muslim, Jew, Buddhist, and Confucian.
—Mahatma Gandhi, preeminent political and ideological leader of India
during the Indian independence movement (1869 to 1948)

Level of Risk

Medium

Background and Purpose

In improv, empathy is important because it helps us to understand that there are different types of personalities and styles of performing onstage. For example, it was a very different experience performing with Jason Sudeikis (*SNL*) than it was with Tim Meadows (*SNL*) or Martin Short (*SNL*). Every performer has a different way of communicating and responding. As an improviser, I have to know the people I am playing with and how I can best support them so that everyone on stage feels like a rock star. When this happens, everyone including the audience enjoys the show.

As improvisers, one person might like more of an ensemble feel, while another performer just attacks the stage and you have to "hang on" for the ride; others like teamwork and play more slowly, developing the scene as they go. No matter whom I am communicating with onstage, I have to understand how they work and how I can make them look good. And if they look good, not only did I do my job but I look good too.

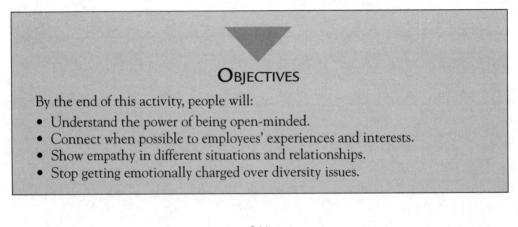

OBJECTIVES

By the end of this activity, people will:

- Understand the power of being open-minded.
- Connect when possible to employees' experiences and interests.
- Show empathy in different situations and relationships.
- Stop getting emotionally charged over diversity issues.

Mini Lecture

Diversity relates to many things including race, gender, age, disability, religion, job title, physical appearance, sexual orientation, nationality, competency, training, experience, and personal habits. In a global environment where many competitive and marketing strategies are geared toward diversity, we can capitalize on our differences and work with our colleagues by being more creative and open to change. Some ways to manage diversity include the ability and willingness to:

- Expand your knowledge of groups other than your own.
- Recognize there are many things you may not fully understand.
- Understand that marginalized people have the right to define themselves and their issues.
- Recognize that equality does not mean sameness; and fairness does not mean treating everyone in exactly in the same manner.
- Strive to meet the distinctive needs of individuals—for example, employees with disabilities have different requirements from employees with no disabilities.
- Create a safe and engaging work environment that models openness and safety.
- Use relevant exercises to engage employees and help them "step outside themselves" and see things from a different perspective.
- Know that some diversity-related topics are more highly emotionally charged than others and be aware of hot-button issues.
- Take advantage of teachable moments that arise as a result of the resistance by some employees to diversity-related learning that addresses strongly held beliefs.

Working recently with the Veterans Association, we realized that many functional changes had to be made in hospitals that were used to working primarily with male patients. As we enter more and more into a global economy, diversity is the norm. When we handle it with ease, we build a successful workforce that is united by our differences.

Overview of Activity

Participants play this activity as an animal of their choice. They are stranded on an island. In teams they find a way to get off the island.

Time

Instructions—4 minutes
Each round—2 to 3 minutes
Debriefing—8 minutes
Total time—27 minutes

STEPS TO FOLLOW

Round 1

1. Have participants get into groups with five to six participants in each. Tell them they are all animals stuck on an island that they want to get off, as in the movie *Madagascar*, so they can talk and function like human beings. This island is lush with trees and shrubs and also a few objects that have washed up on the shore:
   - One empty one-gallon milk carton
   - Two beach balls
   - Two belts
   - Three empty plastic grocery bags
2. Ask the participants to choose an animal they would like to role-play in this activity—it can be any animal they have some knowledge about.
3. Ask them to tell their group their chosen animal—it's okay if two or three of them choose the same animal, but there must be at least four different species within the group.
4. Now instruct each group to have a 10-minute meeting to discuss a plan to get off the island.

Rules

- Every animal's skill and ability should be utilized in the project somehow.
- Everyone must have a role.

Round 2

Have each group either present or play out their scenario of how they would escape from the island.

BENEFITS TO LOOK FOR

The ideas below echo the Diversity approach:

- **Question some of your basic assumptions.** Sometimes we believe that our way is the only way or that our culture was the one who invented everything. Sometimes we forget that, for example, China has been the source of many significant inventions including papermaking, the compass, gunpowder, and printing. Or that the early Egyptians figured out the human anatomy and that the pulse was somehow related to the heart! Everyone has something to offer.

- **Value differences.** Rather than pretend that differences do not exist, it is best to value the differences. When we work with our partners from Cairo, Australia, or South Africa, we learn so much; from food to music to religious beliefs, there is much to learn and be interested in. Not only that, we learn different marketing and competitive approaches to business.
- **Whose job is it?** Understand that it is not the job of minority employees to help coworkers understand issues such as prejudice, exclusion, and discrimination. Yes, it may be useful to understand about Europe by questioning a European colleague, but when cultural diversity touches on hot buttons, we need to have empathy and show respect.

Discussion Points

- **Q: In terms of diversity, what was difficult or empowering about the animal you chose?** (*I chose an animal that wasn't very strong, and so I felt I had to rely on the other animals. My animal was very big, and so it naturally became the leader—it was fun. My animal actually didn't really have any skills, so I felt I held back a bit more than I would normally do. The empowering part of my animal was its skill in building—we built a raft!*)
- **Q: Did some of you feel that your needs were not heard or met?** (*I felt useless because I was a mouse. If I did this activity again, I would be a lion or something that had a bigger voice.*)
- **Q: What helps you understand and work with diversity?** (*I need to show empathy. I need to have respect. I need to see people's positive attributes and look for opportunities in them. I need to learn about their culture and gain knowledge that will hopefully bring understanding. I need to listen more and judge less.*)

Participant Action Plan

Have participants pair up with someone they don't know very well and share what they intend to do as a result of this activity. Provide all the participants with a copy of the following action plan. Ask them to complete it, and set up a time to review their results one week later. At that time, ask them what has worked and what has not worked. What do they need to do to improve?

Diversity Actions

The actions I will take as a result of the Diversity activity are:

_____

_____

_____

_____

ONE WEEK LATER: What results have I gained from the Diversity activity?

_____

_____

_____

_____

Activity 72

Ethics

Grub first, then ethics.

—Bertolt Brecht, German poet, playwright, and
theater director (1998 to 1956)

Level of Risk

Medium

Background and Purpose

Where do improvisers come up with their characters and ideas for sketches? The answer is by observing the world around them. Obviously, the best observations come from real life. Whether you are sitting on a park bench, reading Noam Chomsky, or eating Thanksgiving dinner at Aunt Mildred's, improvisers keep their eyes open for new, fresh, and exciting material.

Sometimes it doesn't always happen that way. Often you will see young improvisers taking mental notes of their role models; quite literally they will stare at them. The next day you'll see that student try the exact same character in class. Now of course, no one is harmed by this, so in terms of ethics, it's not that bad. And this actually happens a lot. The longer you are an improviser, the more you will see the same character or the same moves being made onstage. And to be honest, it is hack and gets boring real fast.

I always encourage my students to find new characters by observing real life. Yes, it's a little bit scarier because you are the first person trying it onstage, but the payoff is huge. Plus, no one can fault you for being a hack or stealing someone's character.

▼

OBJECTIVES

By the end of this activity, people will:

- Identify ethical and unethical behaviors in the workplace.
- Explain how ethics are developed.
- Learn the importance of transparency and accountability.

Mini Lecture

Business ethics is about educating employees to do the right thing for the good of others and the company as a whole. Ethics training is important because employee actions reflect on the company, which can then be held legally and financially responsible for their actions. For that reason, 70 percent of companies train their people in ethics; yet only 55 percent of people report unethical behavior they happen to see.

Common unethical behaviors include abusive or intimidating behavior, lying, and misrepresenting actual time worked. Several factors influence ethical behavior, and the first is whether the employee's manager cares about personal standards or just the bottom line. The second is whether the organization's culture values profit above all else, and a third is the external environment including laws, regulations, and beliefs.

The following eight behaviors are key components that help create ethics in the workplace:

1. Professional dress code
2. Effective communication (online and offline)
3. Attitudes: cooperation, politeness, initiative, assertiveness, and integrity
4. Respect
5. Punctuality
6. Responsibility
7. Transparency and accountability
8. Honesty

Ethics in the workplace focuses on making the right choices; although the selection of the right action may not always seem beneficial, it must be made. For example, how should a store clerk respond if he sees a friend shoplifting? Obviously, the store clerk should prevent the theft, but what if the friend pleads with him to play along? And if the friend continues to shoplift, does the store clerk report them?

How people respond to others who claim that honesty is not necessary is part of developing a code of ethics that translates into the workplace. Doing the right thing for the good of others is not just about ethics. How we behave in the workplace and relate to others affects our mental health and our general feeling of well-being.

Overview of Activity

Participants form groups of 6 to 10 people, and a "conductor" directs them in a common activity for which they would never need an instruction manual. In the final round, they create an instruction manual for ethics.

Time

Instructions—4 minutes
Each round—2 to 3 minutes
Debriefing—8 minutes
Total time—21 minutes

STEPS TO FOLLOW

Round 1

1. Have players form groups of 6 to 10, and tell them to form a U shape. Ask for a volunteer to become the Conductor of that group standing in the middle so that every player can see him or her. Inform the groups that they will be creating an instructional manual together using the Conductors. How? Each Conductor will lead his or her group in writing, creating, and improvising this instruction manual by pointing to the players one at a time. Whoever the Conductor points to will speak. When that speaker points to another player, he or she will pick up where the last player left off. It is as if the players are one author.

2. Tell the Conductors that they can take the players to different chapters, for example: "How to Use," "Different uses for," "Warranty," foreign language translations, and so on. The Conductors will simply say, "And now we cut to Chapter X."

3. Assign each group to write about a mundane activity for which they would never actually need an instruction manual. For example:
   - Taking a walk
   - Watching TV
   - Eating breakfast
   - Reading a book

Round 2

Have the participants repeat round 1 with a new Conductor, and now have the manuals be about objects that do need manuals. For example:
   - Emergency exiting of an airplane
   - Fixing a flat tire
   - Operating an oven
   - Using an iPhone or similar device

Round 3

Now that they have got the hang of it, tell them they will now write an ethics manual. This time, however, it will be a performance, meaning that each group will get to hear the other groups' manuals. Group by group, each group will come up to the front of the room and, in front of the whole group, write a manual on ethics.

Round 1 Example

Conductor points to Player D:

Player D: "The first step you do when you're learning how to walk is …"

Conductor points to Player A:

Player A   "Stand up. You cannot learn to walk sitting down or from your bed."

Conductor points to Player B:

Player B: "Once you have stood up, go to step number 2. Tell your right leg to move forward."

Conductor points to Player E:

Player E: "And stand on that right leg. Put all of your weight on that leg. Then …"

Conductor points to Player C:

Player C: "Tell your other leg to do the same …"

BENEFITS TO LOOK FOR

The ideas below echo the Ethics approach:

- **Learn about ethical behavior.** We learn ethical behaviors from the people and groups we interact with—parents and other family members, peer groups, religious groups, and sectors of societies we operate in.
- **Listen for the warning bells.** You may be on "thin ethical ice" if you hear anyone say: "Well, maybe just this once." "No one will ever know." "It sounds too good to be true." "Everyone does it." "Audit will never catch it." "We have always done it this way."
- **Use decision-making tools.** Ask yourself what a reasonable person would do or what your role model would do. Think about how you would be perceived by your decision or action. Think of someone whose moral judgment you respect: what would that person do? How would my family perceive my actions? Evaluate the options, issues, and consequences of the action. If you are uncertain, talk with someone you trust.

Discussion Points

- **Q: How was it to create instructional manuals?** *(Funny. It was interesting to see what other people said that I forgot. I realized that I need to communicate more because we were not on the same page. I really had to let go of what I wanted in the manual because someone took it to a totally different place.)*
- **Q: Did you have to listen in this exercise?** *(Yes, I had to stop talking to myself; otherwise, I'd miss everything and get lost.)*
- **Q: How was it to create the ethics manual?** *(I had never really thought about what ethics are, and I had assumed that we are all on the same page, but clearly we are not. I really had to think about what I was saying and what I wanted in the manual!)*
- **Q: Why do you think you missed some elements in your ethics manual?** *(I block my creative ideas because I get embarrassed. I'm too polite because my ideas are often quite good. I wait too long to say something and then someone else comes up with my idea.)*

Participant Action Plan

Have the participants pair up with someone they don't know very well and share what they intend to do as a result of this activity. Provide all the participants with a copy of the following action plan. Ask them to complete it, and set up a time to review their results one week later. At that time, ask them what has worked and what has not worked. What do they need to do to improve?

Ethics Actions

The actions I will take as a result of the Ethics activity are:

_____

_____

_____

_____

ONE WEEK LATER: What results have I gained from the Ethics activity?

_____

_____

_____

_____

Activity 73

The Interviewing Process

Never take a job where winter winds can blow up your pants.

—Geraldo Rivera, American attorney, journalist, writer,
reporter, and former talk show host

Level of Risk

Medium

Background and Purpose

Interviewing characters onstage in short-form games like the game Panel of Experts is fantastic. You get to learn about the characters in a short, effective amount of time. Each player is given a magazine theme from the audience on which they are an expert. It's always fun for me because being a woman, the audience often yells something like, "Auto mechanic!" which, of course, I know nothing about but will have to act as if I do. When all of us onstage have gotten our suggestions and we know what our expertise is, the players and I are then asked random questions from the audience. In a matter of seconds we have to create the expert's history, interests, addictions, and everything else under the moon.

I literally have to make it up on the spot and hope that it's interesting, engaging, and funny. If it's not, I'll sit there onstage for an eternity wishing I were somewhere else. If I make one bad comment that doesn't make sense, or if I stumble or pause too long to answer the question, I look scared and incompetent. The audience will never ask me another question, and I'll have to work doubly hard in the next game to win them back, which usually is impossible. The same is true for job interviews.

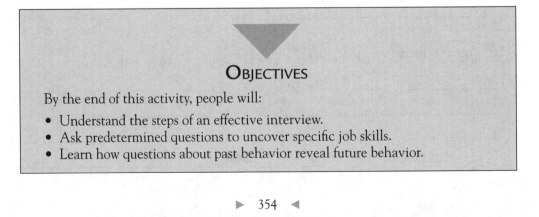

OBJECTIVES

By the end of this activity, people will:

- Understand the steps of an effective interview.
- Ask predetermined questions to uncover specific job skills.
- Learn how questions about past behavior reveal future behavior.

Mini Lectures

Past behavior is a good predictor of future behavior. Asking questions reveals how prospective employees can solve job-related problems; it's also a great way to match the right person to the job. For example, if the job requires a person to find solutions to problems, the interviewer can say, "Tell me about a problem you uncovered in your previous job." And follow up with, "What steps did you take to find a solution?"

Behaviors, also called *competencies*, are a way of reviewing the job description and requirements. Whether it's the interviewer asking the questions or the interviewee knowing which answers to provide, reviewing competencies will help prepare for the interview. Here is a sample of the kind of behavioral questions that will help uncover past behaviors as related to a job's requirements:

"Tell me about a time when you set a goal and were able to achieve it."

"Give me an example of when your presentation skills influenced an opinion."

"Explain how you went above and beyond the call of duty to get a job done."

"Tell me about when you had too many tasks and how you prioritized them."

"Give me a specific example of when you had to make a split-second decision."

"Describe a conflict situation you had and your way of dealing with it."

"When was the last time you showed initiative and took the lead?"

"How do you go about anticipating potential problems and developing preventive measures?"

"How do you manage if you are forced to make an unpopular decision?"

Interviewing is a planning process. The first task is to make a list of specific competencies and behaviors needed for the job. The second task is to plan the questions that will uncover these predetermined skills. The third task is to ask very pointed questions to determine if the candidate possesses those skills.

Overview of Activity

Participants choose a character from either children's book or cartoon characters, celebrities, famous or infamous people, and/or historical figures. They then interview each other.

Time

Instructions—4 minutes
Each round—2 to 3 minutes
Debriefing—8 minutes
Total time—18 minutes

STEPS TO FOLLOW

Round 1

1. Have participants choose a character for themselves that they feel they are a knowledgeable about. Choose from children's book or cartoon characters, celebrities, famous or infamous people, and/or historical figures.
2. Ask them to write down their character's strengths, qualities, accomplishments, philosophies, and weaknesses.
3. Based on the characters they have chosen, ask them to choose an appropriate job or position within the company that they wish to interview for,
4. Have participants find a partner. One will be Partner (A) and the other (B). Have them tell each other the desired job (not the character) they wish to interview for. Based on their partner's job, each partner will then write six questions they will ask their partners in an interview process.
5. Now the interview will begin. In round 1, Partner (B), will interview Partner (A) for the job they chose using the six questions he or she came up with.

   Note: After they finish, see if Partner (B) can guess what character Partner (A) chose.

Round 2

Change roles. Partner (A) will now interview Partner (B) for the job they chose using the six questions that Partner (A) previously wrote down.

Note: After they finish, see if Partner (A) can guess what character Partner (B) chose.

BENEFITS TO LOOK FOR

The ideas below echo The Interviewing Process approach from the interviewee's perspective:

- **Predict questions.** No one can predict the exact questions that an interviewer will ask, but rehearsing and getting an idea of a few important questions that may be asked is helpful— for example: "Tell me about your professional life?" "What do you know about our company?" "Why are you interested in this position?"

- **Do.** Arrive 15 minutes early. Answer the actual questions that are being asked. Get the interviewer to describe the position and responsibilities early in the conversation so you can relate your skills and background to the position throughout the interview. Stress the accomplishments that are most pertinent to the job. Be aware of what your body language is saying. Smile, make eye contact, don't slouch, and maintain your composure. Anticipate tough questions, and prepare in advance so you can turn apparent weaknesses into strengths. Dress appropriately, and make your first impression a professional one. Ask questions—the interview should be a mutual exchange of information, not a one-sided conversation. Last but not least, listen.
- **Don't.** Never interrupt. Don't chew gum. Don't place anything on the interviewer's desk. Don't be overly familiar. Don't wear heavy perfume or cologne. Don't ramble. Don't answer with a simple "yes" or "no." Don't lie—answer questions as truthfully as possible. Do not make derogatory remarks about your present or former employers or companies.

Discussion Points

- **Q: What kind of questions did you ask, and what answers did you miss?** (*I thought I asked pretty good questions until I heard my partner's. I missed asking about their past behaviors, how they had handled a problem in the past.*)
- **Q: Is finding out about past experiences of interviewees important?** (*Yes, because past behaviors are one of the best indicators of future behavior or performance. People can and do change, so it's good to give people a chance.*)
- **Q: How can you find out how interviewees handle problems?** (*I can ask them to describe a recent problem they had. I can ask them to tell me about how they handled the problem and how they resolved it.*)
- **Q: Why is it important to probe deeper into interviewees' answers with more questions?** (*I need to ask follow-up questions to uncover the issues in more detail. If the interviewee is not telling the truth or exaggerating his or her expertise, I'll discover that by asking more questions.*)

Participant Action Plan

Have participants pair up with someone they don't know very well and share what they intend to do as a result of this activity. Provide all the participants with a copy of the following action plan. Ask them to complete it, and set up a time to review their results one week later. At that time, ask them what has worked and what has not worked. What do they need to do to improve?

The Interviewing Process Actions

The actions I will take as a result of The Interviewing Process activity are:

_____

_____

_____

_____

ONE WEEK LATER: What results have I gained from The Interviewing Process activity?

_____

_____

_____

_____

Activity 74

Harassment

I've been ... chased by paparazzi, and they run lights, and they chase you and harass you the whole time. It happens all over the world, and it has certainly gotten worse. You don't know what it's like being chased by them. It is harassment under the guise of, you know, "We are the press, we are entitled." When people are having a private moment, they should be allowed to have a private moment.

—Tom Cruise, American film actor and producer, three Golden Globe Awards, nominated for three Academy Awards

Level of Risk

Medium

Background and Purpose

If I were a stand-up comedian, I'm sure I'd have many stories about audience hecklers. Fortunately, I'm an improviser, and we rarely get harassed by audiences. The only times it does happen is at college events where alcohol is the star and young men and women feel empowered to act like buffoons. But even then the harassment rarely happens in the scenes or games. The type of harassment I'm talking about usually comes in the audience suggestions. I was a host of an improv game one time when I asked for a suggestion, and the response I got was very much potty humor. I took the suggestion and played to the top of my intelligence, which basically affirmed to the whole audience that I don't play in the "gutter." Usually the suggestions after that will not be as bad.

What I've found to be true with most of the audience members who shout out things is that it's not so much that they want to harass the improvisers as it is that they want to impress their friends and/or be a part of the show. Either way, I'm lucky because I have a supportive team around me, and I also have my intelligence.

OBJECTIVES

By the end of this activity, people will:

- Understand the definition of *harassment* in the workplace.
- Identify ways to prevent harassment.
- Know what to do in the event of experiencing harassment.

Mini Lecture

If someone works in an intimidating, hostile, or offensive work environment and cannot reasonably do his or her job due to certain behaviors of his or her management or coworkers, that is called *harassment*. Harassing behavior is any unwelcome verbal, written, or physical conduct that either denigrates or shows hostility or aversion toward a person on the basis of his or her race, sex, color, national origin, religion, sexual orientation, age, veteran status, political affiliation, or disability. Harassment can include such behaviors as a boss or coworker's being rude, yelling, or annoying; making overt and discriminating remarks; and physical conduct.

In legal terms, harassment can result in an employee's suing for wrongful termination or for creating an environment that causes severe stress to the employee or affects employment opportunity and compensation. Obviously the best defense against harassment in the workplace is prevention, and the best way to do that is to promote sound management practices that include:

- Maintaining respectful interpersonal communication
- Managing the staff fairly
- Taking quick and appropriate action to manage conflict
- Clearly defining the responsibilities and tasks of each employee
- Creating an efficient procedure that allows confidential reporting of harassment
- Using specialized resources to help put a stop to a psychological harassment situation and prevent other such situations from arising

Depending on the severity of the harassment, managers should verbally warn the person very clearly that their wish is to see such behavior cease immediately. Many times this will stop the behavior in its tracks, but sometimes it will not. If it continues, managers should bring the matter to the attention of upper management, who must put a stop to it by taking appropriate steps.

If a person experiences sexual harassment, he or she should report it. He or she should simply write down a brief synopsis of what happened and submit it to the boss and the other proper channels at the workplace.

Overview of Activity

In teams of four to five, the players will discuss harassment issues.

Time

Instructions—2 minutes
Round 1—10 minutes
Round 2—10 minutes
Debriefing—8 minutes
Total time—30 minutes

STEPS TO FOLLOW

Round 1

1. Have the participants form groups of four or five. Each group will have 10 minutes to share and discuss their points of view or experiences about harassment issues.
2. Each group has one minute to choose one harassment issue they believe creates the most problems.
3. Each group then has five minutes to create a one-minute TV commercial campaign designed to overcome the group's chosen issues of harassment. Tell the groups to incorporate a celebrity spokesperson, a slogan, and a jingle in this commercial. Everyone must be involved in the commercial.

Round 2

The groups will each have one minute to act out their commercials.

Note: This is not about solving the harassment issues. This is about having awareness of harassment issues and exploring possible ways of dealing with them. If someone is having sexual harassment issues, he or she needs to address those issues outside of this activity.

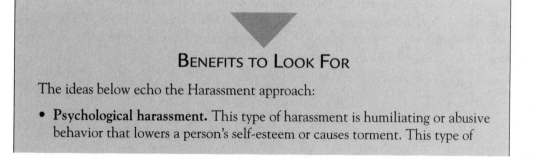

BENEFITS TO LOOK FOR

The ideas below echo the Harassment approach:

- **Psychological harassment.** This type of harassment is humiliating or abusive behavior that lowers a person's self-esteem or causes torment. This type of annoying behavior manifests itself in the form of conduct, verbal comments, actions, or gestures characterized by the following four criteria:

- ○ Repetitive
- ○ Hostile or unwanted
- ○ Affects the person's dignity or psychological integrity
- ○ Results in a harmful work environment
- **Sexual harassment.** This is behavior that exceeds what the person considers being appropriate and reasonable in the performance of his or her work.
- **Management rights and normal conditions of employment.** Psychological harassment must not be confused with the normal exercise of the employer's management rights, in particular his or her right to assign tasks and his or her right to reprimand or impose disciplinary sanctions. If an employer does not exercise these rights in an abusive or discriminatory manner, his or her actions do not constitute psychological harassment.

Discussion Points

- **Q: What were your main feelings about this activity?** (*I realized that people have different ideas about harassment. I am glad that we don't have much harassment in our team. However, we need to make sure we always treat each other with respect.*)
- **Q: What is the best way to prevent harassment?** (*Open communication. Respect. Treating each other fairly. Clearly defined responsibilities and tasks. Escalate problems to HR if needed.*)
- **Q: How effective are verbal warnings against harassment?** (*It depends on the situation. If it's a really bad case of harassment, it's best just to report it. Sometimes warning someone will stop the person because he or she may not have realized what he or she was doing.*)

Participant Action Plan

Have participants pair up with someone they know very well and share what they intend to do as a result of this activity. Provide all the participants with a copy of the following action plan. Ask them to complete it, and set up a time to review their results one week later. At that time, ask them what has worked and what has not worked. What do they need to do to improve?

Harassment Actions

The actions I will take as a result of the Harassment activity are:

_____

_____

_____

_____

ONE WEEK LATER: What results have I gained from the Harassment activity?

_____

_____

_____

_____

Activity 75

Maintain the Improv Culture

The longer I live, the more I realize the impact of attitude on life. Attitude, to me, is more important than facts. It is more important than the past, than education, than money, than circumstances, than failure, than successes, than what other people think or say or do. It is more important than appearance, giftedness or skill. It will make or break a company ... a church ... a home. The remarkable thing is we have a choice every day regarding the attitude we will embrace for that day. We cannot change our past ... we cannot change the fact that people will act in a certain way. We cannot change the inevitable. The only thing we can do is play on the one string we have, and that is our attitude. I am convinced that life is 10 percent what happens to me and 90 percent how I react to it. And so it is with you ... we are in charge of our Attitudes.

—Charles R. Swindoll, American author, clergyman,
educator, and radio preacher

Level of Risk

Medium

Background and Purpose

There are many reasons why I fell in love with improv, and one of them was the culture. The improv community is one that feels like family and one that is always inclusive. I have felt supported, and I have been given ample opportunities to learn and grow. People enjoy each other's company, and the atmosphere is always one of creativity.

The power of improv goes far beyond the stage because it utilizes so many competencies. It helps people generate productive relationships, find connections, be active, be adaptable, be flexible to change, try new things, take risks, be present in the moment, be great listeners, respond instead of react, think ahead, multitask, and be good storytellers, just to name a few. The list is really endless. In the words of Charles Darwin, "In the long history of humankind, those who learned to collaborate and improvise most effectively have prevailed."

▼

OBJECTIVES

By the end of this activity, people will:

- Encourage a culture of improv.
- Create an environment of "yes, anding."
- Remain open and flexible to change.
- Suspend judgments.
- Be supportive.

Mini Lecture

The improv culture creates people who work together in teams and respond to each other organically and successfully in real time. The skills that improvisers learn help them to listen, focus, and cooperate with others. Onstage, they connect people and ideas; in the business environment they create a heightened awareness of the marketplace and help companies develop new product ideas and successfully manage change.

Improvisers listen closely, pay attention to the environment, and are willing to stay open to alternative agendas and change as needed. They put existing things together in new combinations and hold large goals in mind. They cultivate the practice of accessing their own intuition in real time. As human beings, we often sense patterns before we can articulate them consciously; having access to the part of the brain that offers an unexpected, unplanned, but coherent and often brilliant next move is key to contributing rapidly and successfully.

Here are a few of the top characteristics of an improv culture:

1. **Clear goals.** In an improv culture, the goals are clear, which encourages people to use their talents and focus to grab opportunities in the moment.
2. **Group flow.** There is heightened consciousness in the team that fosters great creativity and very high engagement.
3. **Innovation.** Innovation rises from the bottom up, often from random encounters with potential customers asking radical questions.
4. **Collaborative creativity.** It feels like "jamming"—it's energizing and unpredictable, and it produces great results.
5. **New ideas.** Even ideas that aren't ultimately used are seen as positive contributions to the group.
6. **"Yes, and."** Ideas and practices aren't criticized. They are built upon. Time and energy aren't wasted blaming others. The group members jump straight into what they like to do, planning and guiding it in a positive direction with positive questions about how to make it fit the group's larger goals.

Create a culture of improv by being more playful. Begin with what you can control: your own response to life. Watch a funny video. Read some humor. Get a joke book. Turn the first minor challenge of the day into a game. If you face an obstacle, make a joke of it and write down some possible responses. Exaggerate them and make them ridiculous. You don't have to share what you've written; the act of writing down possible responses will, in and of itself, diffuse fears and tension around the task.

Treat the players on your daily stage as just that—players. Say "yes, and" to colleagues, coworkers, and even difficult employees, and see what happens. "Yes, and" is a simple tool that can have amazing and positive impacts. It is really great at removing obstacles and creating collaboration and enthusiasm.

Overview of Activity

In a six-round activity, participants determine what creates a "yes, and" environment and what eliminates barriers. The participants create a six-month strategy to ensure successful and effective communication.

Time

Instructions—6 minutes
Each round—10 to 15 minutes
Debriefing—10 minutes
Total time—60 minutes

STEPS TO FOLLOW

Note: For each round a different person must take the lead.

Round 1. What Is Improv?
In small groups, have participants take a few minutes to determine and describe the improv culture.

Round 2. Barriers
In the same groups, have participants determine at least five things they see happening right now in the workplace that go against the improv culture. Have them focus on things that make relationships, productivity, and communication less effective.

Round 3. Environment
Have the participants create ways to inspire "yes, and" in others so that people can present their ideas and information to people who will give them a "yes, and" response.

Instructions

- Have the participants create specific actionable things the group can do.
- Have the participants identify two to three things that would generate an effective "yes, and" environment.

Round 4. "Yes, and" Coach

Have the participants define and identify the role of the "yes, and" coach—both within the group and outside of the group.

Round 5. Measurements

1. Have the participants create measures that can be used for the next six months to ensure that the team is following the ground rules, achieving success, and inspiring others with "yes, and."
2. Have them think of fun ways to check that the barriers are reduced and effective communication is the norm.
3. Ask them to describe what success looks like. How will they know the group is "yes, anding"?

Round 6. Create a News Show

Have the participants create a one- to two-minute news show that "reports" on the ideas generated in the preceding five rounds.

▼

BENEFITS TO LOOK FOR

The ideas below echo the Maintain the Improv Culture approach:

- **Group flow.** Improv is about working in a team and "giving and taking" so that the whole group profits. Group flow is a particular state of heightened consciousness that fosters great creativity and very high engagement. Group flow is about being authentic, truthful, and at the same time, playful.
- **Innovation.** Sometimes an unexpected opportunity comes from customers complaining about a product or service. When a company listens to what the customers say, it can create a more effective or efficient product. When employees are open to innovation, they make the most of random encounters with potential customers asking radical questions.
- **Jamming.** Collaborative creativity feels like "jamming." It's energizing and unpredictable, and it produces great results. When adults have fun at work, it doesn't mean that they are not productive. It just means that they are enjoying their jobs. And people who enjoy their jobs are more effective in producing good results.

Discussion Points

- **Q: What is improv?** (*We decided that it is about being in the moment, in the now! It's about listening to other people and reacting with positive actions. It's about working together as a team. It's fun!*)
- **Q: What barriers to improv did you discover?** (*Being fearful. Close-minded. Saying "no" all the time. Not listening.*)
- **Q: How important is "yes, and"?** (*It's about giving other people energy. It's a basic rule of improv. It generates a good feeling.*)
- **Q: Did anyone volunteer to be a "yes, and" coach?** (*No one did, but I would like to be the coach. It would be great to have a coach.*)
- **Q: How did the news shows go?** (*We generated lots of good ideas about maintaining a culture of improv. We decided to continue to have fun at work. We want to be collaborative and build a team spirit.*)

Participant Action Plan

Have participants work in groups of three to four and share what they intend to do as a result of this activity. Provide all the participants with a copy of the following action plan. Ask them to complete it, and set up a time to review their results one week later. At that time, ask them what has worked and what has not worked. What do they need to do to improve?

Maintain the Improv Culture Actions

The actions I will take as a result of the Maintain the Improv Culture activity are:

_____

_____

_____

_____

ONE WEEK LATER: What results have I gained from the Maintain the Improv Culture activity?

_____

_____

_____

_____

Index

About the Authors

Val Gee has published four books with McGraw-Hill—*The Winner's Attitude, Super Service*, first and second editions, *The Customer Service Training Tool Kit*, and *OPEN Question Selling*—and she is delighted to have coauthored this book with her daughter Sarah. Entrepreneur and business owner, Val has developed and facilitated hundreds of employee training programs for companies such as Motorola, Hyatt Hotels, Siemens, Baxter Pharmaceutical, Computer Associates, GE Financial, Pepsi, Xerox, Advocate Healthcare, and McDonald's. Val is a member of the Authors Guild, the American Society for Training & Development (ASTD), the American Management Association (AMA), eWomenNetwork, and the British American Business Council. Before making the United States her permanent home in 1983, Val studied in the United Kingdom at Lords Commercial College, St. Aldate's Business College Oxford, and Bedford College.

Sarah Gee graduated from Saint Mary's University of Minnesota with a BA in theater. Before becoming an alum of the Second City, Las Vegas, she appeared in thousands of shows with the Second City Tour Company and on the stages of iO Chicago and iO West in Los Angeles. She is also a facilitator, consultant, coach, and instructional designer for companies such as HSBC, Vodafone, GE Healthcare, Veterans Association, CIB, Farmers Insurance, Heineken, Wrigley, Hyatt, Cemex, General Motors, United Airlines, and ConAgra Foods. She has worked with executive MBA students at the University of California (UCLA), Anderson School of Management, Duke University Fuqua School of Business, and Columbia College. Sarah is a member of the Screen Actors Guild, the Actors Equity Association, the National Speakers Association, ASTD, and AMA.